First in Freedom

⬦⬦⬦⬦⬦⬦⬦⬦⬦⬦⬦⬦⬦⬦⬦⬦⬦⬦⬦⬦⬦

Transforming Ideas Into Consequences for North Carolina

⬦⬦⬦⬦⬦⬦⬦⬦⬦⬦⬦⬦⬦⬦⬦⬦⬦⬦⬦⬦⬦

John Locke
FOUNDATION

Raleigh, North Carolina

2012

www.johnlocke.org

ISBN Number: 978-0-9855878-1-9
Library of Congress Control Number: 2013900784

Printed by ECPrinting
Eau Claire, Wisconsin

Cover Design by Metro Productions
Raleigh, North Carolina

Contents

An Intellectual Tradition Brought Home

by John Hood

In 1948, the University of Chicago Press published one of the foundational texts of the modern conservative movement: *Ideas Have Consequences*. Coming just a few years after another foundational text, Friedrich Hayek's *The Road to Serfdom*, which described the social and economic costs of expansive government, *Ideas Have Consequences* focused more on issues of culture and morality. Its main argument was that by embracing relativism over absolute truth, the West had set the stage for its own decline. The consequences would be not just political and economic chaos but also the loss of individual liberty and social order.

The book's publication gave the conservative movement one of its most enduring intellectual concepts and marketing slogans. Since the early 1950s, few conservative or libertarian organizations have failed to proclaim that "ideas have consequences," and many have included the phrase in their mission statements, stationery, and websites. The publication of *Ideas Have Consequences* also launched its author, a previously obscure professor of English at the University of Chicago, into the forefront of the postwar debate about the future of American culture and politics.

His name was **Richard Weaver**. Although he spent much of his career in Chicago, Weaver was a proud North Carolinian. His family had deep roots in the Tar Heel State. In fact, his hometown is actually named Weaverville, in Buncombe County.

After obtaining his Ph.D. in English from Louisiana State University in 1943, Weaver took his first teaching job at North Carolina State University in Raleigh, after which he relocated his academic life to the University of

Chicago. Still, Richard Weaver never really left North Carolina. It was more than just a birthplace to him. He purchased a home in Weaverville and spent most of his summers there. That's where his mother lived, and where the extended Weaver clan would gather for an annual reunion – an event that often featured a learned discourse by Weaver himself. Heavily influenced by the prewar Southern Agrarians such as Donald Davidson and Robert Penn Warren, Richard Weaver believed that to cultivate ancestral land by hand was also to cultivate personal virtue. The family's garden in Weaverville was plowed by mule well into the 1960s.[1]

During the 1950s and early 1960s, Richard Weaver wrote many other books and articles as a leading spokesman for the traditionalist strand of the conservative movement. He became one of the early contributing editors to William F. Buckley's new magazine *National Review* in the mid-1950s, and in 1957 wrote the first article of the first issue of *Modern Age*, a journal created by conservative scholar Russell Kirk. The latter publication would later move to the Intercollegiate Studies Institute, also an organization in which Richard Weaver played an important early role.

A Movement's Tar Heel Roots

American conservatism – a fusion of free-market economics, traditional values, and constitutionalism – owes a great deal to North Carolina. Richard Weaver is but one of many prominent scholars, authors, journalists, and political leaders with significant ties to the Tar Heel State who have played major roles in building what has become the modern conservative movement. I will mention just a few examples. **Thomas Sowell**, a Gastonia native, is one of the country's most prominent free-market economists. His many books, articles, and columns explore a wide range of issues, from fiscal and regulatory policy to education, affirmative action, and economic history. **Vermont Royster**, a Raleigh native and graduate of the University of North Carolina at Chapel Hill, became editor of *The Wall Street Journal* and two-time winner of the Pulitzer Prize for commentary. His editorial direction and erudite, elegant columns helped make the *Journal's* editorial page a must-read for conservatives everywhere – and for those who would understand the American Right.

In political life, as well, North Carolina made at least two notable contributions to conservatism in the mid-20th century: U.S. senators **Sam**

Ervin and **Jesse Helms**. Ervin, a Morganton native and member of the North Carolina Supreme Court before his appointment to the Senate in 1954, was one of the last and best exemplars of the Southern Democratic tradition. A fierce advocate of constitutional government and civil liberties, Ervin came to national fame as chairman of the U.S. Senate committee investigating the Watergate break-in. By then, of course, he had been joined in the U.S. Senate by Republican Jesse Helms, a Monroe native and former Southern Democrat whose election in 1972 – along with **Jim Holshouser**'s to the Governor's Mansion and future Gov. **Jim Martin**'s to Congress – signified the arrival of the Republican Party as a competitive force in North Carolina politics.

While Ervin and Helms agreed on some matters, such as federal spending and the Equal Rights Amendment, they disagreed on others, such as prayer in public schools. Similarly, Richard Weaver's traditionalism included a suspicion of commercial life that was markedly in tension with views of Thomas Sowell and Vermont Royster. The modern conservative movement is a coalition made up of people who agree on enough to work together but disagree on enough to make the work interesting, to say the least. To be more precise, modern conservatism is actually a mixture – or perhaps a better term would be *conversation* – between tradition and liberty.

During the 19th and early 20th centuries, traditionalists and classical liberals in North Carolina and beyond disagreed on the proper relationship between church and state, the rise of industrialization as a challenge to agrarian communities, and the role of race and sex in public and private life. During the 1930s and 1940s, however, the triumph of progressive politics in the New Deal and the challenges posed by World War II and the ensuing Cold War served to push the traditionalists and classical liberals together. They found common ground, and a common foe in the social democrats and leftists who now called themselves "liberals."

Indeed, some leaders of the emerging movement, such as *National Review*'s Frank Meyer, actively sought a fusion of tradition and liberty – a sense that conservative goals such as social order and strong families might best be advanced through libertarian means, and that libertarian goals such as smaller government and personal freedom might best be advanced through conservative means.

President Ronald Reagan gave a talk about Meyer's Fusionism shortly after taking office in 1981:

> *It was Frank Meyer who reminded us that the robust individualism
> of the American experience was part of the deeper current of
> Western learning and culture. He pointed out that a respect for law,
> an appreciation for tradition, and regard for the social consensus
> that gives stability to our public and private institutions, these
> civilized ideas must still motivate us even as we seek a new economic
> prosperity based on reducing government interference in the
> marketplace. Our goals complement each other. We're not cutting
> the budget simply for the sake of sounder financial management.
> This is only a first step toward returning power to the states and
> communities, only a first step toward reordering the relationship
> between citizen and government.*[2]

Thus the intellectual work that helped form modern American conservatism owes a great debt to North Carolina's own Richard Weaver, in that Frank Meyer specifically credited *Ideas Have Consequences* as the book that inspired him to construct his Fusionist model in the first place.[3]

Carolinians and Conservatism Today

North Carolina's influence on the conservative movement and the national political debate has hardly been limited to the writers and politicians I've already mentioned, the ones who came to prominence in the middle decades of the 20th century. The tradition extends as far back as colonial times, when Edenton lawyer **James Iredell** wrote the influential political essay *Principles of an American Whig* just before the American Revolution that established his reputation as one of America's leading thinkers. In 1790, President George Washington appointed James Iredell to the U.S. Supreme Court, making him one of the first justices – and at 38 years of age, the youngest – on the nation's highest court. **Nathaniel Macon,** a native of Warrenton, served as Speaker of the U.S. House during the presidency of Thomas Jefferson and was one of America's most forceful proponents of the Jeffersonian philosophy of limited government. **Andrew Jackson**, born in the Waxhaw community on the border between the two Carolinas, and his protégé **James K. Polk**, born near present-day Pineville, were both Jeffersonian Democrats who served as presidents of the United States. (Polk was also the first and only UNC-Chapel Hill graduate to win the nation's highest political office.)

4

A couple of generations later, North Carolinians played significant roles in responding to the political rise of the Populist and Progressive movements of the late 19th and early 20th centuries. A good example is **Walter Hines Page,** co-founder of Doubleday publishing house and editor of *The Atlantic Monthly* and *World's Work.* His father, Frank Page, was a successful businessman who founded the North Carolina towns of Cary and Aberdeen. Walter attended Duke University and spent some time as a newspaper publisher in Raleigh before rejoining the New York publishing world in the 1880s. While critical of some elements of Southern culture, Page was a classical liberal who championed Jeffersonian tradition over the new prairie populism of William Jennings Bryan. He used the pages of his magazines to celebrate entrepreneurs such as Great Northern Railway president James J. Hill and his battles with federal regulators and subsidized competitors.[4]

Conservatives and libertarians with strong North Carolina ties are also among the leading lights of the movement today. **Terry Eastland,** former publisher of *The American Spectator* and current publisher of *The Weekly Standard,* began his journalism career at what is now the Greensboro *News & Record,* where he rose to the post of editorial-page editor. **Nina Owcharenko,** one of the top domestic policy analysts at the Heritage Foundation in Washington, is a Charlotte native and UNC-Chapel Hill graduate. **Robert V. Young,** a professor of English at North Carolina State University, is a widely read author and the current editor of *Modern Age,* the previously mentioned conservative journal that published Richard Weaver in its inaugural issue. The new president of the libertarian Cato Institute, Charlotte-area native **John Allison,** is the former CEO of BB&T in Winston-Salem and an alumnus of UNC-CH and Duke. One of Cato's adjunct scholars, **Michael Munger,** is a Davidson College graduate and former chairman of Duke's political-science department. The new editor of one of the libertarian movement's oldest and most-revered journals, *The Freeman,* is **Max Borders,** another Charlotte native and a graduate of Appalachian State University in Boone.

And I would humbly suggest that the John Locke Foundation – founded by North Carolina business and community leaders in 1989 – has become one of the nation's best-known state policy think tanks precisely by emulating the Fusionist model of bringing conservatives and libertarians together to advance a 21st-century agenda for reform and renewal based on timeless principles. Consider how we describe our organization's vision and mission:

> **Vision** — *The John Locke Foundation envisions a North Carolina of responsible citizens, strong families, and successful communities committed to individual liberty and limited, constitutional government.*
> **Mission** — *The John Locke Foundation employs research, journalism, and outreach programs to transform government through competition, innovation, personal freedom, and personal responsibility. JLF seeks a better balance between the public sector and private institutions of family, faith, community, and enterprise.*

As you can see, we focus our efforts on those policies where the interests of traditionalists and libertarians overlap. Since JLF opened our doors in February 1990, we have used research, journalism, and outreach programs to promote greater public understanding of issues such as education, fiscal policy, health care, business regulation, and transportation. Our first research papers in 1990-91 quantified the effects of regulation on housing prices, outlined an "entrepreneurial school" model for education reform that later became known as charter schools, and proposed public-private partnerships to build new highways using electronic toll collection. In 1995, we published the first in a series of alternative state budgets that recommended savings in all departments and activities of state government, including the creation of a Department of Public Safety and other means of rationalizing the state's organizational chart. In 1996, JLF began its Agenda project, which provides political candidates a briefing book on state issues every two years. Later, we added a biennial briefing book on city and county issues.

The John Locke Foundation doesn't spend much time on social-policy issues such as abortion and marriage, other than providing news coverage on our blogs and in *Carolina Journal*, our media project. That's not because we think these issues are unimportant, or because JLF staff members lack strong opinions about them. There are two reasons for this decision. First, there are many other public-policy organizations that cover these issues – and cover them well. We recognize the wisdom of comparative advantage, of playing to one's strengths rather than trying to be all things to all people. Second, while JLF folks have strong opinions about social policy, they are not always shared opinions. In the interest of promoting a Fusionist approach to building and strengthening the conservative movement in North Carolina, we have chosen to devote our attention to fiscal and economic issues.

Keep in mind, however, that Fusionists informed by both the libertarian and traditionalist strands of the conservative movement don't see fiscal and economic issues as simply a matter of dollars and cents. The affordability of government and the health of the economy are directly related to the preservation and vitality of the two-parent family as the institution most likely to rear the next generation of healthy, educated, diligent, sober, and self-sufficient adults. To the extent that families fail to form and thrive, and government programs supplant the traditional roles of parents, other relatives, friends, religious institutions, and local communities, there will be lower economic growth, fewer economic opportunities, and greater demand for costly government services.

Back in 2001, I wrote a book called *Investor Politics* that made this argument in the context of federal and state entitlements.[5] I pointed out that as programs such as Social Security, Medicare, and Medicaid offered a promise – an unfunded and impossible promise, as it turns out – to take care of Americans in disability or old age, they eroded the relationships that traditionally existed across generations. In the natural order of things, parents take care of their children, often with the help of other relatives, after which the grown-up children take care of their parents and other elderly or disabled relatives. To insert impersonal (and inefficient) government programs in place of these relationships was to deal a blow to the traditional model of family. In a sense, these entitlements became programs to benefit *nonrecipients*, such as the 40-something child who would otherwise need to take care of the 70-something parent. Government programs aimed at the needs of children often have a similar effect, a disruption of the parent-child relationship and the natural responsibilities that drive parents to work harder, stay together, and adopt patterns of behavior most likely to help them provide for their families.

None of this is to suggest that government should have no role in providing temporary assistance to needy families (to coin a phrase), delivering long-term assistance to the physical or mentally disabled who lack family resources, and ensuring that workers set aside sufficient money so that future events such as injuries, illnesses, unemployment spells, or retirement do not turn them into permanent wards of the state. But surely the intervention of government should not come – and, given the already staggering size of government's unfunded liabilities, cannot come – at the expense of personal freedom and personal responsibility. At the state and local levels, the John Locke Foundation has called for a more limited, economical, and effective government, not for its abolition. We believe that conservative policy prescriptions, while reflective of powerful philosophical ideas, are also rooted in practicality. Based on hundreds of years of experience with constitutional government, and on the changeless facts of human nature, they have the strongest of all possible selling points: **They work.**

A Window of Opportunity

About a year ago, it became evident that 2013 might be a window of opportunity for North Carolina conservatives. Political trends seemed likely to place the legislature, governor's office, and supreme court in the hands of public officials more sympathetic to conservative ideas than ever before in modern history. Our assumption wasn't that the new generation of leaders would be of one mind on every issue. Republican lawmakers haven't been unanimous in the past. The incoming governor, Pat McCrory, brings his own ideas and experiences as the longtime mayor of the state's largest city. Nevertheless, we saw the prospects for conservative reforms of the tax code, state budget, education, regulatory agencies, health care, and government operations as greater in 2013 than at any time since JLF's founding.

We responded to the challenge by adding two book projects to our normal mix of programs and services. Last summer, JLF published *Our Best Foot Forward: An Investment Plan for North Carolina's Economic Recovery*, a book I wrote to provide historical context and the broad outlines of a conservative reform agenda for the state.[6] The book you are holding now is the logical follow-up to the first one. *First In Freedom* offers analysis and specific recommendations from the JLF Research team on the biggest fiscal and economic issues facing North Carolina in 2013. In the first chapter, the Vice President for Research at JLF, Dr. Roy Cordato, proposes that lawmakers adopt a new model for taxation that ends the current bias against savings, promotes true tax fairness and transparency, and makes North Carolina a more attractive place to invest and create new jobs. In Chapter Two, former JLF fiscal policy analyst Fergus Hodgson makes the case for inserting a Taxpayer Bill of Rights in the constitution to limit the growth of state spending over time and clean up the state's messy balance sheet, which contains tens of billions of dollars in unfunded liabilities for pensions, health care, and capital needs. In Chapter Three, Dr. Terry Stoops proposes a comprehensive agenda for improving North Carolina education by offering parents more choices among competing educational providers. Stoops, a former schoolteacher who directs JLF's education policy studies, is also the author of Chapter Four, which describes a conservative reform agenda for district-run public schools based on higher academic standards, changes in teacher tenure and compensation, and the more-efficient use of tax dollars. Jon Sanders, the director of regulatory studies at JLF, wrote Chapter Five to offer policymakers ideas for bringing transparency and accountability to the rulemaking process and limiting the regulatory burden on job-creating businesses. In Chapter Six, adjunct policy analyst Sean Riley gives North Carolina policymakers detailed advice on how to respond to the challenges posed by President Obama's health care plan. And in Chapter Seven, I offer my views on the best way to reorganize the state's electoral and governmental systems to strengthen accountability to voters, strike a better balance between the legislative and executive branches, and improve the governance of North Carolina's public schools, community colleges, universities, and transportation system.

Some of the ideas you will encounter in *First In Freedom* may be new to you. I hope you find them interesting, appealing, and worthy of action. But I must tell you that they aren't really new ideas. JLF has advanced a consistent, coherent set of conservative policy reforms for more than two decades. Furthermore, many of the recommendations in this book are based on successful programs or policies already in place in other states or countries.

Most importantly of all, the policies we propose in this book are really just the state-level application of ideas that conservatives and libertarians have fashioned, studied, and debated on the national stage for a long, long time. Many of these pioneering thinkers, as you now know, were actually born right here in North Carolina or spent significant time in the state as children, students, or practitioners of their craft. Isn't it about time that North Carolina actually begin to implement the very ideas that these native or adopted Tar Heels have so long and so brilliantly espoused?

It would be fitting if, starting in 2013, North Carolina were to become a national leader in the cause of limiting and reforming government. The very phrase "First in Freedom," which once adorned the license plates of North Carolina drivers, speaks to an old and venerable tradition of North Carolinians standing up for liberty. In May 1775, a group of Mecklenburg County leaders met in Charlotte to fashion a response to escalating tensions between the American colonies and the government of King George III. As they gathered for the meeting, news arrived in town of the battles of Lexington and Concord a month earlier in Massachusetts. Worried and angered, the Mecklenburg leaders decided to set up their own institutions of government. In a document later published as the **Mecklenburg Resolves,** they stated that British military action had resulted in the colonies entering "a state of actual rebellion" and that "all laws and commissions confirmed by or derived from the authority of the King and Parliament are annulled and vacated, and the former civil constitution of these colonies for the present wholly suspended." Some believe that the Mecklenburg committee went further still, issuing a formal Declaration of Independence on May 20, the first of its kind in America. But even if the Mecklenburg Resolves was the only document approved by the delegates, it was still a startling and courageous act of resistance against tyrannical government and deserves the veneration still evident on the state flag and state seal of North Carolina.

The revolutionary fervor was hardly limited to Mecklenburg. Political leaders in counties and towns across North Carolina expressed their resolve to fight for liberty over the subsequent months. By April 1776, they met as the Fourth Provincial Congress in Halifax to decide what North Carolina's position should be at the upcoming Continental Congress in Philadelphia. Three of the participants in Mecklenburg's May 1775 action – Robert Irwin, John Phifer, and John McKnitt Alexander – were members of the Fourth Provincial Congress. In the resulting **Halifax Resolves,** the assembled state leaders decided to instruct the North Carolina delegation in Philadelphia to pursue formal independence from Britain – the first such decision in America. The date of the Halifax Resolves, April 12, is the other date honored on the North Carolina seal and flag.

So there is a strong case to be made that the Tar Heel State led the way on American independence. But that was more than two centuries ago. The challenges facing our economy, our families, our liberty, and our tradition of constitutional government are serious and immediate. Again, it is time to act. At the John Locke Foundation, we believe it is time for North Carolina to reclaim its heritage and resume its leadership in the cause of liberty. It is time for our state to become First in Freedom once more.

Endnotes

1. Fred Douglas Young, *Richard M. Weaver: A Life of the Mind*, Columbia, MO: University of Missouri Press, 1995, pp. 14-15.

2. Ronald Reagan, "Address to the Conservative Political Action Conference," March 20, 1981.

3. Jonathan Adler, "Frank Meyer: The Fusionist as Federalist," *Publius: The Journal of Federalism*, Vol. 34, No. 4, Fall 2004, pp. 51-53.

4. H. Roger Grant, "World's Work: 1900-1932," in Ronald Lora and William Henry Longton, eds., *The Conservative Press in Twentieth-Century America*, Westport, CT: Greenwood Press, 1999, pp. 47-51.

5. John Hood, *Investor Politics: The New Force That Will Transform American Business, Government & Politics in the Twenty-First Century*, Radnor, PA: Templeton Foundation Press, 2001.

6. John Hood, *Our Best Foot Forward: An Investment Plan for North Carolina's Economic Recovery*, Raleigh, NC: John Locke Foundation, 2012.

Chapter One

‹‹‹‹‹‹‹‹‹‹‹‹‹‹‹‹‹‹‹‹‹‹‹‹‹‹‹‹

The Time Is Right for Sweeping Tax Reform

by Roy Cordato

Vermont Royster, the North Carolina native who served as a correspondent, columnist, and editor at The Wall Street Journal for decades, covered countless fiscal-policy debates in Washington. He told his readers not only what was happening with federal spending, but what its likely consequences would be for families, businesses, and the economy. After one particularly reckless budget passed Congress, Royster wrote that "government is not only running out of money but also out of all the 'easy' ways of raising money in the mammoth sums required."

Under Royster's leadership, the editorial staff of The Wall Street Journal became one of the centers of innovative thinking about fiscal policy during the 1960s and early 1970s. His successor, Journal editor Robert Bartley, would help form these ideas into a coherent plan for tax reform that included lower marginal rates, fewer layers of taxation on savings and investment, and the elimination of special-interest spending disguised as tax "breaks." In this chapter, Roy Cordato applies the principles of pro-growth tax reform to North Carolina's problematic tax code.

In a free society, one that respects individual liberty and freedom of choice, taxation has one and only one purpose, to raise the revenues necessary to fund the government. And this should be done while minimizing the damage that the tax system does to both the economy and individual freedom of choice.

The tax system in North Carolina has strayed dramatically from this fundamental idea. The state relies on a tax code that discourages some choices and businesses, often in the name of saving the environment or protecting people's health, while subsidizing others, typically in the name of economic development. The task of this chapter is to discuss how all this can be changed through tax reform that is informed by sound economic analysis and sound principles of democracy and good government.

Where Are the Problems?

The problems are everywhere you look. North Carolina relies primarily for its revenues on two different taxes — the personal income tax, which accounts for 51 percent of revenues, and the sales tax, which makes up 31 percent of revenues. The third-largest revenue raiser is the corporate income tax, at a much smaller 5 percent of total revenue. Added to this mix is a host of less significant taxes, at least in terms of total revenues generated, which includes estate taxes, excise taxes on items like alcohol and cigarettes, and business franchise taxes. Both the income tax and the sales tax need extensive reform in order to come into compliance with sound principles of taxation, while the the corporate income tax really has no place as part of a tax system in a free and democratic society.

Even a cursory look at the system of taxes in North Carolina reveals that it has been constructed in a completely ad hoc manner with little if any attention to the basic principles of either a free society or efficient taxation.

The principles to which I refer can be subsumed under two broad categories. The first is economic efficiency, which focuses on what economists call "neutrality," or the idea that a tax system should not penalize some activities and reward others. It should, to the extent possible, be neutral with respect to people's decision making.

Figure 1: Share of North Carolina State Revenue

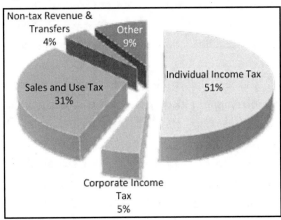

Non-tax Revenue & Transfers 4%

Other 9%

Sales and Use Tax 31%

Individual Income Tax 51%

Corporate Income Tax 5%

For an economist, a market is efficient when it accurately reflects actual conditions of supply and demand, that is consumer preferences and resource scarcities. So a neutral tax system is one that interferes with this as little as possible.

The second is transparency, which is important because, in a democracy, people should have a clear idea of what government is costing them. Taxes are the most obvious indicator of this. If the amount of the taxes being paid is hidden from the people who are actually paying them, decision making at the ballot box is impaired. A transparent tax system is a prerequisite for an informed citizenry.

North Carolina's most important revenue raisers — the income, sales, and corporate income taxes — violate both of these principles. In what follows, I will examine each of these taxes and their problems in detail. I will also assess other, less consequential taxes that plague and ultimately corrupt our system of revenue-raising. Ultimately this chapter will examine and evaluate alternatives for reform of the system.

North Carolina's Income Tax

Since its inception in 1921, the North Carolina income tax has had a graduated, or progressive, rate structure. (The desirability of this will be discussed below.) What this means is that, as incomes increase, specified increments to income are taxed at increasingly higher rates. For example, in 1924 North Carolina had a relatively straightforward system. With each increment in taxable income (after deductions) of $2,500 up to $10,000, the rate was increased by 0.75 percent. So the first $2,500 was taxed at 1.25 percent. If a person had $5,000 in taxable income, the first $2,500 was taxed at 1.25 percent and the second was taxed at 2.0 percent. This was continued up to a taxable income of $10,000. Income above $10,000 was taxed at 4.5 percent.[1]

The term "marginal tax rate" refers to the rate that is being paid on the last increment of income. So, in the 1924 example, a person earning $10,000 would face a "marginal rate" of 3.5 percent on the last $2,500 increment between $7,500 and $10,000, while a person earning $14,000 would face a "marginal rate" of 4.5 percent on the $4,000 above $10,000.

As an aside, $10,000 in 1924 would be equivalent to an income of over $126,000 in 2010 dollars, which would be taxed at a marginal rate of 7.75

percent today. It should also be noted that, while rates at the federal level have trended downward over the last 40 years, except for the expiration of a statutorily temporary increase in the rates in 2007, there has never been a lowering of the structure of marginal rates for the entire history of the North Carolina income tax. Every change since 1924 that was not instituted specifically as a temporary measure to deal with a transient problem has resulted in a rate increase. Most recently in 2001 a temporary top rate of 8.25 percent was instituted for two years and extended for an additional two years to deal with a budget deficit caused by excessive spending in the 1990s.

Penalizing productivity and growth

The current rate structure goes from a bottom rate of 6 percent (1.5 points higher than the top rate when the tax was put in place in 1921) to a top rate of 7.75 percent. Except where distinctions are made in the federal code, such as IRAs and other specially designated savings accounts, the North Carolina income tax system makes no distinction between different kinds of income. For example, all returns to saving and investment, such as capital gains, interest, and dividends, are considered to be ordinary income and are taxed at the same rates as other forms of income. This is partly at odds with the federal system, which taxes capital gains, and with recent changes dividends, at lower rates. I will argue below that by taxing returns to investment and saving, North Carolina introduces double taxation into its tax code and creates a bias against investment activities.

With some notable exceptions, primarily the taxation of capital gains and now dividends, North Carolina's income tax is modeled after the federal income tax. This means that it defines "taxable income" in the same way and, by and large, "piggy-backs" on the federal tax code when determining what are and are not deductible expenses. Because of this, our state income tax system suffers the same problems as the federal system in that it is dramatically biased against work effort relative to leisure and saving and investment relative to consumption spending. These biases, which violate the neutrality principle, stifle both economic growth and job creation.

The economic biases, or "non-neutralities," created by the North Carolina income tax system are generated by both its rate structure and the way it defines taxable income, i.e., its base. As noted previously, North Carolina has a rather steeply progressive tax rate structure that biases against work effort and productivity, and the tax base is defined in such a way that it double, and in some cases triple, taxes the returns on saving and investment.

In the academic literature on the economics of taxation, there is a well-known saying that "people aren't taxed, activities are." The technical way of saying this is that nearly all taxes have an "excise effect." Taxes are generated by siphoning off revenues from one form or another of economic activity. Because taxation reduces the rewards or increases the costs associated with these activities, it discourages them. For example, a tax on cigarettes discourages smoking, a tariff discourages the importation of foreign-made products, a tax on gasoline discourages gasoline consumption, etc.

What is often not recognized is that the income tax also has an excise effect. It places a tax penalty on all income-generating activities — work effort, entrepreneurship, saving, and investment. These are the activities that generate economic growth, productivity and employment opportunities. The North Carolina income tax is no exception. When compared to income taxes of other states, its anti-productivity bias is particularly egregious.

Taxing work effort

This tax penalty on productive activity is most easily demonstrated when analyzing how the income tax has an impact on work effort. People pursue economically productive activities because of the income that they generate. The greater the rewards to these activities, the more likely that they will be pursued. In any particular instance, when deciding how much they are willing to work, people will weigh the satisfaction that they expect to receive from doing other things (what we will generically call leisure) against the income that they would receive from pursuing the work-related activities. These kinds of decisions are made on a regular basis. When people are deciding to work overtime, to take a second job, or to go back to school to get higher degrees or additional training, they assess the additional income that can be gained from these additional efforts and weigh it against the other activities in their lives that they will have to give up.

Income taxation distorts this value judgment in favor of leisure activities. It reduces the financial return to the work activity while leaving the inherently non-pecuniary rewards to leisure untouched. In the terminology of public finance, income taxation drives a "wedge" between the rewards to work effort and the rewards to non-work activities. The higher the tax rate, the greater the wedge, i.e. the greater the penalty against additional economic productivity, and the more distorting the tax.

Here's an illustration. Imagine an income tax system imposing one flat rate of 100 percent with no deductions (i.e., both the marginal and average rate are 100 percent). It is obvious that people, at least for public record-keeping purposes, would put no effort into income-generating activity. As the tax rate fell from 100 percent, the wedge would be reduced and the mix of leisure and work activity would shift. At a tax rate of zero, the wedge would disappear. Given people's true needs and preferences, work effort and productivity would be maximized, and the efficient mix of work and leisure would occur. This mix is guided purely by the interaction of individual preferences and the wages that employers are willing to pay (driven by the value of output produced) as compensation for services rendered.

North Carolina's income tax system enhances this tax penalty, both absolutely and relative to other states, in two different ways. Its income tax rates are high relative to the national average and are particularly high relative to other states in the Southeast with which we are economically most competitive. Not only is North Carolina's top marginal rate of 7.75 percent the highest among states in the region (see Figure 2), but our bottom rate of 6 percent is, except for South Carolina, equal to or higher than the top rate in all other Southeastern states. It should also be noted that Florida and Tennessee have no state income tax.

Adding to this anti-productivity bias is North Carolina's steeply progressive rate structure. That is, the marginal tax rate increases as incomes

Figure 2: Top Marginal State Income Tax Rates

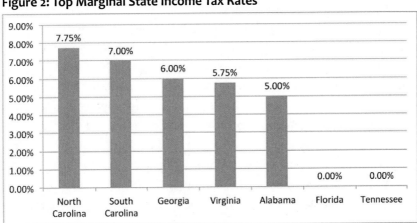

increase. A progressive rate penalizes increased productivity by taking a greater percentage of additions to people's income as they earn more. People climb the economic ladder, in terms of raises and job and career changes, by making themselves more productive. Progressive taxation punishes people for making productivity enhancing changes in their lives, adding an additional bias against economic growth and wealth creation.

Penalizing saving, investment, and entrepreneurship

The income tax penalty on savings, investment, and entrepreneurship is analogous to the penalty against work effort. It follows from the fact that the tax is biased against all income-generating activity, which, in a market economy, is the engine of economic growth and prosperity. The easiest way to see this is to first note that the broad choice facing an individual with a certain amount of after-tax income is to either spend that after-tax income or to save and invest it. Like the leisure/work choice discussed previously, the consumption/saving choice is distorted by the income tax. Under the typical income tax system, the returns to saving, such as interest, are taxed, while the rewards to consumption, which relate to personal satisfaction and are non-pecuniary, are not. The tax system, therefore, penalizes saving and investment by reducing the returns to those activities relative to consumption.

An alternative and more useful way of viewing this bias, in terms of identifying approaches to tax reform, is by showing that income taxation, using the traditional terminology, "double taxes" saving relative to consumption. (This terminology is somewhat misleading. More accurately, the tax reduces the returns to saving twice, while reducing the returns to consumption just once.) This can be demonstrated with a simple example.

Start with an individual who has $100 of pre-tax income. In the absence of taxation, this person has $100 available for either saving/investment or consumption (the purchase of goods and services). If the interest rate is a simple 10 percent per year, then the person can decide whether he prefers to spend $100 or save the $100 and have $110 available for spending a year from now. The decision will be based on his needs and desires and the needs and desires of those who depend on him.

Now assume that the individual faces a 10 percent income tax. His $100 is reduced to $90. This reduces the amount available for consumption by 10 percent and, likewise, it reduces his returns to saving by 10 percent. If the $90 is saved, his interest income is reduced to $9.00. In the absence of further taxation his choice is between spending $90 now or waiting a year and having the opportunity to spend $99. But under an income tax, the returns to saving get hit again. The $9.00 in interest gets taxed by 10 percent also. The return to saving is reduced to $8.10. The tax reduces these returns twice: first, from $10 to $9.00 when the initial $100 is taxed and second, from $9.00 to $8.10 when the interest is taxed. The return from consumption is only reduced once, from the level of satisfaction that could be obtained with $100 to the level that could be obtained with $90. The tax on interest or other returns to investment, including the taxation of dividends and capital gains, biases the decision against saving, investment, entrepreneurship, and business expansion and in favor of consumption spending.

If we apply North Carolina's top marginal rate and look at its actual impact on investment returns — including interest, dividends, and capital gains — we discover that, while reducing the rewards to current consumption by 7.75 percent, it reduces investment returns by about 15 percent. In other words, North Carolina has an implicit top marginal rate on saving and investment of almost double its statutory rate. By taxing saving and investment, North Carolina has a strong anti-productivity bias in its tax code, which stifles entrepreneurship and ultimately job creation. This anti-growth bias does not exist in states like Florida and Tennessee, which have no income tax.

North Carolina's Sales Tax [2]

North Carolina's sales tax, which applies to non-food products and no services, is the second largest revenue generator in the state's tax arsenal. It was instituted in July 1933. The story behind the tax is a familiar one. The new tax was set at 3 percent and, of course, was "temporary." It was set to expire in 1935.[3] It should come as no surprise to anyone familiar with new revenue proposals in North Carolina that the original purpose of the tax was "to help fund education" during the lean years of the Great Depression when local property and income tax revenues were down. After several extensions of this "temporary" tax, it was finally made permanent after extending the expiration date to 1939.[4] The rate stayed at 3 percent until 1991 when it was increased to 4 percent.

Then in 2001 it was raised "temporarily" to 4.5 percent. Not surprisingly, given the history of the tax, when it was about to expire in 2003 it was extended to July 2005. The 4.5 percent rate was made permanent. In 2009 the rate was raised 1.25 percent, a penny of which was not permanent and was allowed to expire in 2011. While the rate currently stands at 4.75 percent, the total tax in most counties is between 7 and 8 percent due to local-option sales taxes. The exemption for food items not eaten on the premises began in 1996 but was eliminated in July 1997. This exemption has been instituted and rescinded many times over the 70 years that the tax has been in place.

The most important problems with North Carolina's sales tax center around its base — what is and isn't subject to the tax. The "fix" for these problems, unlike the "fix" for the income tax to be addressed in the section that follows, is implicit in their identification.

North Carolina's sales tax violates the neutrality principle by excluding some categories of purchases that should be included and including categories that sound principles of taxation suggest should be excluded. In other words, the sales tax base is too narrow in some areas and too broad in others. The reason for this is that, as with the income tax, there has been little to no thought put into whether or not the tax conforms to sound, basic principles of taxation. And unfortunately this problem continues to this day.

In 2009, the General Assembly formed a Joint Finance Committee on Tax Reform (JFCTR). The directive from the legislature simply stated:

> *The President Pro Tempore of the Senate and the Speaker of the House of Representatives authorize the Finance Committees of the Senate and the House and other designated members to meet during the interim to study and recommend legislation to reform North Carolina's sales and income tax structure in order to broaden the tax base and lower the State's tax rates.*[5]

While using the term "reform," this language simply directed the JFCTR to come up with recommendations for a particular set of changes. It gave no indication that the changes should be rooted in what anyone who has rigorously thought about tax reform would recommend. The directive does not address whether such changes would be sensible in terms of making the tax system more efficient from an economic perspective or more just from an ethical perspective. In other words, it gives no reason for making those changes. The issue that policymakers and the JFCTR have focused on the most is the fact that North Carolina's sales tax is imposed only on goods and does not, at least directly, include services. And certainly that is what was meant to be the focus by the JFCTR when it was directed to come up with recommendations for broadening the base. By services I not only refer to haircuts, lawn care, house painters, etc., but also professional services such as legal, accounting, and medical. As an aside, we will see below how most of these services are taxed, to some degree, indirectly.

The reason why the focus has been on expanding the tax to services is that it tends to be seen as having significant revenue-raising potential. It is not often presented as part of an overall strategy of making the sales tax conform to the sound principles of taxation discussed above. For example, in testimony before the JFCTR, Michael Mazerov from the Washington, D.C.– based Center for Budget and Policy Priorities stated, "there is enormous revenue-raising potential in the sales taxation of services." In fact, Mazerov estimates that North Carolina could raise an additional $1.5 billion a year by extending the current sales tax to services purchased by households.[6] But from the perspective here, tax reform should not be about increasing tax revenues but about fixing the tax system so as to conform to sensible, economic growth-enhancing principles of tax policy. In this respect, extending the tax to services should be one part of a reform package, but reform that did only this would not be an improvement.

In fact, the sales tax includes one important element in its base that actually makes it too broad, the sales of goods from one business to another. That is, it taxes goods that are sold as inputs to other production processes. The problem with taxing business-to-business sales is that all of these taxes are ultimately paid by the consumers of these goods in the form of higher prices. This means that these taxes are hidden from the consumers who are actually paying them, fooling consumers into believing that the total sales tax they are paying is less than it actually is. In the process, the system hides the true cost of state government from voters. Furthermore, since consumers are paying explicit sales taxes on the full prices of the products they buy, which includes business-to-business sales taxes on products that were inputs into their production, they are paying a tax on a tax. The system is, to some extent, taxing the same purchase twice.

It is because of the business-to-business tax that we cannot say that consumer services are completely untouched by North Carolina's sales tax.

For example, the haircutting services of a barber are not directly taxed, but the clippers, combs, shampoo, barber chairs, and cash registers are when purchased by the business owner. As noted, the customer bears the cost of these taxes in the form of higher prices. This is why I noted above that services are, to some degree, taxed indirectly.

Any reform of the sales tax would have to include not only extending the tax to services but also abolishing all taxes on business-to-business sales. To proceed with the former without the latter, would extend double-taxation, which is probably the most egregious problem with North Carolina's tax system as it violates both basic principles — neutrality and transparency.

North Carolina's Corporate Income Tax

In addition to the problems discussed above with the personal income tax, North Carolina further punishes investors with a separate tax on corporate income. First, it should be pointed out that the corporate income tax does not tax corporations. A corporation is a legal and accounting entity and as such cannot pay taxes. All taxes "paid" by a corporation must ultimately come out of someone's pocket. These individuals come from one of three groups — corporate stockholders, who pay in the form of lower dividends or capital gains; the corporation's employees, who pay in the form of lower wages or fewer jobs; or customers, who pay in the form of higher prices. A mix of these three groups will always pay corporate taxes. So they add a third layer of taxation on stock dividends and capital gains from the sale of stocks. They also add additional layers of taxation on workers and reduce the purchasing power of shoppers. Corporate taxes are hidden from those who actually pay them and are a particularly dishonest form of taxation.

The hidden nature of corporate taxation also makes the taxes easy to demagogue by those who want to raise taxes while making people think that someone else — such as a "greedy" corporation — is paying. Furthermore, North Carolina's corporate income tax, at a rate of 6.9 percent, is not only the highest in the region but also the 21st highest in the nation.

In addition to these problems, politicians use it as a negative slush fund. Statutorily the rate is 6.9 percent, unless you are a politically favored business and have a niche carved out for you in the law. It is riddled with special breaks and exemptions for those who carry out their business the way the government wants them to.

Figure 3: Corporate Income Tax Rates, North Carolina and Nearby States

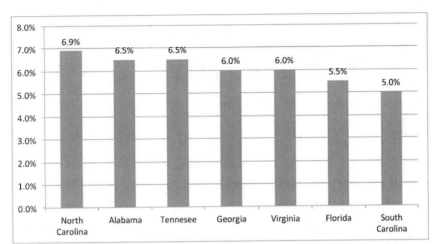

Because of all of these problems, our belief is that the there is no point in reforming the corporate income tax and that it should be repealed as part of any overall tax reform, which will be discussed below.

And the Rest

North Carolina has several other taxes, some worse than others. Together they make up 8 percent of the state's general fund revenues. These include estate taxes, franchise taxes, special excise taxes on tobacco and alcohol, and a few others. Strictly speaking none of these conform to the principles of neutrality or good government outlined above, and I will not discuss all of them here. But clearly there is one that should be singled out in terms of penalizing investment and economic growth — the estate tax.

North Carolina's estate tax, sometimes referred to as the death tax, kicks in after $3.5 million of inheritance. This mimics the federal estate tax. Above this threshold the tax is steeply progressive maxing out at 16 percent, which applies to estates above $10 million.

Estate taxes are a second, and in many cases a third, layer of taxation on the same income. Typically income is from accumulated investments and the returns on those investments, often in building a business or farm, or in property that is used to generate income. Much of this income was taxed first before it was ever invested. On top of that, the returns on the investments were taxed (see the previous discussion of the income tax) and, with the estate tax, it is taxed again when it is left to one's children or other heirs.

These accumulated tax penalties discourage entrepreneurship and economic growth.

The franchise tax, levied on capital stock or property, is levied on company owners "for the privilege of doing business in North Carolina," as the Department of Revenue website puts it.[7] Everything that was said about the corporate income tax applies to the franchise tax. It is an additional layer of taxation on investment, which, if you're counting, could be as many as four, and is completely hidden from those who actually pay it.

Finally, I want to mention excise taxes. These are basically sin taxes on sales of tobacco and alcohol. These are additions to the sales tax meant to disproportionately and negatively influence the freely made choices of North Carolina citizens. Not only are they an example of poorly conceived and inefficient tax policy, but they are inconsistent with the role of government in a free society.

What Direction for Reform?

If North Carolina could start from scratch, what would be the best possible tax system in terms of raising the revenues needed for government operations while meeting the objectives of economic neutrality and good government? In other words, how can we construct a tax system that does not disproportionately discourage work effort, saving, and economic prosperity and also makes clearer to citizens how much they are paying?

A simple, single-rate tax levied only on income used for final consumption will come closest to meeting these criteria. Above we showed how the current income tax is harming North Carolina's economy by double-taxing saving and investment, thereby discouraging entrepreneurship. With some adjustments, North Carolina's income tax base can be reformed such that it only includes income used for consumption purposes. In other words, it can be converted from an income tax to a consumption tax, while legally keeping the structure of our current tax system.

Since, with the exception of charitable giving, all income is either spent on consumption goods and services or saved and invested, we can convert the income tax into a consumption tax by subtracting net savings from the tax base. This new tax system would treat all savings and investment in the same way that IRAs and 401(k) retirement investment plans are currently treated, except that there would be no penalties for withdrawing funds before any legally specified length of time. The interesting feature of such a tax is that, in fact, it doesn't mean, as one might think, that the returns to saving go untaxed. Instead both consumption and saving are taxed equally.

This can be demonstrated by making reference to the example on page 18. What if we took out of the tax base all income used for saving, with the tax and interest rates remaining at 10 percent? If the person in the example decided to spend his $100 in pre-tax income, he would be subject to the 10 percent tax immediately and would have $90 available for consumption purposes. But if instead he decided to save the $100 for a year, he would not be taxed on it until it was taken out of savings and used for consumption. At the end of a year, if he chose to withdraw the money from savings or to cash in his investment, the original $100 and the return of $10 would be taxed at a rate of 10 percent. This would leave him with $99 for consumption purposes, or the equivalent of a full 10 percent return on $90. If you recall from the previous example, the returns to saving/investment were reduced once when the income was first taxed and before it was directed toward saving, and then those returns were taxed or reduced a second time when the interest was taxed. By taking saved income out of the tax base, both the principal and the interest are taxed, but only once when they are ultimately spent. Public-finance economists call this a "consumed income tax." It is also referred to as the Unlimited Savings Allowance, or USA, tax, which is how it will be referred to for the remainder of this chapter.

Functionally, this would be the equivalent of a perfectly constructed sales tax, i.e. a sales tax that eliminates all of the problems that are discussed above. Like the sales tax, the USA tax would also only tax income that is used for consumption purposes. The key difference is not analytical but practical. The responsibility for collecting and ultimately paying the sales tax is not with the earner of the income, the individual consumer, but with all of the separate businesses with which the consumer is doing business. And instead of it being paid all at once, it is collected piecemeal, at each individual point of sale. The sales tax unnecessarily adds a middleman to the process with all of the associated extra burdens.

This year the North Carolina General Assembly has an opportunity to take positive action and pass meaningful comprehensive and principled tax reform. Based on the analysis and ideals discussed above, the John Locke Foundation is offering two possible proposals. The centerpiece of both of these reforms is the transformation of the current state income tax — which we believe is the tax that is doing the most damage to our economic system — into the consumed income or USA tax as outlined above. We are not indifferent between these proposals and discuss them as being our "first-best" and "second-best" alternatives. On the other hand, we believe that either proposal would be a vast improvement on North Carolina's existing tax code. Furthermore, empirical analysis provided by the Beacon Hill Institute at Suffolk University in Boston demonstrates that either proposal would have a positive impact on the state's economy.[8]

Our "first-best" proposal

Ideally North Carolina would replace all of its current tax revenue with a single rate USA tax. This would eliminate the biases against saving and investment and reduce the bias against work effort found in the existing income tax. But realistically that is not likely to happen. The most important reason for this is that the North Carolina state constitution specifies that income tax rates cannot go above 10 percent.[9] For legal purposes, the USA tax would still be considered an income tax, not a consumption tax, even though in reality and for purposes of economic analysis it is clearly the latter. This means that, on a revenue-neutral basis, it would be legally impossible for all tax revenues to be replaced by just this tax since to do so would likely require a rate above the constitutional limit. This is why our "first-best" proposal would not replace all of the taxes collected by North Carolina's state government. Our focus is on eliminating those taxes that especially penalize saving, investment, and economic growth.

Given this, our "first-best" recommendation is to abolish the personal income tax, the sales tax, the corporate income tax, and the estate tax, replacing them all with a single rate USA tax. This would eliminate the most significant biases against productivity in the income tax plus the uneven taxation of purchases as represented in the current sales tax.

A few other specifics should be noted about this plan. First, in addition to direct savings and investment, we propose a tax exclusion for educational savings and expenditures. The logic is that at least some share of education spending acts as an investment in what is called "human capital." It is not current consumption, like buying a stereo or going to a Broadway show. Spending on education is expected to yield a future return, much of which will be monetary. For this reason, we provide for education savings accounts (ESAs) in which people would not only be allowed to make pre-tax contributions — as would be the case with other saving accounts — but also not be taxed on withdrawals as long as the money were spent on tuition, tutoring, or other education expenses. North Carolina already has a similar arrangement for college tuition with its 529 college savings plan.

In addition to allowing parents to deduct educational savings and spending, our plan also allows individuals to take 40 percent of their current federal personal exemptions and includes full deductibility for charitable giving. This proposal would also institute three major changes with respect to the tax treatment of home ownership sales. Households could use their USAs to accumulate pre-tax funds for making a downpayment. Interest, dividends, and capital gains would build up in savings accounts without extra layers of taxation. Then, after making a taxable withdrawal to use as a downpayment, households would never pay income tax on any capital gains from the subsequent sales of the home. This would apply to all home sales, not just primary residences, with no cap on the amount of gains that are realized. This would eliminate any double taxation on that portion of a home that acts as an investment for the home owner. What will be paid for out of after-tax income will be mortgage interest, insurance, maintenance, and other operating costs of the home. This would treat the purchase of a home like what under current tax law is called a Roth IRA. Under a Roth IRA, after-tax income is used for savings or other investment purposes while the returns on the investment are exempt from taxation. With the tax reform being proposed here, a home would be purchased with after-tax income while any investment return, the capital gains on the sale, would be tax-exempt.

What do the numbers say?

As noted, an analysis of the John Locke Foundation's consumed-income tax proposal has been conducted by a team of economists at Suffolk University's Beacon Hill Institute. They have calculated the USA tax rate that would be necessary to replace all tax revenues currently collected via the income tax, sales tax, corporate tax, and estate tax, leaving all others in place. This is what is known as a "revenue-neutral" tax rate.[10] Their study concludes that the flat rate would need to be about 9 percent (remember, the state's retail sales-tax rate in this scenario would be zero). This is a "static calculation," which means that it is not extrapolating from any expansionary effects on economic growth that the tax reform might have.

The Beacon Hill Institute has also calculated a second, dynamic revenue-neutral rate given this same tax base. The dynamic rate takes into consideration the economic growth effects that would be associated with the tax reform, which are significant. Consistent with the economic theory discussed above, Beacon Hill concludes that there will be very significant positive economic growth effects from adopting a consumed-income tax, which will in turn expand the tax base. In fact, they estimate that taking this approach to tax reform would increase North Carolina's GDP by over $11.76 billion in the first year and by almost $13 billion after four years with an immediate first year increase in employment of 80,500 jobs and an employment increase of 89,000 jobs by 2017.

If these impacts are taken into account then the revenue-neutral USA tax rate falls to 8.5 percent. We recommend that the legislature, in considering this proposal, targets the dynamic rate. To assume no growth effect of making such a transition would be unreasonably conservative and inconsistent with good economic analysis. If the legislature were to entertain a proposal closer to the 9 percent static rate then it should be written into the law that any surpluses that are generated due to the dynamic effects of tax reform should be earmarked for USA tax rate reductions.

Why Not Reform the Sales Tax?

One might question why we suggest reforming the current income tax by transforming it into a consumption tax rather than abolishing it completely and reforming the sales tax, as some are suggesting. While conceptually the sales tax could be reformed to conform to the principles outlined above, there are several problems that arise due to the fact that the tax is collected at point of sale. The USA tax automatically taxes all consumption equally by taxing it as a **category**. Consumption spending is reduced by the tax rate. This would also be the case with an "ideal" sales tax, but reaching or coming close to that ideal is much more difficult with the sales tax than it is with the USA tax. With the USA tax, the nature of individual consumer purchases are irrelevant and are less likely to come into play as part of the political process.

Because the sales tax is collected at each point of sale, it becomes more susceptible to political manipulation. It is much easier to exempt some goods or services or to differentiate rates for one industry or another based on that industry's political clout or on public sentiment. In transforming the current sales tax into an efficient and transparent consumption tax, especially in extending the tax to services, each individual industry will become a special interest group arguing that the tax should not apply to it or that it should face a reduced rate. And when one considers that many of these groups already have considerable political clout — for example, lawyers, doctors, hospitals, and bankers — the probability of having to fight a host of individual political battles seems quite high. Also, because individual venders do not collect the USA tax, administrative and logistical problems like those that are encountered when dealing with Internet purchases disappear. Purchases at brick-and-mortar retailers would automatically be treated the same as online purchases, without any action needed by Washington.

A "Second-Best" Proposal

If full-bore adoption of a USA tax proves impossible, the next-best solution would be to replace the revenue from the personal and corporate income tax and the estate tax with a USA tax while leaving the existing sales tax in place. This would remove what are clearly the three most economically damaging taxes from the current system. While the sales tax has certain problems, as discussed above, it is fundamentally a consumption-based tax and does not have the punitive effects on investment that the other taxes have. We also believe that it would not be politically practical to attempt to make the necessary changes to reform the sales tax properly while at the same time transforming the income tax into the USA consumption tax, again for reasons discussed above.

The Beacon Hill Institute has also estimated both static and dynamic revenue neutral rates for the USA tax for this proposal given that the revenue from the current sales tax remains as part of the base. They estimate that the static USA tax rate would fall to 5.78 percent, from the 9 percent required under our "first-best" proposal. Under this "second-best" scenario, the state sales tax rate would continue at its current rate of 4.75 percent.

In examining the dynamic impacts, we asked the Beacon Hill team to estimate the growth effects of a revenue-neutral tax reform package that would maintain a 6 percent USA tax rate and, instead of keeping the state sales tax rate as is, reduce it to 4.5 percent. While this too would have positive growth effects for the state, they would not be as significant as the effect found with our "first-best" proposal. Real GDP for the state is predicted to rise by about $4 billion in 2013 and by about $5.8 billion by 2017. The economic growth will produce about 10,000 jobs in 2013 and nearly 14,000 by 2017.

If the political will is not there to move forward with our first-best proposal, then we believe that this approach, with a 6 percent USA tax rate and a 4.5 percent sales tax rate, would be a reasonable alternative. We would also like to point out that all of these estimates assume no change in revenue to the state and therefore no reductions in spending. We clearly do not believe that government spending in North Carolina is optimal. Indeed, we have consistently advocated lower levels of spending. With spending cuts could come lower rates which would, in turn, further boost economic growth and, depending on the size of the cuts, increase job creation by many thousands in both of the scenarios here outlined.

Administering a North Carolina USA Tax

Under these reforms, regardless of whether the sales tax is jettisoned or kept, the process of filling out state tax returns would not change a great deal. Anyone required to pay income tax in North Carolina would start with the relevant share of adjusted gross income (AGI) from his federal tax return (which currently accounts for deposits into tax-sheltered accounts.)

From AGI, tax filers would first take their personal exemptions, which in our plan would be calculated by multiplying their federal personal exemptions by .4 (40 percent). They would then deduct charitable contributions. Finally, they would deduct all other net savings — additional income placed in savings accounts and other investment vehicles, including stocks, bonds and mutual funds, and any interest and dividends that are rolled over minus the amount taken out of any of these accounts and not reinvested (unless the withdrawals were used for educational expenses, as previously discussed).

If the federal government had a more sensible income tax system — a flat tax with an unlimited allowance for net savings — then adopting such a system in North Carolina would be simple. Instead of the current set of IRAs, 401(ks), 529 plans, ESAs, and HSAs, with their wide variety of limitations and specifications, the federal system would allow all households to put unlimited amounts into these savings vehicles using pre-tax dollars. Because the accounts are already subject to annual reporting to the Treasury

Department on the net inflow-outflow of funds (such as Forms 5498 and 1099-4), it would be easy for households and the government to compute the appropriate amount of tax deduction for net savings. For example, if you put $7,000 into your IRA for retirement and $2,000 into an ESA for your daughter's future college expenses, and took out $3,000 from your USA to use as a downpayment on a car, your net savings that year would be $6,000. North Carolina could piggy-back on the system, using the inflow-outflow reporting to compute the net-savings deduction for state income tax.

Obviously, that is not the current situation. While North Carolinians can and do exclude the pre-tax savings currently allowed under federal law for IRAs, ESAs, and other savings vehicles, a properly structured consumed-income tax wouldn't put caps on annual deposits or exclude some households from participation based on income, as current federal law requires. So in order to adopt a true consumed-income tax in North Carolina, we will have to supplement current federal tax reporting with something else.

One option would be simply to allow all those filing income tax in North Carolina to compute and report their net savings every tax year, relying on the honor system and the risk of audit to ensure that taxpayers do not abuse the system — by faking or double-counting the amount saved, for instance. While North Carolina currently enforces other state tax provisions this way, many policymakers would be understandably wary of such an approach given the significant sums and revenue implications involved.

Fortunately, there is another option. North Carolina can authorize a new savings vehicle available to all taxpayers who file income tax in the state. It would function just like the current federal IRA, except that deposits would be unlimited and withdrawals prior to retirement would be subject to tax only, not penalties. Banks, mutual-fund companies, and other financial firms would be allowed to offer these accounts — let's call them Carolina USAs — to anyone whose earnings subject them to income tax liability in the state. They would be required to send annual inflow-outflow statements to depositors as well as the state Department of Revenue.

Would these Carolina USAs have some compliance costs associated with them? Certainly, but not significantly different from the kinds of reporting requirements already associated with IRAs and the like. Moreover, the administrative costs would obviously be far lower, and more limited in scope, than those associated with broadening the scope of the retail sales tax to include entire service industries that previously had no responsibility to collect and remit state sales taxes.

The Carolina USA solution is logical and practical. Still, if there are any unforeseen and fatal flaws with the proposal, there remains one final option. Rather than treating all net savings in North Carolina as if it occured within a traditional IRA — in which you get deductions going in and pay tax on what comes out — we could treat net savings like a Roth IRA. That is, we could tax the principal of all investment going in and then exempt the return on that investment. In other words, we could change North Carolina tax law to treat interest, dividends, and capital gains as non-taxable forms of income. There are actually good reasons to prefer the Carolina USA model, both practical and political, but the point is that policymakers should not allow enforcement issues to prevent the adoption of a sensible tax policy for North Carolina.

Conclusion

North Carolina's tax structure penalizes economic growth and is a factor inhibiting our state's success in the 21st century economy. Saving, investment, and entrepreneurship, which are the engines of capital formation and economic growth, are double-taxed — and sometimes, because of the corporate income and estate taxes, they are triple-taxed.

The principles and economic analysis discussed here are a well-established part of the ongoing national discussion of the economics of taxation. And, in fact, over the years, the federal income tax code has moved, albeit slowly and in a piecemeal fashion, in the direction of applying these principles. Traditional IRAs, Roth IRAs, and 401k and 403b plans are all examples of this. So are Health Savings Accounts and college-savings plans.

At lower levels of government, some states have historically pursued a different course, levying a sales tax but no income tax, at least on wage income. In our region, both Tennessee and Florida have this model. It should be pointed out, however, that both of these states continue to penalize investment activity. They both have a corporate income tax. In addition, while Tennessee does not have an income tax on regular income, it does tax investment income from stocks and bonds. Furthermore, the sales tax in both states violates the neutrality principle by not including services in the tax base. On the other hand, both Florida and Tennessee should be commended for not including business-to-business sales in their sales tax bases.

As discussed, the principles behind the "sales tax only" approach to reform are the same as those endorsed in this chapter, tax neutrality and transparency. But, as discussed above, we believe that for North Carolina the political practicalities of moving in this direction, given our current system, would be insurmountable and end up producing a special-interest frenzy with very little accomplished in terms of real tax reform.

It is our belief, backed up by economic theory and quantitative analysis, that the proposals made here to transform North Carolina's income tax into a consumption-based USA tax, while abolishing the state's corporate and estate taxes, has the potential to generate strong incentives for businesses in the state to expand while attracting and stimulating new investment, economic growth, and job creation.

The elimination of the corporate income tax would make North Carolina one of only four states with neither a corporate income tax nor a gross receipts tax and the only state in the eastern half of the US with neither tax. This would make the state very competitive, acting as a magnet for economic expansion.

The politics of making such significant changes will not be easy to navigate. There will be special interests that benefit from the current tax code and will resist change. But for the general welfare of North Carolinians, state policymakers should resist these pressures and be willing to make some difficult but constructive choices.

Endnotes

1. Historical information provided by the N.C. Division of Revenue.
2. For a more extensive narrative of this history see presentation titled "History of State and Local Taxes in North Carolina" by Roby B. Sawyers, Ph.D., CPA, NC State University. http://bit.ly/UhBLHs.
3. Robert Murray Haig and Carl Shoup, *The Sales Tax in America*, New York: Columbia University Press, 1934, pp. 186-193.
4. Neil Jacoby, *Retail Sales Taxation*, New York: Commerce Clearing House, 1938.
5. Study of North Carolina's Sales and Income Tax Structure, Interim Joint House and Senate Finance Committees.
6. Michael Mazerov, "Sales Taxation of Services: Options and Issues," presentation to the Interim Joint House and Senate Finance Committees, North Carolina General Assembly, December 1, 2009, http://www.ncleg.net/gascripts/DocumentSites/searchDocSite.asp?nl=56&searchCriteria=mazerov.
7. NC Department of Revenue, *Franchise Tax Information*, "Who Should File," #9, "Franchise Tax Payable in Advance," http://www.dor.state.nc.us/taxes/franchise.
8. David Tuerck, Paul Bachman, and Michael Head, "A Consumed-Income Tax Proposal for North Carolina," Beacon Hill Institute, Suffolk University, December 2012.
9. North Carolina State Constitution, Article V, Section 2, Subsection 6. www.ncleg.net/Legislation/constitution/ncconstitution.pdf.
10. As noted this assumption of revenue neutrality should not be taken as an endorsement of current levels of state spending. Indeed we believe that the state budget should be significantly cut. Our proposals for budget cutting can be found in the most recent John Locke Foundation alternative budget. See Joseph Coletti, "Protecting Families and Businesses: A Plan for Fiscal Balance and Economic Growth," John Locke Foundation, Spotlight #408, February 2011, http://www.johnlocke.org/research/show/spotlights/259.

⬦⬦⬦⬦⬦⬦⬦⬦⬦⬦⬦⬦⬦⬦⬦⬦⬦⬦

Aligning State Spending With the Will of Constituents: A Taxpayer Bill of Rights for North Carolina

by Fergus Hodgson

North Carolina has produced many political leaders known for their fiscal conservatism. Both Democrat Sen. Sam Ervin and Republican Sen. Jesse Helms were frequent critics of wasteful spending in Washington, for example. More than a century earlier, native Carolinian Andrew Jackson resisted pressure from Whigs and fellow Democrats to expand the size, scope, and cost of the federal government. As president, he went beyond simply opposition and actively worked to reduce spending and taxes. "Every diminution of the public burdens arising from taxation," Jackson once remarked, "gives to individual enterprise increased power and furnishes to all the members of our happy confederacy new motives for patriotic affection and support."

As North Carolina faces daunting fiscal and economic challenges, some policymakers believe that state government is too small, and state taxes too meager, to meet the needs of the 21st century. Former JLF analyst Fergus Hodgson couldn't disagree more. In this chapter, he argues that North Carolina should set a firm cap on state spending growth to keep tax rates low and ensure that taxpayer dollars are spent only on high-priority programs.

Constitutionally limited government is at the heart of the American ideal, and explicit constraints at the state level have proved themselves popular among constituents. That is likely because they communicate constituent preferences even when elections and elected officials might fail to do so.

In the case of balanced budgets, 45 states, including North Carolina, have some form of constitutional mandate.[1] As testament to the positive incentives generated for fiscal prudence, those states with the strictest mandates faced 35 to 45 percent smaller budget gaps during the Great Recession.[2]

Support for such a constitutional provision at the federal level is also overwhelming, at between two-thirds and three-quarters of respondents in national polls.[3] In light of four straight years of trillion-dollar plus deficits, this further highlights the enormous disconnect, and need for resolution, between constituent wishes and the actions of elected officials.[4]

This chapter will examine the historical and public choice basis for a specific constitutional amendment in North Carolina. The one for consideration, a Taxpayer Bill of Rights (TABOR), would require voter approval for growth in state spending and taxation beyond inflation and population growth.

Reagan and the Genesis of TABOR

The term "taxpayer bill of rights" or "TABOR," broadly speaking, can refer to any one of a variety of tax and expenditure limits, both statutory and constitutional. In 2005, the Americans for Prosperity Foundation found 30 in existence across the states — including a statutory one in North Carolina.[5] However, such was the variation across states that AFP Foundation

Figure 1: Federal Expenditures as a Percentage of GDP

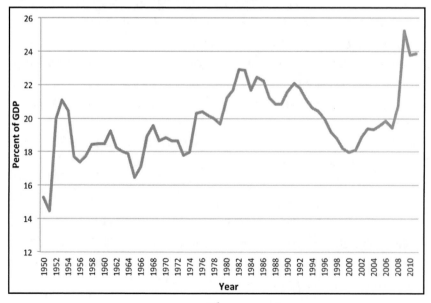

struggled to categorize them. They've not attempted a comparable ranking since.[6] These limits differ widely in what they propose to achieve and what they actually achieve. With hindsight on our side, though, this chapter offers a precise model of a TABOR for North Carolina, drawing on both the success and the shortcomings of experiences here and in other states.

The earliest relevant tax and spending limit, at least in proposal form, dates back to 1972 and the Ronald Reagan administration in California.[7] At that time, the growth of government and its instability had become apparent. So, too, had the need for a new solution. As the National Tax Limitation Committee stated, "For much of the nation's history, taxes and government spending were not a problem. As recently as the mid-1920s government at all levels taxed and spent but 10 percent of the national income, 3 percent federal, 7 percent state and local." By comparison, 2011 federal spending alone reached 26 percent of national income, and the deficit was 9 percent.[8]

Even these comparisons have a downward bias and can be misleading. In order for the measure to rise — expressed as a percentage of national income, or GDP — government spending has to grow at a faster rate than the economy. Should it stay the same in inflation-adjusted dollar terms, it would appear to fall, since it would constitute a smaller proportion of a growing economy. The North Carolina experience over the past 40 years demonstrates budget growth both in percentage and absolute-value terms, and this trend will receive attention in the next section.

Many theories exist to account for growth in the size and scope of government in the United States. One deserves particular mention, though, as we shall see when we examine how to handle fluctuations in the business cycle. In *Crisis and Leviathan: Critical Episodes in the Growth of American Government*, Robert Higgs documented that crises generate periods of vulnerability towards growth of government.[9]

Predictably, crises foster emergency measures, often measures never attempted before. Since the onset of the Great Recession in 2008, for example, federal officials have acquired unprecedented equity in at least 707 formerly private institutions.[10] Once over, however, the tendency is for government officials to retain or at least partially retain the powers or spending levels they claimed necessary to overcome the crisis. They manage to do this in part because the targeted beneficiaries form lobbies to defend their shares of the now-expanded government.[11]

Higgs describes this pattern as the "ratchet effect," and it explains why Milton Friedman's saying rings true, that there's nothing so permanent as a temporary government program.[12] It also explains why temporary federal aid, once rescinded, leads to state and local tax increases rather than the end of the revenue flow to beneficiaries.[13] In the case of North Carolina, state elected officials used one-time federal "stimulus" funds for government education, including teacher positions, in 2010 and 2011.[14] Then after that federal funding expired, state legislators increased the number of state-funded teacher positions but still faced criticism, since the total number declined.[15]

In an effort to stop this ratcheting-up of government spending in California, then-Gov. Ronald Reagan established the Governor's Tax Reduction Task Force. The task force brought many worthy intellectuals together, including the previously-mentioned public choice specialist James Buchanan and Milton Friedman of the University of Chicago.[16]

They presented their findings in December 1972, recommending a constitutional amendment to limit the growth of spending and taxation each year. Getting that into politically viable legalese, though, proved to be a challenge, so it went through 44 drafts before submission to the legislature.[17]

With this intellectual backing and refinement behind him, Reagan held great confidence in the initiative — Proposition One. "Frankly," Reagan said, "I believe our revenue limit holds the promise of assisting the legislature in its determination of spending priorities so that state government can, once and for all, reverse the trend toward higher and higher taxes and permit the people to keep a larger share of the earnings to use as they wish."[18]

Unfortunately, in the 1973 special election, California voters rejected Proposition One by a 54 to 46 percent margin.[19] In subsequent decades, those residing in the state have gotten precisely what Reagan foresaw and sought to avoid. He feared that "no" votes would convey a spending mandate to politicians — that people did not care about their tax burden.[20]

"Government must realize that it cannot indefinitely tax the people at constantly increasing levels without destroying the people's ability to support themselves and their families," Reagan said. "In the end they will wind up defenseless, at the mercy of a vast special interest-oriented government bureaucracy they unwittingly helped to create."[21]

Today, California has become one of the most highly taxed and least-free states in the union. It comes in 48th on the Tax Foundation's State Business

Tax Climate Index and 48th in the Mercatus Center's Index of Personal and Economic Freedom.[22] California has also witnessed a long-term exodus to other states with "chronic economic adversity" as the leading explanation. Since 1990, net migration has amounted to a loss of 3.4 million Californians.[23]

While the amendment failed in California, it established a TABOR example for others to replicate and build on. Proposition One included a limit on state spending to the prevailing percentage of state personal income—8.5 percent at the time. However, a two-thirds majority and a vote of constituents were sufficient for an override. Proposition One also excluded a variety of revenue streams, such as federal funds and gifts to the state.

With concern for fluctuations in the business cycle — periods of growth and periods of economic downturn — Proposition One provided for both a surplus fund, to be refunded to taxpayers, and an emergency fund, to be available should the governor declare an emergency. Foreseeing a shift of burden to local governments, Proposition One also required all property tax increases, administered at the local level, to have voter approval. At the same time, the state could not impose unfunded mandates on local governments.

The fundamentals of the ideal TABOR have not changed markedly since Proposition One, proposed nearly 40 years ago. However, the specifics do matter, and vigilance regarding compliance remains essential. As the National Tax Limitation Committee has observed, "experience has demonstrated that state governments are very creative in the ways they circumvent this discipline. [A TABOR] is not a substitute for but an addition to every other fiscal constraint in any state."[24]

Put simply, a TABOR says "here's the total amount you may spend this year; you decide how to allocate it and how to raise it"—nothing more.[25] One subsequent TABOR, Colorado's, stands head and shoulders above the others for relative success in achieving this outcome. Its implementation and continuation have not come without challenges, and these suggest the need for further refinements if other states are to adopt Colorado's example in a sustainable manner. Before we get to those, though, let us clarify why such a measure is so necessary in North Carolina.

North Carolina a Fitting Candidate

North Carolina's total state spending (from all revenue sources) has grown steadily for the past four decades, both on an inflation-adjusted,

Figure 2: State Spending Per Capita, 2012 Dollars

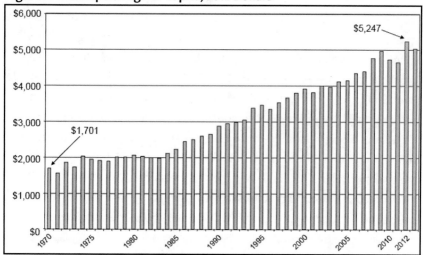

per-capita basis and as a percentage of personal income. In fact, fiscal year 2012 was a record for both metrics: $5,247 per resident and 14.4 percent of personal income. That compares to $1,701 — less than one third of the 2012 level — and 10.9 percent of personal income in 1970.

With minor variations, this trend remains the same across all of the major sectors of spending, including education, corrections, health and human services, transportation, and debt service. All have more than doubled since the mid-1970s in inflation-adjusted, per-capita terms.[26]

To compound the problem, many items such as infrastructure and executive branch activities ought to be able to benefit from economies of scale. In other words, the state can spread those expenses across a higher population. North Carolina has enjoyed a considerable immigration influx and population growth — 46 percent between 1990 and 2011, compared with 25 percent nationally.[27] Yet, this influx appears to have had little if any impact on the per-capita level of spending. State spending growth has proceeded at an even-faster pace.

For three key reasons, since the turn of the millennium, this expansion has failed to garner accurate media attention:

- The growth has occurred primarily outside of the General Fund, which many media and policy outlets confuse and refer to as simply "the state budget."[28] In 2012, the General Fund was 38 percent of total state spending, down from 59 percent in 2000.[29]

- North Carolina has become more dependent on federal funds, which have enabled the growth outside of the General Fund. In 2012, 36 percent of state revenue was from federal aid, up from 24 percent in 2000.[30]
- State officials have not accurately reported their expenses associated with future liabilities, particularly government employee pension and health care retirement benefits. These unfunded liabilities — deferred expenses — are now officially worth $37.5 billion, but more realistic accounting places them at $81.8 billion.[31]

The expanded state apparatus in North Carolina is working directly contrary to a government of limited powers and the desire of North Carolinians to retain more of their earnings. North Carolina has the highest tax burden of all neighboring states and places 44th in the nation on the Tax Foundation's State Business Tax Climate Index.[32] While other sectors of the economy have become more efficient and affordable over time, state government has gone in the opposite direction.[33]

The public has noticed. Consider the response to a poll question from the Civitas Institute in December 2009.[34] (See Figure 3) Respondents had to be eligible voters in North Carolina.[35] A total of 54 percent strongly or somewhat supported a spending cap, with just 24 percent opposed. If half of the unsure respondents were to give support as well, that would equate to an almost two-thirds majority of 65 percent — comfortably stronger than the 61 percent voter approval for North Carolina's 2012 marriage amendment.[36]

Also note that the proposed amendment did not mention exceptions or voter approval for additional increases. It proposed a straight cap on state spending, and presumably an amendment with the flexibility of voter approval could garner even higher support.

By contrast, North Carolina's present statutory TABOR, which the legislature enacted in 2001 and then replaced in 2006, might as well not exist.[37]

This legislation (§143C-4-6), perhaps the epitome of fecklessness, caps General Fund spending at 7 percent of total state personal

Figure 3

Do you support or oppose amending the state constitution to limit the growth in state spending to equal the increase in population and inflation?	
Strongly Support	28%
Somewhat Support	26%
Somewhat Oppose	9%
Strongly Oppose	15%
Not sure	22%

Figure 4: North Carolina State Spending Versus Inflation and Population Growth Limit Since 2000[41]

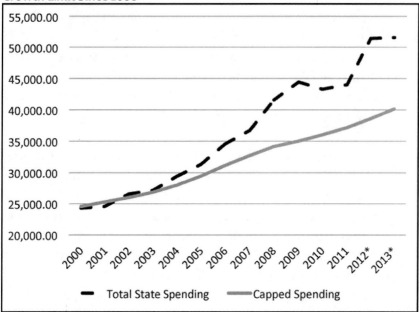

income.[38] However, the General Fund is less at 5.6 percent of state personal income.[39] The TABOR excludes everything outside the General Fund, such as capital expenditures, one-time expenditures due to natural disasters, federal mandates, and the costs of providing health insurance for state employees. The legislature can also repeal it whenever it sees fit to do so.

From 1995 through the recent 2011-2012 session, North Carolina legislators have proposed TABORs with substance, including initiatives for an amendment to the state constitution.[40] However, none has succeeded in getting to the ballot. The most recent version, despite four prime sponsors and 37 cosponsors in the N.C. House, failed to exit a Judiciary Subcommittee.[42]

This version (H.B. 188) merits attention, particularly because it includes many valuable components in line with model legislation. It ties General Fund spending to population and inflation growth, submits a constitutional amendment for voter approval, and refunds all excess revenues beyond an emergency reserve. Lawmakers can and should take this language and build on it for a new bill in 2013, along the lines discussed in the remainer of this chapter.

For example, the complexity of H.B. 188 — due to many revisions — is likely to confuse and dissuade voters. Key vulnerabilities include the limitation to the General Fund only, a lack of clarity on how to refund surplus revenues, no protection against mandates on local governments, and the authority for a two-thirds legislative override. As noted earlier, recent growth in state spending has occurred outside of the General Fund. In fact, between 2003 and 2013, inflation-adjusted per-capita spending in the General Fund went down by 5.7 percent.[43] In other words, at least over the last 10 years, a restriction on the General Fund alone would have had no effect — while during the same period total spending grew by 27.7 percent.[44]

Regardless of the vulnerabilities of the previous bill (H.B. 188), North Carolina is a prime candidate for a TABOR that can actually subject state spending growth to the will of the public. North Carolina suffers from persistent growth in state spending and the associated tax burden, constituent support is on the side of a TABOR, and numerous North Carolina legislators have already demonstrated their interest with a TABOR bill in committee from the most recent full session.

Lessons from Colorado

Before proposing precise model legislation for North Carolina, we can learn a great deal from Colorado's experience with a TABOR, which 54 percent of voters approved in 1992.[45] It has been by far the closest to ideal of any in existence in the United States — perhaps the only one with any meaningful impact — and the Americans for Prosperity Foundation gave it an A- in their 2005 ranking.[46] The AFP report rated Colorado's TABOR positively for covering all General Fund spending, its limit to population growth and inflation, its voter-approval requirement for tax increases, and its automatic refunds of surplus revenues.

Colorado TABOR Limit = (Previous Fiscal Year Spending) x
(1 + Inflation + Population Growth) + (Voter-Approved Revenue Changes)[47]

The next-best states, Florida and Missouri, also have constitutional limits and received B grades. However, Florida's limit only applies to corporate income taxes.[48] Missouri's "Hancock" amendment, which ties revenue to a percentage of state income, has proved too generous and too open to evasion, as legislators have discovered ways to exempt specific revenue streams.[49]

Colorado's TABOR remains an excellent model, but it does not include the approximately 57 percent of state spending that occurs outside of the General

Fund.[50] It has also faced political challenges that threatened its sustainability. In fact, in 2005 voters suspended it for five years and weakened the formula.[51] Further, TABOR opponents are suing the state in federal court with the claim that by limiting legislative control over fiscal measures, Colorado has violated the United States Constitution.[52] Their argument is that the TABOR imposes direct democracy and prevents a republican form of government.[53]

The court case is spurious, as the Colorado-based Independence Institute has shown.[54] However, a federal judge has allowed the case to go to trial, and it indicates the depth of opposition that the TABOR faces from those who want to expand state government without approval from constituents.[55]

So what actually happened in the decade after passage of Colorado's TABOR, prior to its weakening? Aside from the data, a couple of actions on the part of opponents have been revealing.

First, they pursued a temporary suspension of the TABOR in 2005 (Referendum C), rather than its outright repeal.[56] Perhaps, foreseeing the slim margin of victory — 52 to 48 percent — they realized that the TABOR remained popular. And even that result came after supporters of Referendum C outspent their opponents in the lead-up to the vote by almost three-to-one.[57] That explains the need for a court case, rather than a simple citizens' initiative to repeal it. Keep in mind, this is in a presidential swing state that gave its Electoral College votes to Barack Obama in both 2008 and 2012.[58]

Second, those campaigning against the TABOR resorted to misleading hyperbole and outright dishonesty.[59] The Washington, D.C.-based Center on Budget and Policy Priorities, for example, released a video in 2005 which, among other incorrect statements, claimed that the TABOR made "drastic cuts inevitable."[60] The fact is that the Colorado TABOR allows state General Fund revenue and spending to increase in line with population and inflation, and it can increase further with voter approval. Besides, as Penn Pfiffner of the Independence Institute explains, "The State's general (tax) fund rose every year except during the recession [of the early 2000s], when nearly every state in the Union retrenched. Even so, *total spending for the state government has never gone down in any year,* including during the recession."[61]

This tactic suggests that an accurate overview upholds the TABOR's effectiveness at achieving its stated objectives. "By understanding the truth," Pfiffner continues, people in other states "will note that they have nothing to fear from passing their own TABOR."

Figure 5: Pre-TABOR and TABOR Comparison[62]

	1983-1992	1993-2002
Population Growth + Inflation	40.1 percent	62.6 percent
General Fund Revenue Change	82.7 percent	61.8 percent
General Fund Spending Change	73.4 percent	75.9 percent

The positive news for Colorado, and for others considering a TABOR, is that it worked. It brought public accountability and restrained increases in the state's General Fund spending. Consider the comparison between the decade before and the decade after approval of the TABOR. Whereas in the first period, General Fund spending and taxation grew at almost twice the rate of population growth and inflation, under the TABOR period it stayed fairly consistent with the legal limit.

In six of the years between 1993 and 2005, Colorado also experienced TABOR surpluses, when revenues exceeded the constitutional limit. State legislators returned $3.3 billion of the surpluses to taxpayers via 21 different mechanisms. Current law now provides for three: a sales tax refund, an earned income tax credit, and a temporary income tax rate reduction.[63]

Beyond the policy outcomes, a simple compilation of economic data is favorable towards Colorado's TABOR years. They've been a far cry from the "formula for decline" moniker that opponents have sought to spread.[6]

Alongside the sharp rise in per-capita personal income, the tax burden fell in percentage terms. So disposable income — at least after state and local taxation — increased by nearly 43 percent, or 3 percent on an annual basis. The relative prosperity attracted a healthy stream of immigration with a measured population increase of more than 33 percent, more than twice the national average of about 16 percent over the same period.[71]

Of the five measurements, the only one to worsen was Colorado's ranking for unemployment. That was despite the rate falling by almost a full

Figure 6: Colorado's Indicators Before & After TABOR (national ranks)[65]

	1992	2005
Per Capita Personal Income[66]	$27,548 (16)	$38,795 (8)
Gross State Product[67]	$114.0 billion (23)	$217.3 billion (21)
Unemployment Rate[68]	6.0 percent (12)	5.1 percent (31)
Population[69]	3.5 million (26)	4.7 million (22)
State and Local Tax Burden[70]	9.6 percent (25)	8.5 percent (14)

percentage point. Basically, it converged over the 13 years to become equal with the national average of 5.1 percent in 2005.[72]

At this point you're probably wondering how Referendum C, which suspended the TABOR for five years and adjusted its formula, managed to achieve majority approval. The momentum for the suspension arose in the aftermath of the recession in the early 2000s. Critics highlighted what they saw as a flaw in the formula, a "ratchet-down effect" during recessionary periods, and this concern does have substance to it.[73]

Prior to Referendum C, the TABOR limit followed from the previous year's General Fund spending and reserve increase, with the adjustment for population growth and inflation. During the recession in 2002, however, revenues fell well below that permitted level.[74] Going by the prevailing formula, the following year's limit then started from and imposed a lower revenue and spending cap than the previous year's.

Voters could have approved increases at that point. However, lobbying proved sufficient to get Referendum C instead. It changed the formula to be based on the previous year's limit, rather than the previous year's spending level (which included revenue diverted to reserves). That eliminated the ratchet-down effect and made the TABOR cap rigid against both increases and decreases.[75] The formula change was not essential, but it appears to have given Colorado's TABOR a more sustainable form politically. The TABOR, now back in effect since 2011, is slightly less inclined to restrain spending and looks unlikely to do so for another two years. At the same time it is less vulnerable to the negative publicity that may come with the ratchet-down effect and the need for frequent ballot measures, particularly during sensitive crisis or recessionary periods.

Given a desire for a sustainable and realistic amendment, this refinement to the formula appears to be prudent and the key lesson from the Colorado experience. Otherwise, Colorado has provided a successful example of a TABOR — except that it still doesn't apply to non-General Fund spending. In North Carolina, most state spending is now outside the General Fund.

TABOR Mechanics and Explanation

TABORs — or "tax and expenditure limitations," as they are often called — were popular with the American Legislative Exchange Council (ALEC) right from the founding meeting in 1973, soon after Reagan's Proposition One in California.[76] ALEC is the nation's largest nonpartisan association of state legislators, and its members have modeled and refined the proposal.[77]

The model bill in the chapter appendix draws from the Colorado example and the work of ALEC and the National Tax Limitation Committee.[78] It offers a constitutional provision with the objective of accountability for constituents via a voter-approval requirement to protect against undesired growth in state spending. It includes the following key provisions:

- A *revenue and spending limit* at inflation and population growth plus whatever level receives explicit voter approval. The model legislation refers to a limit on all non-federal and unemployment insurance revenues, but so long as North Carolina maintains a constitutional rule for a balanced budget, it equates to a cap on spending as well.

  To apply the TABOR to federal funds would be to venture into uncharted waters. It would also generate legal challenges, given the limited control that state legislators may have over use of such funds. North Carolina's heavy use of federal funds means, however, that excluding this money — 36 percent of the 2012 budget — places a much less onerous requirement on the state.[79]

  Should there be a temptation to target the TABOR further and exclude additional items such as user charges or gifts to the state, the most important consideration should be for the General Fund. At no point should any part of the General Fund receive exemptions or discriminatory treatment. To do so would be a recipe for the undoing of the TABOR, since it would set the stage for some spending components to crowd out others. It would also further concentrate the challenge of complying with TABOR on fewer people.

  The formula for the TABOR cap should be equal to: (Previous Fiscal Year's TABOR Limit) x (1 + Inflation + Population Growth) + (Voter-Approved Revenue Changes). This means the first year of TABOR implementation will determine the initial base for the formula and will continue on as such until a voter-approved change occurs.

  The calculation uses the Consumer Price Index, since it is the most widely used and understood measure of inflation in the United States.[80] An alternative measure, the GDP Deflator from the Bureau of Economic Analysis, would be preferable, since it is a broader measure of the underlying value of the US Dollar. The GDP Deflator also tends to give a lower measure of inflation and would be more restrictive by about 0.4 percent each year.[81] However, a lack of understanding and familiarity may cause confusion among lawmakers and the public.

Of more importance than the distinction between those two measures, though, is that legislators avoid targeted measures of inflation such as those specific to state and local government. These confuse the value of the dollar with the prices faced within a specific sector. That is particularly problematic when state and local government policies may themselves be the causes for particular price trends, as opposed to the value of the dollar. In other words, increased state spending is likely to cause prices for those particular goods and services to rise. That does not reflect a devalued dollar but an increased government sector demand.

- *An automatic diversion of surplus funds* to the North Carolina Savings Reserve Account.[82] All revenues that the state collects beyond the TABOR limit must be unavailable for spending except under a declared emergency. This money will remain in the already-existing Savings and Reserve Account, which at present is severely underfunded at 1.6 percent of the General Fund's value.[83] Once the Savings and Reserve Account reaches 10 percent of the previous year's General Fund value, a refund to taxpayers of additional surpluses is required.

- *A Budget Stabilization Fund* that will hold revenues for automatic rebates or to fund temporary tax-rate reductions of equal value. This will only occur when revenues exceed both the TABOR limit and the 10 percent reserve fund maximum. This money is available for no other purpose, even in the case of emergencies, except with voter approval. This fund is particularly important, since it holds money purely for being returned to taxpayers and must be safe from any political gamesmanship.

- *A prohibition against unfunded mandates* on local governments. With limited revenues coming in at the state level, or at least less money permitted to be spent, state officials would be more likely to mandate programs at the local level without funding. Since the money must come from somewhere, that would simply be a transfer of the tax collection role and burden to local counties or municipalities. A transfer of the tax burden is not the goal of the legislation, so Section 7 simply requires that all state mandates come with sufficient funding.

Concluding Remarks

The growth of state spending in North Carolina has been bipartisan, reaching record levels in 2012. As state spending consumes a larger and larger share of the economy, a constitutional remedy is necessary to transfer greater authority back to the people and place North Carolina on a sustainable path.

Fortunately, a clearly defined TABOR is a proven remedy yet to be implemented in North Carolina. While federal funds complicate state efforts at accountability, within the discretion that state legislators do have, the TABOR is perhaps the most powerful tool available. It would advance North Carolina as a national leader in fiscal responsibility, stability, and accountability. Most importantly, it would better align the actions of state officials to serve the will of their constituents.

Appendix: Model Taxpayer Bill of Rights for North Carolina

Section 1. *{Election Provisions}* For any fiscal year that commences on or after____ North Carolina state must have voter approval in advance for any new tax rate increase, mill levy above that for the prior year, valuation for assessment ratio increase for a property class, or extension of an expiring tax, any markup on products sold through state-controlled enterprises, or a tax policy change directly causing a net tax revenue gain to any district. Voter approval is also required for creation of any multi-fiscal year direct or indirect district debt or other financial obligation without adequate present cash reserves pledged irrevocably and held for payments in all future years, except for refinancing district bonded debt at a lower interest rate or adding new employees to existing district pension plans. Voter approval is also required for suspension of the spending limits imposed by this Act.

Section 2. *{Definitions}*

(A) "Inflation" means the Consumer Price Index (all items) for the United States of America, or the subsequent index, as computed by the Bureau of Labor Statistics.

(B) "Population" means the number of people residing in the state, excluding armed forces stationed overseas, as determined by the United States Bureau of Census.

(C) "Fiscal year spending" means the total amount of monies appropriated by the state or local government district except:

(1) appropriations funded monies received from the federal government;

(2) appropriations funded by unemployment and disability insurance funds;

(D) "Fiscal year" means any accounting period consisting of 12 consecutive months.

(E) "Per capita expenditures" mean the quotient derived from dividing expenditures of the state for a fiscal year by its population on the first day of that fiscal year.

(F) "Emergency" means an extraordinary event or occurrence that could not have been reasonably foreseen or prevented and that requires immediate expenditure to preserve the health, safety, and general welfare of the people.

(G) "Total state revenues" means all monies derived from North Carolina's own revenue sources.

(H) "Local government district" means any local governmental jurisdiction, including cities, municipalities, counties, school districts, and special districts.

(I) "Bonds means any form of multi-fiscal year indebtedness, including non-recourse, limited tax general obligation bonds, or limited liability bonds.

(J) Voter approval means approval by a majority of eligible voters participating in an election.

Section 3. {Spending Limits}

(A) For any fiscal year that commences on or after North Carolina state spending shall grow at no more than the previous fiscal year's rate of inflation plus the percentage change in state population in the prior calendar year, adjusted for revenue changes approved by voters as required in section 1 of this Act. Population shall be determined by annual federal census estimates and such number shall be adjusted every decade to match the federal census.

(B) The maximum annual percentage change in each local government district's fiscal year spending equals inflation in the prior calendar year plus annual "local growth".

Section 4. (Revenue Limits)

(A) If the amount of total state revenue for the prior fiscal year exceeds the amount of total state revenue for the next preceding fiscal year, the maximum amount of total state revenues shall be the amount of total state revenues limit for the prior fiscal year plus the product of the applicable amount and the sum of inflation and the percentage change in state population in the prior calendar year.

(B) If the amount of total state revenues for the prior fiscal year is less than the amount of total state revenues for the next preceding fiscal year, the maximum amount of the total state revenues shall be the amount of total state revenues limit for the most recent year for which the amount of total state revenues exceeded the amount of total state revenues for the preceding fiscal year.

(C) The maximum annual percentage change in each local government district's property tax revenue equals inflation in the prior calendar year plus annual "local growth," adjusted for property tax revenue changes approved by voters.

Section 5. {Savings Reserve Account}

(A) For any state fiscal year that commences on or after _____ the state treasurer shall transfer revenues in excess of the total state revenues limit determined pursuant to section 4. of this Act, to the savings reserve account, to the extent necessary to ensure that the balance of the fund at the end of the fiscal year is an amount up to 10 percent of the total state revenue limit. The state shall is required to transfer at least one-fourth of any unreserved General Fund balance at the end of the fiscal year other than revenue in excess of the total state revenues limit to the savings reserve account.

(B) Monies in the state savings reserve account may be expended for declared emergencies only. 'Emergency' means an extraordinary event or occurrence that could not have been reasonably foreseen or prevented and that requires immediate expenditures to preserve the health, safety, and general welfare of the people. 'Emergency' does not mean a revenue shortfall or budget shortfall. Appropriation from the fund can only occur upon a two thirds vote of all elected members of each house of the Legislature concurring therein. Interest or other income earned on the emergency reserve fund shall accrue to the fund.

Section 6. {Budget Stabilization Fund}

(A) For any state fiscal year that commences on or after _____, if revenue from sources not excluded from total state revenues exceeds the limit on total state revenue calculated in accordance with section 3, for that fiscal year the excess shall be reserved or refunded as follows:

(B) The state treasurer shall first transfer the excess to the savings reserve account to the extent necessary to ensure that the balance of the fund at the end of the fiscal year is an amount no more than 10 percent of the total state revenues limit for the fiscal year as required by section 3 of this Act. The state treasurer shall not transfer any monies other than the revenues in excess of the total state revenues limit to the fund. Interest or other income earned on the budget stabilization fund shall accrue to the fund.

(C) For any state fiscal year that commences on or after ____ if the amount of the total state revenues is less than the amount of total state revenues for the prior fiscal year, the state treasurer shall have the authority to transfer money from the budget stabilization fund to the general fund in an amount equal to the difference between the amount of total state revenues for the prior fiscal year and the amount of total state revenues for the fiscal year. Under no other circumstances shall the state treasurer transfer moneys from the budget stabilization fund to the general fund.

(D) Any excess that remains after the state treasurer has made the transfers available in paragraph (B) of this section shall be reserved in the current fiscal year and refunded during the next fiscal year through temporary income or sales tax rate reductions or rebates.

(E) On or after ____ transfers of state cash fund principal from any state cash fund to the general fund, other than transfers from the emergency reserve fund or the budget stabilization fund to the general fund are prohibited. On or after ____ state cash fund appropriations that either supplant any state general fund appropriation, or that, if not made would necessitate a state general fund appropriation are prohibited. For purposes of this paragraph, a state cash fund appropriation that is funded by user charges or fees imposed on goods or services that do not exceed the cost of the goods or services provided shall not be deemed to be an appropriation that supplants any general fund appropriation.

Section 7. {*Mandated and Shifted Costs*} The state shall not impose upon any local unit of government any part of the total costs of new programs or services, or increases in existing programs or services, unless a specific appropriation is made sufficient to pay the local unit of government for that purpose. The proportion of state revenue paid to all local units of government, taken as a group, shall not be reduced below that proportion in effect at the adoption of this article. Where costs are transferred from one unit of government to another unit of government, either by law or court order, the limitation imposed by Section 3 shall be adjusted and transferred accordingly so that total costs are not increased as a result of such transfer.

Section 8. {Severability Clause} If any expenditure category, or revenue source, shall, by a court of competent jurisdiction in a final order, be adjudged exempt from this Article, the process of computing the expenditure limitation shall be adjusted accordingly and remaining provisions shall be in full force and effect.

Section 9. {Implementation} The legislature shall enact legislation that may be necessary to implement and enforce the provisions of this Article.

Section 10. {Conclusion} Whereas the said proposed amendment was adopted by three-fifths of all members elected to each House of the Legislature.

Now, therefore be it enacted by the legislature of the state (three-fifths of all members elected to each House thereof concurring therein):

The said proposed amendment is hereby concurred in and adopted, and shall forthwith become a part of the Constitution of the state.

Section 11. {Repealer Clause}

Section 12. {Effective Date}

Endnotes

1.   W. Gardner Selby, "Sen. John Cornyn says 49 states have a balanced budget amendment in their state constitutions," *Tampa Bay Times*, St. Petersburg, FL, http://www.politifact.com/texas/statements/2010/dec/25/john-cornyn/sen-john-cornyn-says-49-states-have-balanced-budge. "State Balanced Budget Provisions," National Conference of State Legislatures, http://www.ncsl.org/issues-research/budget/state-balanced-budget-requirements-provisions-and.aspx.

2.   Matthew Mitchell, "State Budget Gaps and State Budget Growth: Between a Rock and a Hard Place," Mercatus Center, August 02, 2010, http://mercatus.org/publication/state-budget-gaps-and-state-budget-growth. Note that, unless stated otherwise, spending and taxation references are for fiscal rather than calendar years.

3.   Michael Watson, "CNN Poll: Americans like Balanced Budget Amendment," Accuracy in Media, July 22, 2011, http://www.aim.org/on-target-blog/cnn-poll-americans-like-balanced-budget-amendment. Jonathan Strong, "Poll: Large majority support balanced budget amendment to Constitution," The Daily Caller, May 27, 2011, http://dailycaller.com/2011/05/27/poll-large-majority-support-balanced-budget-amendment-to-constitution.

4.   Fergus Hodgson, "Four Consecutive Years and Going Strong: Trillion Dollar Plus Deficits," *The Locker Room*, The John Locke Foundation, November 6, 2012, http://lockerroom.johnlocke.org/2012/11/06/deficits.

5.   The legislature repealed the statute (S 143-15.4) in the 2006 legislative session., http://www.ncga.state.nc.us/EnactedLegislation/Statutes/PDF/BySection/Chapter_143/GS_143-15.4.pdf. The original text can be found in this copy of the budget manual from 2001: http://www.osbm.state.nc.us/files/pdf_files/complete.pdf pp. 32, 33.

6.   Barry Poulson, "A Fiscal Discipline Report Card: Grading the States' Tax and Expenditure Limits," Americans for Prosperity Foundation, June 2005, http://www.scstatehouse.gov/archives/citizensinterestpage/SpendingCapsStudyComm/AmericansForProsperity.pdf.

7.   Barry Poulson and Lewis K. Uhler, "Tax and Expenditure Limits: From Roots to Current Realities," The National Tax Limitation Committee, Presented at the National Taxpayers Conference in Washington D.C. June 11-13, 2009. http://www.docstoc.com/docs/130952032/tax-and-expenditure-limits-roadmap-to-fiscal.

8.   Julie Ni Zhu, "Raising Taxes Won't Help," American Institute for Economic Research, September 3, 2012, https://www.aier.org/article/7815-raising-taxes-won%E2%80%99t-help. Definition for Gross Domestic Product, http://www.investopedia.com/terms/g/gdp.asp#axzz2BqVANRZB.

9.   Robert Higgs, *Crisis and Leviathan: Critical Episodes in the Growth of American Government*, Oxford University Press: New York, NY, 1987.

10. Fergus Hodgson, "Unprecedented Federal Ownership Compels State Defense," John Locke Foundation, Fiscal Insight, August 14, 2012, http://www.johnlocke.org/newsletters/research/2012-08-14-nqm5a1nvfjj82l40ttu074jtv6-fiscal-insight.html.

11. Robert Higgs, "The Economic Recovery: Washington's Big Lie," Ludwig von

Mises Institute, October 11, 2010, http://mises.org/media/6060/Governments-Response-to-the-Crisis-A-Fantastic-Success-for-Government.

12. Robert Higgs, Internet Videoconference Interview with Jeffrey Tucker, http://www.youtube.com/watch?v=67eelZustMk. Dr. Eamonn Butler, "Nothing is so permanent as a temporary government program," Adam Smith Institute, August 13, 2010, http://www.adamsmith.org/blog/tax-and-economy/nothing-is-so-permanent-as-a-temporary-government-program.

13. Russell Sobel and George R. Crowley, "Do Intergovernmental Grants Create Ratchets in State and Local Taxes?: Testing the Friedman-Sanford Hypothesis," Mercatus Research Summary, http://mercatus.org/sites/default/files/publication/Sobel_Research_Summary.pdf.

14. Terry Stoops, "Education Spending Debate Requires Context," *Carolina Journal*, August 2, 2012, http://www.carolinajournal.com/daily_journal/display.html?id=9362.

15. John W. Pope Civitas Institute, "N.C. Real Solutions," March 15, 2012, http://www.nccivitas.org/2012/n-c-real-solutions.

16. Poulson and Uhler, "Tax and Expenditure Limits," p. 2.

17. Poulson and Uhler, "Tax and Expenditure Limits," p. 3.

18. *Ibid.*

19. Ronald Reagan, "Reflections on the Failure of Proposition #1 On spending and the nature of government," National Review, December 7, 1973, http://old.nationalreview.com/flashback/reagan200406080927.asp. For results of the 1973 ballot proposal, Proposition #1, see http://ballotpedia.org/wiki/index.php/California_Proposition_1,_Tax_and_Spending_Limits_%281973%29.

20. For reports on the 1973 California Governor's race and Prop #1, see http://www.youtube.com/watch?v=_QroATlRO4k&feature=youtu.be&t=1m27s.

21. Poulson and Uhler, "Tax and Expenditure Limits," p. 3.

22. Scott Drenkard and Joseph Henchman, "2013 State Business Tax Climate," Tax Foundation, October 9, 2012, http://taxfoundation.org/article/2013-state-business-tax-climate-index. Jason Sorens and William Ruger, "Freedom in the 50 States: An index of personal and economic freedom," Mercatus Center, June 7, 2011, http://mercatus.org/freedom-50-states-2011. "California's State and Local Tax Burden, 1977-2010," Tax Foundation, October 23, 2012, http://taxfoundation.org/article/californias-state-and-local-tax-burden-1977-2010.

23. Tom Gray and Robert Scardamalia, "The Great California Exodus: A Closer Look," Manhattan Institute for Policy Research, Policy Report, No. 71, September 2012, http://www.manhattan-institute.org/html/cr_71.htm#.UKPOyfGGG01.

24. Poulson and Uhler, "Tax and Expenditure Limits," p. 5.

25. *Ibid.*

26. Fergus Hodgson, "2012 State Spending at a Record High: Albeit Concealed, State Spending Has Grown for Decades," John Locke Foundation, Spotlight Article, Raleigh, NC, May 8, 2012, http://johnlocke.org/research/show/spotlights/273.

27. NC Quick Facts, State and County Quick Facts, U.S. Census Bureau. Data derived from Population Estimates, American Community Survey, Census of Population and Housing, State and County Housing Unit Estimates, County Business Patterns, Non-employer Statistics, Economic Census, Survey of Business Owners, Building

Permits, Consolidated Federal Funds Report. Last revised September 18, 2012, http://quickfacts.census.gov/qfd/states/37000.html. Richard L. Forstall, "Population of Counties by Decennial Census: 1900 to 1990," Population Division, US Census Bureau, Washington DC. http://www.census.gov/population/cencounts/nc190090.txt.

28. The General Fund is a share of the state's budget that is all from state-derived revenues and is available for discretionary expenditure since it is neither federally controlled nor tied to a particular departmental trust. "State budget negotiations done," *The News & Observer*, Blog posting, June 28, 2012, http://projects.newsobserver.com/under_the_dome/state_budget_done#storylink=misearch. Edwin McLenaghan, "State Investments in Public Services Declining Even as Demand Grows," North Carolina Justice Center, Policy Briefing, December 2011, http://www.ncjustice.org/sites/default/files/BTC%20Brief%20-%20State%20Investments%20Declining.pdf.

29. Hodgson, "Spending at a Record High."

30. *Ibid.*

31. Fergus Hodgson, "State Unfunded Liabilities," The John Locke Foundation, Policy Report, Agenda 2012, Raleigh, NC, http://www.johnlocke.org/agenda2012/1g-stateunfundedliabilities.html. Cory Eucalitto, "State Budget Solutions' third annual State Debt Shows total state debt over $4 trillion," State Budget Solutions, August 28, 2012, http://www.statebudgetsolutions.org/publications/detail/state-budget-solutions-third-annual-state-debt-report-shows-total-state-debt-over-4-trillion.

32. Scott Drenkard and Joseph Henchman, "2013 State Business Tax Climate Index," Tax Foundation, Policy Report, October 9, 2012, http://taxfoundation.org/article/2013-state-business-tax-climate-index.

33. Bureau of Labor Statistics, http://www.bls.gov, consider personal computers and peripheral equipment as one example. Their consumer price index has fallen by more than 60 percent since 2005.

34. "December 2009 Poll Results," John W. Pope Civitas Institute, Question #26, http://www.nccivitas.org/2009/december-2009-poll-results/.

35. Confirmed via email correspondence with President of the Civitas Institute, Francis De Luca.

36. "North Carolina Same-Sex Marriage, Amendment One," Ballotpedia, http://ballotpedia.org/wiki/index.php/North_Carolina_Same-Sex_Marriage,_Amendment_1_%28May_2012%29.

37. Online records of this legislation can be found at http://www.ncga.state.nc.us/EnactedLegislation/Statutes/PDF/BySection/Chapter_143/GS_143-15.4.pdf. "Budget Manual," North Carolina Office of State Budget and Management, http://www.osbm.state.nc.us/files/pdf_files/complete.pdf.

38. Budget legislation can be seen: http://www.ncga.state.nc.us/gascripts/statutes/statutelookup.pl?statute=143C.

39. Fergus Hodgson, "One Way Street for Spending Adjustments: Reverse Logrolling Offers an Alternative," John Locke Foundation, Policy Spotlight, Raleigh, NC, June 28, 2012, http://johnlocke.org/research/show/spotlights/275. David Lenze and Matthew von Kerczek, "Bureau of Economic Analysis News Release," Bureau of

Economic Analysis, September 25, 2012, p. 4, http://bea.gov/newsreleases/regional/spi/2012/pdf/spio912.pdf.

40. Bill status for 1995-96 TABOR can be found at http://www.ncleg.net/gascripts/BillLookUp/BillLookUp.pl?Session=1995&BillID=H129&submitButton=Go.

41. North Carolina Office of State Budget and Management, "North Carolina State Budget: Post-Legislative Budget Summary 2011-2013," p. 280, http://www.osbm.state.nc.us/files/pdf_files/2011PLS_rev.pdf. North Carolina Office of State Budget and Management, "Population Estimates and Projections," http://www.osbm.state.nc.us/ncosbm/facts_and_figures/socioeconomic_data/population_estimates.shtm.

42. Bill status for the 2011-12 TABOR can be found: http://www.ncleg.net/gascripts/billlookup/billlookup.pl?Session=2011&BillID=H188.

43. Fergus Hodgson, "North Carolina Fast Facts (FY 2012-2013)," John Locke Foundation.

44. Ibid.

45. "Article X, Colorado Constitution," Section 20: "The Taxpayer's Bill of Rights," BallotPedia, http://ballotpedia.org/wiki/index.php/Article_X,_Colorado_Constitution#Section_20.

46. Poulson, "Fiscal Report Card," p. 8.

47. "State Spending Limitations: TABOR and Referendum C," Colorado Legislative Council Staff, Memorandum to Long-Term Fiscal Stability Commission, July 6, 2009, p. 2. http://www.colorado.gov/cs/Satellite?blobcol=urldata&blobheader=application%2Fpdf&blobkey=id&blobtable=MungoBlobs&blobwhere=1251601829837&ssbinary=true.

48. "States with a Supermajority Requirement to Raise Taxes," Americans for Tax Reform, http://www.fiscalaccountability.org/index.php?content=supersub1.

49. Dean Stansel, "Missouri's Hancock II Amendment: The Case for Real Reform," Cato Institute, Briefing Paper No. 20, October 17, 1994, http://www.cato.org/pubs/briefs/bp-020.html.

50. "State Spending Limitations: TABOR and Referendum C," Colorado Legislative Council Staff, Memorandum to Long-Term Fiscal Stability Commission, July 6, 2009, p. 4, http://www.colorado.gov/cs/Satellite?blobcol=urldata&blobheader=application%2Fpdf&blobkey=id&blobtable=MungoBlobs&blobwhere=1251601829837&ssbinary=true.

51. Colorado State Spending Act, Referendum C (2005)," BallotPedia, http://ballotpedia.org/wiki/index.php/Colorado_Referendum_C_(2005).

52. Eli Stokols, "Judge gives green light to TABOR lawsuit," FOX 31 Denver, posted July 30, 2012, http://kdvr.com/2012/07/30/judge-gives-green-light-to-tabor-lawsuit/.

53. Tim Hoover, "Federal judge allows legal challenge to Colorado's TABOR to go forward," The Denver Post, July 30, 2012, http://www.denverpost.com/breakingnews/ci_21191886/federal-judge-allows-legal-challenge-tabor-go-forward.

54. Robert G. Natelson, "New II Issue Paper Rebuts Myth that Citizen Review of Laws and Taxes Violates the Republican Form," Independent Institute, October 26, 2012, http://constitution.i2i.org/2012/10/26/new-ii-issue-paper-rebuts-myth-that-citizen-review-of-laws-and-taxes-violates-the-republican-form/. About the Independence Institute," Independent Institute, http://www.i2i.org/about.php.

55. Matt Arnold, "Federal judge allows frivolous Colorado anti-TABOR lawsuit to go to trial," Examiner.com, http://www.examiner.com/article/federal-judge-allows-frivolous-colorado-anti-tabor-lawsuit-to-go-to-trial.

56. "Colorado State Spending Act, Referendum C (2005)," BallotPedia, http://ballotpedia.org/wiki/index.php/Colorado_State_Spending_Act,_Referendum_C_(2005).

57. "Referendum C: Suspension Of Sate Spending Cap," National Institute on Money in State Politics, http://www.followthemoney.org/database/StateGlance/ballot.phtml?si=20056&m=272.

58. 270 to Win, Colorado, http://www.270towin.com/states/Colorado. Timothy Stenovec, "Colorado Election Results 2012 MAP: Presidential and House Winners (Real-Time Map)," The Huffington Post, posted November 11, 2012, retrieved November 19, 2012 http://www.huffingtonpost.com/2012/11/06/colorado-election-results-2012-map_n_2047614.html.

59. This video from the Center of Budget and Policy Priorities is particularly revealing. "Video: The Real Story Behind TABOR," Center on Budget and Policy Priorities, March 2, 2006, http://www.cbpp.org/cms/index.cfm?fa=view&id=2482.

60. Penn Pfiffner, "TABOR Benefits Colorado's Citizens: A response to misleading video," Fiscal Policy Center, p. 1, http://www.i2i.org/articles/taborpfiffner.pdf.

61. *Ibid.*

62. Fred Holden, "A Decade of TABOR: Ten Years After: Analysis of the Taxpayer's Bill of Rights," Independent Institute, Issue Paper Number 8-2003, June 2003, p. 7, http://www.i2i.org/articles/tabor2003.PDF.

63. Kate Watkins, "TABOR Refund Mechanisms," Colorado Legislative Council Staff, Issue Brief Number 10-16, October 22, 2010, http://www.colorado.gov/cs/Satellite?blobcol=urldata&blobheader=application/pdf&blobkey=id&blobtable=MungoBlobs&blobwhere=1251665701857&ssbinary=true.

64. Iris J. Lav and Erica Williams, "A Formula for Decline: Lessons from Colorado for States Considering TABOR," Center on Budget and Policy Priorities, March 15, 2010, http://www.cbpp.org/cms/?fa=view&id=753.

65. One or a lower ranking is the most desirable: higher income, lower unemployment, higher Gross State Output, higher population, lower tax burden.

66. "Per Capita Personal Income by State," Bureau of Business & Economic Research, University of New Mexico, October 12, 2012, http://bber.unm.edu/econ/us-pci.htm. The 1992 dollar value is adjusted for inflation with the GDP deflator, so both are in $USD 2005. ($21,102/76.602)*100 = $27,548. 21 National Data, GDP & Personal Income, U.S. Department of Commerce, Bureau of Economic Analysis, n.d., http://bea.gov/iTable/index_nipa.cfm.

67. Regional Data, GDP & Personal Income, U.S. Department of Commerce, Bureau of Economic Analysis, n.d., http://bea.gov/iTable/index_regional.cfm.

68. "U.S. Unemployment Rates by State," Infoplease, http://www.infoplease.com/ipa/A0931330.html. Again, the 1992 dollar value is corrected to take inflation into account. Both are in $USD 2005 terms. (87,302/76.602)*100 = $113,968 million.

69. "Vintage 2005: National Tables," United States Census Bureau, July 1, 2005, https://www.census.gov/popest/data/historical/2000s/vintage_2005/index.html.

"Time Series of Intercensal State Population Estimates: April 1, 1990 to April 1, 2000," Population Division, United States Census Bureau, April 11, 2002, https://www. census.gov/popest/data/intercensal/st-co/files/CO-EST2001-12-00.pdf.

70. "Colorado's State and Local Tax Burden, 1977-2010," Tax Foundation, October 23, 2012, http://taxfoundation.org/article/colorados-state-and-local-tax-burden-1977-2010.

71. Census Bureau, "Population Estimates."

72. "Labor Force Statistics from the Current Population Survey," Bureau of Labor Statistics, http://data.bls.gov/timeseries/LNS14000000.

73. "State Spending Limitations: TABOR and Referendum C," Colorado Legislative Council Staff, Memorandum to Long-Term Fiscal Stability Commission, July 6, 2009, http://www.colorado.gov/cs/Satellite?blobcol=urldata&blobheader=application%2Fp df&blobkey=id&blobtable=MungoBlobs&blobwhere=1251601829837&ssbinary=true.

74. *Ibid*, p 3.

75. Colorado's Post-Referendum C TABOR Limit = (Previous Fiscal Year's TABOR Limit) x (1 + Inflation + Population Growth) + (Voter-Approved Revenue Changes).

76. Poulson and Uhler, "Tax and Expenditure Limits," p. 6.

77. American Legislative Exchange Council, "Membership," http://www.alec.org/membership/. Adam Wise of the Center for State Fiscal Reform confirmed, via email correspondence, ALEC's relationship with tax and expenditure limitations.

78. For more on the National Tax and Limitation Committee, see http://limittaxes.org/about/our-history/.

79. Hodgson, "Spending at a Record High."

80. Definition for "Consumer Price Index," http://www.investopedia.com/terms/c/consumerpriceindex.asp#axzz2Cg5hCz41.

81. A 1990 to 2010 comparison between the Consumer Price Index and the GDP Deflator reveals average annual rates of inflation of 2.2 and 2.6 percent. In other words, according to the CPI, prices rose by 67.2 percent during the two decades, while according to the GDP Deflator they rose by 53.6 percent. See the Bureau of Economic Analysis and Bureau of Labor Statistics websites for this data, http://bea.gov/itable/, http://www.bls.gov/data/.

82. North Carolina Savings Reserve Account Created in 1991, Fiscal Brief, North Carolina General Assembly Fiscal Research Division, http://www.ncleg.net/fiscalresearch/Fiscal_Briefs/Fiscal_Briefs_PDFs/Savings_Reserve_Issue_Brief_2012.pdf.

83. Hodgson, "One Way Street."

Chapter Three

◇◇◇◇◇◇◇◇◇◇◇◇◇◇◇◇◇◇◇◇

Parental School Choice:
A 'nuts and bolts' guide to choice in North Carolina

by Terry Stoops

In 1955, economist Milton Friedman published an article, "The Role of Government in Education," that many cite as the intellectual origin of the school-choice movement. Friedman argued that while taxpayers might have a financial responsibility to ensure that all children have the means to obtain education, government ought not to be a monopoly or near-monopoly provider of educational services. In subsequent decades, intellectuals, activists, and politicians of diverse views on other issues came together in a reform movement that achieved significant successes in many jurisdictions, including parental choice within public school districts, charter schools, and an array of tax breaks and scholarships assisting families who choose private schools.

One of the strongest advocates of school choice on the national scene today is Gastonia native Thomas Sowell, an economist and author at Stanford University's Hoover Institution. Drawing on his own experiences growing up poor, first in North Carolina and later in Harlem, Sowell has argued that true educational opportunity for disadvantaged students requires greater choice for parents and greater competition among providers. "The education establishment knows that any such reforms have to be headed off at the pass," Sowell once observed, "because once the public has a choice — and especially after it exercises that choice and sees the benefits to the children — there will be no stopping the demand for fundamental changes in the way our public schools function." In this chapter, JLF Research Director Terry Stoops offers policymakers a roadmap for advancing choice and competition in our state.

Few North Carolinians realize that the state has extensive educational options for preschoolers and college students but little for children in the "middle" — the 1.5 million students in district-run public schools. How large is our system of "bookend" school choice? In North Carolina, well over $1 billion in state and federal funding goes to private preschools, childcare facilities, and institutions of higher education every year.

North Carolina's pre-kindergarten and child-care programs are massive state-funded voucher programs. Of the 24,500 children participating in the NC Pre-K (formerly More at Four) program, about one-third choose to attend a private pre-kindergarten facility. Even more impressive is that the state's $400 million subsidized childcare program provides funding for 85,000 children in over 8,000 private facilities and homes.[1]

Last year, the North Carolina General Assembly approved legislation that created a $6,000 per year tax credit for families of special-needs children who receive educational services in a private K-12 school or facility.[2] Even before passage of that bill, however, North Carolina law permitted public school districts to contract with private special education facilities or providers if the district could not provide the necessary services to the child.[3]

In addition, the North Carolina tax code provides parents with deductions for contributions to qualified college tuition savings plans (also called 529 plans) and tax credits for child-care expenses. The combined tax value of the deduction and credit was approximately $56.4 million last year.[4]

The federal and state governments also direct hundreds of millions of dollars to private college and university students in North Carolina. Approximately 38,000 private college and university students received a combined $159 million in federal Pell grants last year. The federal government also distributed $832 million in direct loans to 124,000 North Carolinians enrolled in private institutions of higher education. This year, the state legislature set aside $86 million for grants to low- and middle-income students who choose to attend a private college or university in the state.[5]

Regrettably, children in the "middle" enjoy considerably fewer educational options than their preschool and college counterparts.

Currently, about 50,000 children attend charter schools in North Carolina. Taxpayers spent over $366 million in state, local, and federal funds last year to fund their operations. Even after the approval of 32 new charters last year, however, only a little over half of NC counties will have a charter school at

TYPES OF SCHOOL CHOICE

Tax-Credit Scholarships

Tax-credit scholarships allow individuals and/or corporations to redirect a portion of their state tax payments to a non-profit organization that provides private-school scholarships.

Individual Tax Credits and Deductions

This allows parents to receive a credit or deduction on state income taxes when they pay for approved educational expenses.

Education Savings Account

An education savings account is a tax-free vehicle in which parents can save money to spend on approved educational expenses, such as tuition, textbooks, and tutoring, and into which governments can also deposit tax dollars for these uses.

Vouchers or Scholarships

"Universal" – for all children
"Means-Tested" – for low-income children
"Low-Performing Schools" – for children enrolled in persistently low-performing schools
"Special Needs" – for students who have serious physical, emotional, or mental disabilities

Charter Schools

Charter schools are public schools that are exempt from certain state and local regulations and are governed by a non-profit board of directors rather than an elected school district.

Homeschools

Although state regulations vary, homeschooling allows parents to use a curriculum of their choice to teach their children at home.

Online Schools

Virtual, online, or e-schooling is a type of instruction that allows qualified instructors to deliver lectures, content, and assessments using Internet-based communication tools.

Open Enrollment

Usually limited to public school districts, open enrollment allows parents to place their children in any grade-appropriate public school in the district.

the start of the 2013-2014 school year. Despite the recent removal of the charter school cap, state regulations and the courts continue to impede the replication and implementation of successful charter school models.[6]

During the 2011-12 school year, North Carolina had nearly 80,000 children enrolled in 48,000 home schools and 96,000 children enrolled in non-public schools. Unfortunately, North Carolina does not provide home and private school families options for support.[7] Superb non-public schools have suffered enrollment declines and fiscal woes since the start of the Great Recession.[8]

In sum, taxpayer support for private preschools, childcare facilities, and institutions of higher education has not "privatized" these markets. Rather, it has yielded better results than would have come from government monopoly. It is time for the traditional K-12 system to follow suit by expanding publicly funded educational options for families. We must also commit to making improvements to state laws and regulations that govern charter schools.

School Choice Research and Law in North Carolina

It would be easy to advocate school choice based solely on the belief that competition, freedom of choice, and decentralization are essential elements of any effective and efficient social and economic institution. But it is also important to make the case for school choice based on rigorous research and empirical evidence. Fortunately, North Carolina has been home to choice programs that have attracted the attention of researchers for over a decade. The studies discussed in Appendix A suggest that properly designed and implemented school choice programs will improve academic and social outcomes for participating students.

With regard to the constitutionality of school choice in our state, two legal scholars have examined the issue closely. In a 2006 report published by the North Carolina Education Alliance, Institute for Justice attorney David Roland concluded that school choice is consistent with the Constitution of North Carolina.[9] A subsequent study by Jeanette Doran of the N.C. Institute for Constitutional law agreed with Roland's conclusion.[10] Additional information on the constitutionality of school choice is included in Appendix B.

School Choice Design

The parameters and scope of any school choice program depend on several factors. For most, political and legislative processes come to mind immediately. Equally important, however, are state and federal tax laws and the operation of the public school funding system in the state. In addition, existing laws, regulations, and policies may derail a school choice program, regardless of the quality of the program's design or magnitude of popular support. Simply put, there is no universal blueprint for school choice, or education reform generally, that is immune to criticism or void of the short-term and long-term problems that inevitably plague government created and operated ventures.

School choice expert Herbert Walberg points out that every school choice plan answers four fundamental design questions:

- Should all parents, or only low-income parents, be entitled to receive vouchers? This is a question of *eligibility and scope*.
- Should the plan be implemented all at once or phased in over several years? This question concerns *timing*.
- How should the value of the voucher be set, and should it be the same regardless of the tuition charged by the participating school? This question addresses *finance*.
- What restrictions, if any, should be imposed on participating schools regarding enrollment, curricula, facilities, and other policies? *Regulation and accountability* are the concerns here.[11]

Walberg's useful framework will guide the discussion of school choice options below.

Tax-Credit Scholarships

Currently, eight states operate 10 programs that allow individuals and/or corporations to receive a tax credit for donations to scholarship granting organizations. SGOs are state-approved and state-supervised nonprofits that distribute private school scholarship funds to eligible students.

Fiscal impact studies show that, over time, properly designed tax-credit scholarship programs may save states money. Brian Gottlob of the Friedman Foundation for Educational Choice found that Oklahoma's tax credit scholarship could produce a net gain of resources available in public schools equal to $2,136 per public-school student using a scholarship.[12] Subsequent analyses of tax-credit proposals in other states yielded even more impressive results. In Nebraska, savings could rise to $7,765 per public-school student using a scholarship. A proposed tax credit in Maryland could save taxpayers more than $133 million over 10 years. In Indiana, the state would realize between $300,000 and $4.7 million worth of savings in the first year and up to $8.8 million in the second year. Friedman Foundation assessments of proposed and enacted Tax Credit Scholarships in states such as New Mexico, Kentucky, Idaho, Montana, New Hampshire, Georgia, and Indiana also conclude that there is the potential for substantial savings for states.[13]

Other researchers agreed that tax-credit scholarship programs are economically beneficial. According to a study conducted by the Florida Office of Program Policy Analysis and Government Accountability, the state saved $1.49 for every $1 in revenue lost to the tax credit.[14] Utah State University researchers concluded that a proposed $2,000 tax credit scholarship program in Utah could generate savings to the state of between $754.7 million and $1.18 billion over a 13-year period, provided that parental demand remained strong. Average annual savings for a $2,000 tuition tax credit would be between $53.9 and $84.4 million. A $1,000 tax credit would produce yearly savings of $38.5 to $57.9 million.[15]

In addition to financial savings, there is evidence that tax-credit scholarship programs raise student achievement. For example, an August 2011 study by David Figlio found that low-income students who received a Florida tax-credit scholarship performed at or above the level of the national average for *all* students.[16]

Existing programs

No two states operate their tax-credit scholarship programs in the same way. Arizona operates a three-part tax credit scholarship program. The Personal Tax Credits for School Tuition Organizations permits individual taxpayers to take a dollar-for-dollar tax credit of up to $500 for donations to School Tuition Organizations, or STOs. Married taxpayers filing jointly are entitled to a credit of $1,000 for their donations. Taxpayers may also claim a $200 credit for donating to an extracurricular or character education program in a public school. The state caps the value of a scholarship that an STO may award and the organization establishes its own eligibility criteria.[17]

Arizona's Corporate Tax Credits for School Tuition Organizations allows corporations to receive a dollar-for-dollar tax credit on their corporate income tax liability for donations to an STO. Similar to the individual tax credit program, the state caps the value of the scholarship. Only $10 million in tax credit may be claimed each year. STOs may participate in the individual and corporate tax credit programs but are required to award corporate tax credit scholarships to low-income students who are entering kindergarten or who were previously enrolled in a public school.[18]

Lexie's Law is a corporate tax credit program that provides scholarships to special-needs and foster-care children in Arizona. Special-needs students are required to have a documented disability, and must have been enrolled in a public school for a year prior. The foster-care children eligibile for the program do not have the same enrollment requirement.[19]

Florida's tax-credit scholarship program allows businesses to take a dollar-for-dollar corporate income and insurance premium tax credit on donations to a Scholarship Funding Organization, or SFO. The scholarships are means-tested and require the student to have been enrolled in a public school. The state capped the program at $140 million and a single SFO operates the program. Increases in the cap may be triggered by a participation benchmark, namely 90 percent of tax credit claimed in a given year.[20]

Georgia operates both individual and corporate tax credit scholarship programs. Individual taxpayers may claim a dollar-for-dollar credit of $1,000 and married couples filing jointly may claim a $2,500 credit for donations to a Student Scholarship Organization, or SSO. Corporations may claim a tax credit equal to 75 percent of their corporate income tax liability. Corporate tax credits are capped at $50 million. The cap is adjusted for inflation until 2018. Caps on individual scholarships equal the statewide average per-pupil expenditure (local and state funds only) for the school year. SSOs establish eligibility criteria.[21]

Indiana has an individual and corporate tax credit scholarship program for low-income students. Individuals and corporations may receive a tax credit for 50 percent of their donations to a Scholarship Granting Organization or SGO. The statewide cap on tax credits is $5 million. Students must meet residency, income, and enrollment guidelines to qualify.[22]

In Iowa, individual taxpayers may receive an income tax credit worth 65 percent of their donation to a School Tuition Organization (STO). The statewide cap on tax credits is currently $8.75 million. Up to 25 percent of the statewide cap may be used to provide businesses a corporate income tax credit for donations to an STO. Only low-income students are eligible to receive a tax credit scholarship in that state.[23]

New Hampshire has the nation's newest tax-credit scholarship program. Businesses in New Hampshire may receive a business profits tax credit and/ or the business enterprise tax credit for 85 percent of their donations to a scholarship organization. For the first year, the statewide cap on tax credits is $3.4 million. In the second year, the cap increases to $5.1 million. All public school students are eligible, but the scholarship organization must award at least 40 percent of its funds to low-income students. Low-income private and homeschool students may also receive a scholarship.[24]

In 2012, Oklahoma launched the Oklahoma Equal Opportunity Education Scholarship Act for individual and corporate donations to Scholarship Granting Organizations or SGOs. The $3.5 million private school scholarship program will allow low-income students to receive scholarships ranging from $5,000 for the typical student to up to $25,000 for a special-needs student. Individuals may receive a tax credit for 50 percent of their donations to an SGO. The credit is capped at $1,000 for individuals, $2,500 for married couples filing jointly, and $100,000 for corporations. A $1.5 million tax credit program is available for individuals and corporations who donate to SGOs that distribute "educational improvement grants" to public schools.[25]

Pennsylvania's Educational Improvement Tax Credit Program is the largest tax-credit scholarship program in the nation. Corporations may direct between 75 and 90 percent of their corporate income tax liability to one of two places, either a Scholarship Organization (SO) or an Educational Improvement Organization (EIO). An SO is a private school scholarship granting organization. An EIO provides grants to traditional public schools. The maximum tax credit for each business is $300,000, and the program cap is just under $44 million. Household income and the number of dependents in the household determine student eligibility.[26]

Rhode Island's tax-credit scholarship program provides corporate income tax credits to businesses operating in the state that donate to a Scholarship Organization, or SO. Tax credits range from 75 to 90 percent of the corporation's tax liability, depending on past participation and value of the donation. The state maintains a cap of $100,000 per corporation and $1 million in credits statewide. Only low-income students are eligible to receive a scholarship.[27]

The regulation conundrum

Of the 10 tax-credit scholarship programs in operation (New Hampshire excepted),

- Seven limit scholarships to low-income students,
- Eight have a cap on scholarship amount,
- Three have testing mandates,
- Five allow the taxpayer or corporation to claim 100 percent of their donation,
- Five cap the amount that may be claimed by an individual or corporation, and
- Six have an absolute cap on the total dollar amount that may be claimed each year.

Of the 10 tax-credit scholarship programs highlighted above, Arizona's Personal Tax Credits for School Tuition Organizations is the least regulated. Nevertheless, it is not the largest tax-credit scholarship program in the nation. Nearly 26,500 students received scholarships from Arizona's program in 2010. During the same year, nearly 29,000 students received scholarships from the tightly regulated Florida Tax Credit Scholarship Program. Another program with strong regulations, Pennsylvania's Educational Improvement Tax Credit Program, awarded scholarships to over 38,600 students in 2010. Florida's average scholarship was approximately double the average scholarship amount awarded in Arizona, despite the fact that Arizona had a four-year head start on Florida. Pennsylvania's was the least of the three.

The point is that there is no apparent relationship between the amount of regulation imposed on a tax-credit scholarship program and the size and/ or growth of that program. Obviously, this should not be construed as an invitation to impose regulation *ad infinitum*. But it does suggest that a certain baseline amount of regulation and accountability does not inhibit long-term growth. The question is how much and what kinds of regulatory and accountability measures states should impose on these programs.

State regulation of school choice programs has been debated in the school choice movement for decades. Although more than two perspectives exist, there are two main opposing viewpoints on the issue of how much regulation of tax-credit scholarship programs is appropriate.

Some argue that parents and taxpayers are necessary and sufficient barriers to the misuse of educational funds. This is particularly true with tax-credit scholarship programs, according to Adam Schaeffer of the Cato Institute. Schaeffer argues that layers of government oversight are unnecessary because three layers of accountability are already built into the system. First, parents choose whether their children will attend a given school. Second, the scholarship-granting organization oversees the distribution of funds to parents. Third, taxpayers who donate to a tax-credit program want to ensure that the funds they donate are spent in the most productive way. Unlike traditional vouchers, tax credit funds are private funds, distributed through independent nonprofits. Thus, taxpayers have an incentive to make wise decisions when they donate to a scholarship-granting organization.[28]

Others contend that parents and taxpayers are necessary but not sufficient to ensure accountability. John Kirtley, one of the creators of Florida's tax-credit scholarship program, argues that a well-designed program requires five core components:

- Financial means-testing to focus the resources of the program on students who most need it and can least afford it;
- Portability that will enable parents — not individual schools or scholarship organizations — to own the decisions of where their children attend school;[29]
- Academic accountability that requires scholarship students to be tested, with either the state test or a national norm-referenced test. Further, scores must be reported to an independent research entity that will publish the overall learning gains of the students;[30]
- Fiscal accountability and transparency for scholarship organizations;
- Fiscal accountability for schools that receive scholarship students, such as submitting to the scholarship organization a review by a third-party CPA showing the money was used properly.

Kirtley concludes, "But if the movement hopes to spread choice to a large number of states, a *laissez faire* approach will fail."[31]

At issue are six core areas: student eligibility, funding source, value of the tax credit, testing, requirements for scholarship-granting organizations, and fiscal accountability for participating schools.

Means-tested, universal, or mixed eligibility?

As mentioned above, seven of the 10 tax-credit scholarship programs in operation have income-eligibility guidelines. Arizona (corporate only), Florida,

Indiana, and Oklahoma use eligibility for the federal Free and Reduced-Price Lunch Program as the standard. Iowa and Rhode Island use the federal poverty level. Pennsylvania has guidelines based on household-income range and the number of dependent family members. All three methods are valid ways of determining income eligibility.[32]

But would a means-tested tax-credit scholarship exclude students who need help but do not meet the guidelines? Schaeffer points out that middle-income students who require additional educational services would not be eligible for a scholarship if the program maintained strict income guidelines. Likewise, a child would be ineligible for a means-tested scholarship if the household lost a source of income after filing the previous year's tax return. For these reasons, Schaeffer recommends that states with means-tested scholarships create a carve-out for families who exceed the income cutoff. A tax-credit scholarship approved in New Hampshire in 2012 will allow a scholarship granting organization to use up to 20 percent of its funds for children who do not meet income requirements.[33]

Individual or corporate income tax credit?

Most school choice advocates believe that states should create both individual and corporate tax-credit scholarship programs. Of the two, individual tax credit programs are favored by most advocates because individual income taxes are generally a broader, more stable source of revenue than corporate income taxes. Corporate tax liability is often unpredictable and donations are often too few to guarantee a consistent level of funding for scholarship-granting organizations year after year. (More importantly, the tax plan presented elsewhere in this book would eliminate the corporate income tax.) For students who rely on scholarships for multiple years of schooling, stability is critical.

Taxpayers who have a tax liability and a child that meets eligibility requirements should not be required to donate and apply to a scholarship granting organization in order to receive a scholarship or financial assistance. As described later in this chapter, parents, family members, and others willing to spend their money to assist a qualified child should be able to claim a tax deduction or credit on qualified out-of-pocket educational expenditures for an eligible beneficiary.

Income, sales, or property tax?

Not all states collect individual and corporate income taxes. For example, Alaska, Florida, Nevada, South Dakota, Texas, Washington, and Wyoming do not have state income taxes. Tennessee and New Hampshire tax dividend and interest income only. Thus, Florida, for example, relies on insurance premium tax revenue to fund its tax-credit scholarship program.

Could a tax-credit scholarship program exist in the absence of individual and corporate income taxes? It is possible but has yet to be attempted. One option is to allow individuals to claim a credit on sales taxes for donations to scholarship organizations. This would be achieved by allowing taxpayers to deduct sales taxes paid to their state governments on their federal income tax returns. Another option is to create a system whereby an individual tax credit could be collected at the point of sale.

Adam Schaeffer believes that tax credits based on a portion of property taxes paid could be made available for those who donate to SGOs. Schaeffer admits that his model for claiming a credit on property taxes imposes an additional burden on local governments and may not be constitutional for states that have "uniformity" clauses in their state constitutions.

North Carolina is one such state. Article V, Section 2 of the North Carolina Constitution states, "No class of property shall be taxed except by uniform rule, and every classification shall be made by general law uniformly applicable in every county, city and town, and other unit of local government."[34] Courts in states like Pennsylvania have ruled that a uniformity clause in the state constitution prohibits municipalities from allowing certain citizens to take a tax credit on property taxes paid. In North Carolina, a tax-credit system based on property taxes may encounter a similar challenge.[35]

Proposals for a property tax credit program reveal the complexities involved. For example, a taxpayer would be allowed to take a credit on property taxes but not from property taxes levied for bonded indebtedness or payments pursuant to lease-purchase agreements for capital construction. This would limit the tax credit available to those who live in counties that have significant capital debt for county facilities and/or public schools.

Additionally, the student would be required to be a resident of the school district in which the person is claiming the credit. Residency requirements would have to consider families that have children in custody arrangements that span multiple districts. Most importantly, the question of providing property tax credits to renters, who pay property taxes indirectly, is relevant. If low-income citizens in an area are predominantly renters, then limiting the credit to property owners means that mostly middle- and upper-income citizens benefit from the credit.

Credit value: Dollar-for-dollar or a percentage?

Currently, five states allow taxpayers to claim a tax credit on every dollar donated to a scholarship organization. Others provide taxpayer a credits on their donations ranging from 50 percent to 90 percent.

Adam Schaeffer argues that all individual income tax credits should be equal to 100 percent of qualified education expenses up to a cap on the total amount of tax credits that a taxpayer may claim for each child. For corporate income tax credits, the amount should be a 100 percent credit up to a total program cap. His argument has four parts:

- A reduced credit percentage has serious consequences for establishing and expanding a program. It is necessarily more difficult to raise funds when there is direct cost versus dollar-for-dollar credit.
- The credit percentage appears difficult to change in a positive direction compared to other aspects of tax-credit policy.
- A 100 percent credit implies that the taxpayer, for the good of the state and its citizens, should direct these funds. A less than 100 percent credit implies the taxpayer receives a benefit from the state. In other words, this is not a favor to or benefit bestowed on a taxpayer in the way that other credits are. Rather, it is a way of paying directly for a service the state must otherwise provide itself.
- The fiscal impact can be managed by reducing the number of existing private school children eligible initially instead of reducing the credit.[36]

Schaeffer's points are well taken. Although a dollar-for-dollar credit may be difficult in the short term, a tax credit that covers only a portion of the educational expenses will hamper the long-term growth of the program.

One or multiple scholarship organizations?

The question of the number of scholarship-granting organizations (SGOs) is an important one. Florida maintains a single SGO that is allowed to use up to 3 percent of its donations for overhead after three years of operation. Most

Figure 1: Scholarship Granting Organizations

State	Type	Scholarship Organizations	Overhead Allowances
Arizona	Individual	49	Up to 10%
Arizona	Corporate	17	Up to 10%
Arizona	Special Needs	5	Up to 10%
Florida	Corporate	1	Up to 3%
Georgia	Individual and Corporate	39	Up to 10%
Indiana	Individual and Corporate	4	Up to 10%
Iowa	Individual and Corporate	12	Up to 10%
New Hampshire	Corporate	N/A	Up to 10%
Oklahoma	Individual and Corporate	N/A	Up to 10%
Pennsylvania	Corporate	234	Up to 20%
Rhode Island	Corporate	5	Up to 10%

school choice advocates believe that parents should be able to donate to the SGO of their choice. Misconduct or corruption in a single statewide SGO would destroy the tax credit scholarship program indefinitely. Multiple SGOs neutralize this problem by allowing corporations and taxpayers to direct and redirect funding to high-performing SGOs.[37]Minimum requirements for scholarship-granting organizations should include the following components:

1. Requirements for owners and operators that ensure sound management of the scholarship organization. One recommendation would bar owners and operators who declared personal or corporate bankruptcy anytime in the seven years prior to the start of their tenure.
2. Guidelines that specify and describe appropriate expenditures of scholarship funds
3. Prohibition on earmarking scholarships for specific children, particularly the children of SGO employees and board members, or a single non-public school.
4. Authorization to use student records to confirm eligibility.
5. A cap of 10 percent on overhead or administrative expenses for each scholarship organization. This will allow a diverse group of organizations to participate in the program, rather than those with

the existing funding and infrastructure to take on the additional costs of administering a scholarship program.

6. Requirement that each SGO spend at least 90 percent of its donations on scholarships.

7. Separate accounts for scholarship and operating funds. If the organization is an existing nonprofit, charitable contributions and operating funds independent of the scholarship program should be placed in a separate fund.

8. Annual audits conducted by a certified public accountant, member of the state department of education finance office, or the Department of Revenue. Another way to guarantee financial viability is to require the school to file a surety bond payable to the state in the estimated amount of funding that the school expects to receive from the scholarship program. Non-public schools may also be required to comply with laws for entities receiving scholarship funding, such as using the state's chart of accounts or other reporting requirements.

9. Quarterly or annual reports filed with the Department of Revenue by a date specified in the law.

10. A monitoring requirement for schools that receive a scholarship through the organization.[38]

Academic accountability: Testing or no testing?

How much academic accountability is sufficient? Some argue that tax-credit scholarship programs in Georgia, Pennsylvania, and Arizona suffer from a lack of meaningful data collection and reporting. On the other hand, Florida's program is tightly controlled by a single, minimally funded SGO that requires schools to administer standardized tests to students.[39]

Reasonable accountability and transparency regarding student achievement should be included in any tax-credit scholarship law. North Carolina's current requirement for non-public schools — that they administer a nationally norm-referenced test — is a good starting point.[40] It is critical that nonpublic schools receiving scholarship funds be free to administer any reputable assessment to meet the testing requirement. In addition, participating schools should be obliged to report accountability results on an easily accessible website.

Requirements for nonpublic schools

Qualifications for participating nonpublic schools should rely on existing statutes to the greatest extent possible. Four statutes outline documentation and accountability measures for nonpublic schools, including:

- Maintain annual attendance and disease immunization records for each pupil enrolled and regularly attending classes.[41]
- Administer, at least once in each school year, a nationally standardized test or other nationally standardized equivalent measurement selected by the chief administrative officer of such school, to all students enrolled or regularly attending grades three, six and nine... in the areas of English grammar, reading, spelling and mathematics. Each school shall make and maintain records of the results achieved by its students.[42]
- Administer, at least once in each school year, a nationally standardized test or other nationally standardized equivalent measure selected by the chief administrative officer of such school, to all students enrolled and regularly attending the eleventh grade. The nationally standardized test or other equivalent measurement selected must measure competencies in the verbal and quantitative areas. Each private church school or school of religious charter shall establish a minimum score which must be attained by a student on the selected test in order to be graduated from high school.[43]
- Shall adopt rules for the procedures a person... must follow and the requirements that person must meet to obtain a driving eligibility certificate.[44]

Additional requirements for schools participating in a tax-credit scholarship program are standard fare:

- Comply with state and federal anti-discrimination laws, i.e., certify that the school does not discriminate in admissions on the basis of race, color, national origin, religion, or disability.[45]
- Comply with state and local health and safety laws and codes.
- Possess an occupancy permit.
- Conduct background checks and exclude from employment anyone not permitted by law to work in a nonpublic school.
- Operate the school for three years or post a surety bond or letter of credit equal to $250,000.[46]

In the event that a school has more applications than seats, the school should choose students at random using a lottery. That said, it is reasonable to set aside seats for siblings and students enrolled in previous years.

Other considerations

Based on experience and research, proponents of tax-credit scholarship programs have outlined other suggestions related to the implementation, expansion, and regulation of various aspects of the program:

1. The initial law should cap the tax credit at 2 percent of total state spending on K-12 education. Based on 2011-12 figures, that would be equal to nearly $152,000,000 for North Carolina.[47] It should also include an escalation provision that increases the cap by at least 25 percent if donations reach at least 90 percent of the cap.

2. To ensure that states do not incur crippling initial costs from the program, the education tax credit should initially cover only students switching from public to private school and students just starting school. If the program begins for kindergarten and adds a grade each year, it will take 13 years to phase in the program for public school students.[48]

3. A slow phase-in of students already enrolled in private schools should occur simultaneously, so long as the "deadweight" costs do not compromise the program.

4. The state should not impose additional regulations or accreditation requirements on private schools that participate in the program.

5. Similarly, the state should not impose onerous regulations on scholarship-granting organizations. Statutes governing the reporting requirements of nonprofit organizations should apply to SGOs. The state may enact reasonable requirements governing the monitoring and reporting of scholarship income and disbursements.[49]

A few model bills have been developed to guide lawmakers in developing tax credit scholarship legislation that incorporates best practices from states, and many of them are recommended in this section.[50]

Education Savings Accounts (ESAs)

Providing low- and middle-income families the means to choose their schools would greatly improve their children's prospects for receiving high-quality education. Tax-credit scholarships are one way to allocate those resources. Education savings accounts, or ESAs, are another way. An education savings account is a tax-free vehicle in which parents can save money to spend on approved educational expenses, such as tuition, textbooks, and tutoring, and into which governments can also deposit tax dollars for these uses. In 2011, Arizona became the first state to authorize the use of government-funded education savings accounts.

ESAs are similar to an existing program, federal Coverdell Education Savings Accounts. Coverdell ESAs allow low- and middle-income parents to deposit up to $2,000 a year in tax-deferred funds into an account that can be used for elementary, secondary, or higher education expenses. (Coverdell ESAs will be discussed in great detail later in this chapter.) One major difference between the federal program and Arizona's new law is that in the latter case, state government deposits tax funding in ESAs. Participant Arizona families may add funds voluntarily to their ESAs.

Under the Arizona law, parents must meet eligibility criteria to receive an ESA. The child must be a resident of the state and have a documented disability. The child must also meet one of three of the following requirements:

1. Attended public school full-time for the first 100 days during the prior school year;
2. Received a scholarship from a Student Tuition Organization that receives contributions to provide scholarships to students with disabilities; or
3. Received an ESA in the prior year.

As indicated above, Arizona's Empowerment Savings Account (ESA) program initially targeted special-needs children. In 2012, it was expanded to include other populations including students in low-performing school districts (i.e., those that receive a "D" or below on their accountability report cards), children with an active-duty military parent, and adopted and foster-care children. These additional populations will be eligible for ESAs in 2013. Legislators chose to defer the expansion of the program in order to give the state time to set up financial and administrative capacity. Like Arizona, North Carolina should provide targeted ESAs to the groups of students that may benefit the most. A North Carolina ESA program may also require a phase-in approach considering that the program requires a fairly extensive infrastructure to maintain.

Parents who are approved for an ESA must sign a one-year contact with the Arizona Department of Education. The contract details rules and regulations associated with using the ESA. Among other requirements, parents are obligated to submit quarterly expense reports to the state. Parents must also submit a form to verify that the child will voluntarily withdraw from his public school in exchange for the ESA. Parents may not accept a tax-credit scholarship from a Student Tuition Organization (STO) during the period in which they receive ESA funds.

A weighted funding formula determines how much the state deposits into the ESA, but the parents receive only 90 percent of the per-pupil allocation in their ESAs. This ensures that school districts are compensated for the loss of students. It also allows districts to cover a portion of the fixed costs that remain in the absence of those children. According to the Arizona Department of Education, the average base amount per scholarship is anywhere from $1,500 to $3,700 per child. Funds are added to the base amount according to the circumstances of the individual child. Students with multiple disabilities and severe sensory impairments receive the most funding, while those with mild impairments receive the least (See Figure 2).[51]

Purchases must include instructional materials in five core subject areas — reading, grammar (writing), mathematics, social studies, and science. Qualified expenses include the following:

1. Tuition and fees at a nongovernmental (private) school for preschool, kindergarten and grades one through 12;
2. Textbooks required by the private school or instructional program;
3. Educational therapies or services from a licensed or accredited practitioner or provider;
4. Tutoring services from a state, regionally, or nationally accredited provider;
5. Curricula;
6. Tuition or fees for a private online learning program;
7. Fee for nationally standardized norm-referenced achievement tests, Advanced Placement exams, or any exam related to admissions to a postsecondary institution;
8. Contributions to a qualified College Savings Plan (529 Plan);
9. Tuition or fees at an eligible postsecondary institution; and
10. Bank fees charged for the management of the ESA.[52]

Figure 2: Arizona ESA Weighted Student Funding System

Disability Category - Definition	Weight	Estimated per pupil amount
Hearing impaired	4.771	$15,785.00
Students with multiple disabilities, autism and severe mental retardation placed in resource programs	6.024	$19,931.00
Students with multiple disabilities, autism and severe mental retardation in a self-contained program.	5.833	$19,299.00
Students with multiple disabilities and severe sensory impairments.	7.947	$26,293.00
Students with orthopedic impairments in a resource program.	3.158	$10,488.00
Students with orthopedic impairments in a self-contained program.	6.773	$22,409.00
Preschool students with hearing impairments, visual impairments, developmental delay, preschool severe delay or speech/language impairment.	3.595	$11,894.00
Students with developmental delays, emotional disabilities, mild mental retardation, specific learning disability, speech/language impairment and other health impairment.	0.0093	$10.00
Students with emotional disabilities enrolled in private special ED or intensive district programs	4.820	$15,947.00
Students with moderate mental retardation	4.421	$14,627.00
Visually impaired	4.806	$15,901.00
Students in Kindergarten through third grade	0.060	$199.00
English Language learners	0.115	$380.00

Currently, parents may not use ESA funds for hardware (chairs, desks, computers, pens, pencils, etc.), field trips, or books that are not part of the curriculum purchased by the parent. Jonathan Butcher of the Arizona-based Goldwater Institute recommends that other essential expenses be added to the list of qualified expenditures, including transportation fees, school uniform expenses, educational summer camps, and basic classroom materials, such as pens, paper, and calculators.

The ability to deposit ESA funds into a 529 College Savings Account gives ESAs a major advantage over traditional vouchers. It provides an additional incentive for forward-thinking parents to find the most cost-effective curricula and instructional settings for their children. By doing so, families may retain a larger balance of their ESAs to save for postsecondary education.

Although the Arizona Department of Education employs multiple safeguards against fraud and abuse of ESAs, Butcher recommends additional measures, including:

- Conducting random audits, along with quarterly and annual reviews, and hiring or outsourcing auditing help.
- Creating a fraud reporting system with a telephone hotline and online forms. The state should also commission "compliance buyers," or investigators who pose as parents and try to commit fraud in order to find weaknesses in the system.
- Requiring parents to buy surety bonds using account funds. These bonds are insurance vehicles that would require bondholders to repay any misspent money. Public notaries and construction contractors regularly use these bonds, and the up-front costs are small on an annual basis. Many financial institutions offer this product.[53]

In a recent study, Matt Ladner of the Foundation for Excellence in Education points out that a number of government programs offer guidance about ways to minimize fraud and abuse in an ESA system. Specifically, states could incentivize financial firms to find and prevent the use of ESA funds for bogus or disqualified expenditures. Ladner adds that states could look to the U.S. Department of Agriculture (USDA) for guidance. According to a 2007 General Accounting Office report, the USDA significantly reduced fraud in their massive debit card program, Food Stamps. Analysis of electronic benefits transfer (EBT) transaction data is one of the methods used successfully by the USDA to catch attempted fraud and abuse.[54]

In sum, Butcher offers several recommendations for legislators considering the ESA model for their states. First, he argues that all students should be eligible to receive ESAs, but the complex implementation of the program may require a phase-in approach similar to the one taken in Arizona.

Second, Butcher points out that the school-funding system must be adapted to accommodate ESAs. Specifically, he recommends that states implement systems that allow all education funding to follow the child. ESAs through special appropriations or conventional school funding methods muddle implementation.

Butcher also suggests that legislators carefully define the list of allowable expenditures, taking into account the educational needs of families with school-age children. He affirms the need for states to adopt strong safeguards to prevent fraud and abuse, including those mentioned above. Finally, Butcher outlines recommendations to strengthen ESA programs based on the Arizona experience, including giving parents increased flexibility to invest unused funds, incorporating properly-structured accountability requirements, and finding better ways to identify eligible homeschool families.[55]

Education and the Tax Code

ESAs and tax credit scholarships are designed to assist vulnerable student populations, but all parents have an interest in making investments in the education of their children. As a state, North Carolina should ensure that educational investments, like financial investments, are encouraged, not penalized, by our tax system. As a first step, North Carolina should extend tax deductions for both educational expenditures *and* savings. After all, our concern is not simply who is eligible to receive taxpayer funds to attend home and private *schools*. It is making parents mindful of investments in the *education* of their children.

Deductions for qualified educational expenditures

Currently, a handful of states offer families tax deductions for qualified educational expenditures. Louisiana operates the boldest educational tax deduction program in the nation. The deduction is worth 100 percent of the total amount spent on qualifying educational expenses, including private school tuition and fees. A deduction of 50 percent may be taken for families that incur educational expenses for home or public school education. The maximum deduction is $5,000 per child, and the average deduction taken by the 97,000 participating families in FY2011 was nearly $2,400.[56]

Although the definition of educational expenses is broad, some expenditures do not qualify for the Louisiana education tax deduction. Most notably, taxpayers cannot deduct expenses for pre-kindergarten education, musical instruments, doctor's visits, immunizations, physical examinations, afterschool tutoring, and fees related to extracurricular activities. On the other hand, taxpayers in Louisiana may deduct the cost of school uniforms and accessories such as shoes and socks, so long as they are part of the dress requirements for the school uniform. Furthermore, state law permits taxpayers to deduct the cost of registration fees, textbooks, curricula, other instructional materials, and fees that are incurred as required by certain classes, such as those requiring laboratory or field work.[57]

The fiscal effect of the tax deduction varies by the type of deduction taken. The estimated fiscal impact of Louisiana's Elementary & Secondary School Tuition Deduction, for example, is $17.5 million a year. The fiscal impact of the Educational Expenses for Home-Schooled Children Deduction is trivial — approximately $175,000 a year. Finally, the Deduction for Fees and Other Educational Expenses for a Quality Public Education has a fiscal impact of just under $1.8 million.[58]

So the tax deductions for homeschool and public school educational expenses have little impact on state revenue for Louisiana, although they do provide some relief for parents who invest in educational materials and supplies for their families. Obviously, the Elementary & Secondary School Tuition Deduction is a larger program because it applies to 100 percent of the cost of private-school tuition and fees up to $5,000.

Unlike Louisiana, North Carolina's tax code does not permit homeschool families to claim a tax deduction for educational expenses and contributions to education savings accounts. In order for a homeschool deduction to be successful, state legislators must keep state regulators at a significant distance from homeschools. Tax credits and deductions are not invitations to burdensome regulations and intrusions from the state. Rather, they are acknowledgements of the great financial sacrifices made by families who forgo income and tax dollars to educate their children at home — an investment that generates a future taxable return when their children become adults and begin working and paying taxes.

Deductions for contributions to education savings accounts

As of 2008, 33 states, including North Carolina, offered families tax benefits for deposits of personal income into college-savings accounts or 529 plans. Funds deposited into these accounts have significant advantages for taxpayers. Contributions are tax-deductible and these after-tax dollars accrue tax-free as long as expenditures are made for approved college education costs.[59]

In 2006, the legislature capped deductions for contributions to a 529 plan at $750 ($1,500 on a joint return) and imposed adjusted gross income limitations on eligibility for the deduction. Later, the legislature amended the law to allow all taxpayers, regardless of adjusted gross income, to deduct $2,500 ($5,000 on a joint return) for contributions to North Carolina's 529 College Savings Plan (also called the Parental Savings Trust Fund of the State Education Assistance Authority).[60] Last year, the state fiscal impact for deductible contributions to North Carolina's 529 plan totaled $5.4 million.[61]

Parents may also contribute after-tax dollars to a federal Coverdell Education Savings Account. Like 529 plans, the savings accrue tax-free as long as withdrawals are used for qualifying elementary, secondary, or higher education expenses. Unfortunately, North Carolina does not offer state tax incentives for contributions to Coverdell accounts, i.e., contributions are not tax-deductible.

Coverdell accounts are more restrictive than 529 plans. Coverdell contributions may not exceed $2,000 per year for each beneficiary, whereas contributions to 529 plans can reach up to $13,000 a year without a tax penalty.[62] The contribution limit for Coverdell accounts is reduced for taxpayers that have a modified adjusted gross income (MAGI) between $95,000 and $110,000 (between $190,000 and $220,000 if filing a joint return). Families with a MAGI that is $110,000 or more ($220,000 or more if filing a joint return) cannot contribute to any Coverdell ESA. North Carolina's 529 plan does not disqualify or reduce/prohibit taxpayers from claiming a deduction on contributions based on their adjusted gross income.[63]

As a starting point, North Carolina should offer an income tax deduction for contributions to Coverdell ESAs. It would be the first state in the nation to do so. The tax deduction would be consistent with requirements outlined in federal law and, thus, subject to the following rules:

- Any individual living in the state can claim a deduction on state income taxes for a contribution made into the Family Education Savings Account of a legal beneficiary who at the time of the donation resides in the state.

- The cap on the amount that can be deducted annually is $1,000 per person or $2,000 for a married couple filing jointly.
- A total of $2,000 in contributions into a single child's account can be claimed for the tax deduction per year.
- A contributor can claim only one contribution per year.
- Any individual can make a contribution into the account of any beneficiary regardless of whether the individual and beneficiary are related; however, the beneficiary must consent to receiving the contribution.
- To be eligible for a tax deduction, a contributor must make a contribution into a Family Education Savings Account that is considered a Coverdell Education Savings Account under federal law.
- Allowable uses of funds contributed into the Family Education Saving Account will be regulated by federal rules governing Coverdell Education Savings Accounts.[64]

As a long-term goal, the state should allow families to open and contribute to Coverdell-type accounts for pre-kindergarten, primary, and secondary school expenses. These Coverdell-type accounts should have the tax and regulatory features of a 529 plan.

Contributions to ESAs should be tax deductible up to $7,700 (the estimated average cost of a North Carolina private school) per beneficiary per year for anyone making a qualified contribution to the ESA of an eligible beneficiary.[65] Ideally, contribution limits would not be adjusted based on adjusted gross income and taxpayers would be able to make ESA contributions with pre-tax dollars in the same way that many contribute to health savings accounts, namely payroll deduction.

In the meanwhile, the state may want to consider creating a tax-credit scholarship program for those families who would not qualify for an Arizona-type ESA or reap the benefits of tax deductions for educational expenditures and savings.

Charter Schools

Charter schools, independent tuition-free public schools of choice, are more popular than ever. According to a 2012 survey commissioned by the Center for Education Reform in Washington, D.C., 70 percent of North

Carolina voters agreed that communities should be allowed to create charter schools. Support was consistent across political affiliations and demographic characteristics. A majority of North Carolina Republicans, Democrats, Independents, African Americans, women, and registered voters with school-aged children welcome charter schools in their communities. Previous polls agree with these findings.[66]

Charter school regulations

In response to parental demand and changes in leadership, the 2011 NC General Assembly eliminated the 100-school cap on charters and loosened enrollment growth restrictions.[67] Although both were positive developments, charter school reform is far from complete. The State Board of Education continues to approve heavy-handed rules and regulations that multiply the challenges that new and existing charter schools face. Excessive regulation stifles experimentation, innovation, and customization.

While charter schools have more freedom than district-run public schools, they are required to meet certain state regulations. In addition to participation in the state testing program, charter schools are subject to the following accountability measures:

1. The school is subject to the financial audits, the audit procedures, and the audit requirements adopted by the State Board of Education for charter schools. These audit requirements may include the requirements of the School Budget and Fiscal Control Act.
2. The school shall comply with the reporting requirements established by the State Board of Education in the Uniform Education Reporting System.
3. The school shall report at least annually to the chartering entity and the State Board of Education the information required by the chartering entity or the State Board.[68]

But despite multiple layers of state accountability, there is disagreement about how much autonomy charter schools should have. In the paper that formed the basis of the State Board of Education's vision statement, Edward Fiske and Helen Ladd articulate a vision of charter schools that seeks to limit freedom:

For such options to play such positive roles, however, it is important that they [charter schools and other alternative models] maintain their status as an integral part of the larger state education system. They have a legitimate claim on taxpayer funds to the extent that they further the overall purposes of the state education system. In practical terms, this means that charter schools, virtual schools and other new options must be accessible to all students and held to the same high standards of academic, fiscal and other forms of account- ability as traditional public schools. To justify state support, they must also embrace the central values of the public school system of which they are a part.[69]

According to the State Board of Education's vision, charter schools have a legitimate claim on taxpayer funds only if they embrace the purposes, standards, and values of district-run public schools. In their formulation, charter schools are virtually indistinguishable from traditional public schools.

Consistent with its vision, the State Board of Education has approved multiple layers of charter school regulation since 2006 (See Figure 3).[70] While regulations mandating criminal history checks are reasonable, the State Board of Education designed others to be punitive. Charter revocation remains a

Figure 3: Charter School Policies Approved Since 2006

Policy Title	Date Approved
Policy Regarding Charter Schools Renewal Process	10/05/2006
Policy Regarding Planning Year for New Preliminary Charter Schools	11/02/2006
Policy for Charter Schools on Financial and Governance Noncompliance	04/03/2008
Policy Regarding Criminal History Checks for Individuals Handling Fiscal Matters in Charter Schools	06/04/2009
Charter School Accountability Requirements	12/03/2009
Revocation of Charter for Lack of Academic Performance	12/03/2009
Charter School Application and Review Process	12/03/2009
Policy Regarding Charter Amendments for Existing Public Charter Schools	04/05/2012

valid accountability measure. Yet, it should take more than three years of low academic achievement, as outlined in the "Revocation of Charter for Lack of Academic Performance" policy, to trigger it. As I have noted elsewhere, there is no district-run public school equivalent to that policy.[71] District schools that do not meet the student performance benchmarks outlined in this policy are not subject to closure. In fact, it is just the opposite. The Department of Public Instruction deploys additional resources and support to struggling district schools. All substantive policies approved by the State Board of Education should treat all public schools — district and charter — as equals.

The principle of equal treatment should extend to charter school funding.[72] According to statute, charter schools are entitled to an equal per-pupil share of funds contained in the local current expense fund. Therefore, funds not deposited into local current expense appropriation are off limits to charter schools. A few years ago, brazen officials representing the state's Department of Public Instruction and Local Government Commission recommended that school districts create Fund 8 — an offshore bank account of sorts — to keep funds away from charter schools. Their accounting trick continues to be used to "stash" funds from charters because revenue in Fund 8 is not technically part of the local current expense fund. These problems could be avoided by redesigning the way the state and local governments allocate revenue to charter schools. This may include a system that bypasses the school district altogether. For example, legislators may want to consider a law that mandates all county commissions to direct local education dollars to charter schools that enroll students who reside in their respective jurisdictions.

In addition, the "Policy Regarding Planning Year for New Preliminary Charter Schools" is sensible for school operators, administrators, and board members who have limited experience in operating a school. Yet, experienced charter school operators — those who have operated solvent and academically successful enterprises — should not be required to "redshirt" their schools. Rather, the State Board of Education should outline a process for expediting the charter review and approval process for applicants who want to replicate or "franchise" a charter school that has met high academic and fiscal standards for the previous five or 10 years.

It is possible to hold charter schools to high fiscal and academic standards without imposing additional regulations on them. Indeed, requirements already established in state law provide adequate accountability measures for charter schools. More importantly, charter schools have the most powerful accountability measure – parental choice.

Charter school law

Regulations from the State Board of Education present one problem. Only a major reconstitution of the board and its leadership would produce much-needed regulatory reform. Flaws in North Carolina's charter school law present another challenge. The latter would require passage of legislation that would make significant changes to existing statute. The last time the General Assembly attempted a major overhaul of the state's charter statute, the results were not ideal and a severely limited compromise bill replaced it.[73]

The Center for Education Reform rated North Carolina's charter school law as the 14th weakest of the nation's 42 charter laws. CER identified five principles of high quality charter school laws:

- *Number of Schools & Applications:* The best charter laws do not limit the number of charter schools that can operate throughout the state. They also do not limit the number of students who can attend charter schools. Poorly written laws set restrictions on the types of charter schools allowed to operate (new starts, conversions, online schools), hindering parents' ability to choose among numerous public schools. Strong charter school laws allow many different types of groups to apply to open and start charter schools.[74] In 2011, North Carolina eliminated the 100-school cap on charters. In addition, it raised the student growth allowance from 10 percent to 20 percent per year.[75] Ideally, North Carolina's charter schools would not be subject to restrictions on student growth. Rather, the school would assess the physical limitations of the campus and classrooms and make enrollment growth decisions accordingly.
- *Multiple Charter Authorizers:* States that permit a number of entities to authorize charter schools, or provide applicants with a binding appeals process, encourage more activity than those that vest authorizing power in a single entity, particularly if that entity is the local school board. The goal is to give parents the most options possible, and having multiple authorizers helps reach this goal. Additionally, it is important that the authorizing entities have power independent from one another to prevent creating multiple authorizers "in name only."[76] Technically,

North Carolina has two authorizers, the State Board of Education and the University of North Carolina System.[77] UNC System schools, however, have never used their authorization power. As such, the State Board of Education remains the only entity that approves charter schools. Even charter schools that are granted preliminary approval from local school districts must appeal to the board. At minimum, the state should extend authorizing authority to school districts, qualified non-profit organizations, and/or a charter school review board.

- *Waivers & Legal Autonomy:* A good charter law is one that automatically exempts charter schools from most of the school district's laws and regulations. Of course, no charter school is exempt from the most fundamental laws concerning civil rights. These waivers allow charter schools to innovate in ways that traditional public schools cannot.[78]North Carolina's charter schools have limited autonomy. They must participate in the state testing program and are required to meet minimum teacher certification standards for a portion of their faculty. While few would object to a testing requirement, charter schools should be allowed to choose the test used to assess student performance, as the state's private schools currently do. In addition, charter schools should be given power to hire as many uncertified or unlicensed teachers as they desire.[79] A recent study concluded that inexperienced and uncertified teachers did not have adverse effects on student achievement in new charter schools.[80]

- *Full Funding & Fiscal Autonomy:* A charter school needs to have control of its own finances to run efficiently. The charter school's operators know the best way to spend funds, and charter law should reflect this need. Similarly, charter schools, as public schools, are entitled to receive the same amount of funds as all other conventional public schools. Many states and districts withhold money from individual charter schools due to fees and "administrative costs," but the best laws provide full and equal funding for all public schools.[81] North Carolina school districts have had a history of withholding funds from charter schools. In *Sugar Creek Charter School et al. v. The Charlotte-Mecklenburg Board of Education*, plaintiffs alleged that the Charlotte-Mecklenburg Schools withheld funds that the district was obliged to allocate to charter schools in their jurisdiction. The North Carolina Court of Appeals panel ruled that Charlotte-Mecklenburg

Schools unlawfully withheld reserve fund balances, Hurricane Katrina relief funds, sales tax reimbursements, preschool programs, donations for specific programs, and capital reimbursements. State law should contain safeguards against the illegal practice of denying funds that are statutorily and legally owed to charter schools.[82] Despite this ruling, school districts have found other ways (Fund 8, for example) to deny funds to charter schools.

Charter school governance

Who should oversee charter schools in North Carolina? Although occasionally assisted by a charter school oversight board, the State Board of Education has been the agency responsible for governing the state's charter schools. This places North Carolina in the minority. State education agencies oversee only 19 percent of charter schools nationwide. School districts authorize and regulate more than half of all charter schools.[83]

An alternative would be to empower independent chartering boards to authorize and monitor charter schools. Currently, there are 10 independent chartering boards in the 41 states with charter school laws. These boards have varying degrees of autonomy and power. Hawaii and Utah have quasi-independent advisory boards, while Arizona and D.C. have boards that exercise substantial authority over charter schools. Independent chartering boards oversee 15 percent of all charters.[84]

Unfortunately, independent chartering boards have a losing record in the courts. State courts have upheld the constitutionality of an independent chartering board in Colorado. State courts have declared two others — Florida and Georgia — unconstitutional, although Georgia voters recently approved a constitutional amendment that will allow a statewide charter school commission to authorize charter schools.[85]

At minimum, the General Assembly should amend the charter school law to give school districts full authorizing authority, but charter authorization need not be limited to the State Board of Education, state universities, or an independent charter school board. Authorizers may include for-profit companies, county commissions, city councils, mayors, or boards of trustees of two- or four-year institutions of higher education. Ideally, each of these entities would be an authorizer in its own right and would not have to receive final approval by the State Board of Education. But with great power comes great responsibility. All authorizers would be held to high standards and be required to follow specific protocols before approval, including public hearings and transparency.

Transportation and food service

Currently, charter schools are not required to provide student transportation or food service, although many do so voluntarily. Some advocacy groups claim that low-income families are discouraged from applying to the handful of charter schools that do not provide these services. Without a doubt, the public deserves to know how many low-income families have cited transportation and food service as reasons why they don't apply to charter schools. The state should take accusations of inequitable access seriously.

If there is evidence of a widespread problem, the state could implement a tax credit for charter school transportation. A Florida law provides tax credits for corporations that donate a portion of their tax liability to a scholarship-funding organization. The law requires these organizations to use donations for the transportation, food service, or instructional materials of children who qualify for a free or reduced price lunch.[86] Otherwise, charter schools should receive state and local allotments for transportation and food service that are comparable to funding received by school districts for these purposes.

To date, however, there has been no evidence that transportation and food service limitations are systemic barriers for low-income families in North Carolina. Charter schools have been in existence in the state for 16 years, so there has been sufficient time to examine the problem and reach conclusions about its plausibility. At this point, the idea that transportation and food service are barriers to low-income families is pure speculation.

Facilities

Charter schools do not receive funding for facilities or capital needs. Yet, the strong demand for charter seats, combined with the loosening of restrictions on enrollment growth, will place additional pressure on charter facilities.

Many existing charter schools do not have the physical capacity to keep up with demand, and some have called upon legislators to consider amending state statute to either 1) allow school districts and county commissions to voluntarily contribute capital funds to charter schools, or 2) create a revenue stream for charter school facilities. Without a doubt, the second option is much more controversial than the first.

The Center for Education Reform recommends that states adopt a simple funding formula for charter school facilities. They advise calculating a per-pupil facilities funding average for the resident school district and multiplying that amount by the number of students attending the charter school.[87] There are three concerns with this approach, however. First, the per-pupil facilities funding average may be artificially inflated (or deflated) due to a temporary influx or outflow of funding from a bond or other form of indebtedness. Using a multi-year average would provide charter schools a more consistent and predicable level of capital funding. Second, a funding mechanism would need to be in place for students crossing district lines to attend a charter school. In this way, the facilities funding should follow the child from his resident district to his destination charter school. Finally, legislators would have to modify the state lottery law to redistribute a portion of the funds earmarked for school construction.

Two states and the District of Columbia provide charter schools a level of facilities funding that is comparable to district schools. Each represents a different way to structure the distribution of facilities funds to charter schools. Michigan state law includes a provision that simply funds charter facilities in the same way the state funds district facilities. In Missouri, charter schools are considered to be their own school district, thereby making them eligible to receive funding in the same way that traditional districts do. Washington D.C. employs formulas that allocate capital funding based on the characteristics of students enrolled. The formula-based approach is the least desirable of the three because it the one that is most prone to manipulation.[88]

Conclusion

The purpose of school choice is not to ensure that all children attend a private, charter, or home school. Most proponents of school choice have little interest in dismantling public schools or privatizing primary and secondary education. Rather, they envision an education system that ensures that all families have the means to choose the school that best meets the needs of their children regardless of provider. The way that those funds are collected and delivered may vary, but the principle remains the same. Families, not bureaucrats, should be in charge.

Appendix A: Research on the Benefits of School Choice

According to the Friedman Foundation for Educational Choice, there is overwhelming evidence that school choice has a positive academic impact on participating students nationwide. To date, of ten studies that used a random assignment or experimental research design, the "gold standard" in social science research, nine found that voucher recipients had statistically significant increases in performance and one yielded inconclusive results.[89] More than twenty studies found that vouchers also provide traditional public schools various academic and financial benefits.[90]

Likewise, most studies of school choice in North Carolina continue to find positive effects for student achievement.[91] In an August 2000 evaluation of the Charlotte Children's Scholarship Fund, Jay Greene found that low-income, predominantly African-American, scholarship recipients had combined reading and math scores six percentile points higher than the control group after only one year of schooling.[92] In a follow-up study published in the November 2007 issue of *Policy Studies Journal*, Joshua Cowen found comparable gains for recipients of vouchers from the Children's Scholarship Fund.[93] On the other hand, Michael Patrick Wille's study of two large-scale choice programs, the Milwaukee Parental Choice Program and the Charlotte Children's Scholarship Fund, concluded that choice students in Charlotte did not benefit academically from the program. Wille warned, however, that his analysis was compromised by a small and limited sample of Charlotte Children's Scholarship Fund students.[94]

Education researchers Comfort Okpala, Genniver Bell and Kwami Tuprah evaluated an intradistrict school choice program in an unidentified southeastern school district in North Carolina.[95] They found that, between 1997 and 2001, students who exercised school choice had significantly higher scores on state achievement tests than their counterparts in traditional schools. The authors speculated that socioeconomic factors may account for the difference, but their statistical methodology was not able to corroborate or refute that theory.

A number of studies have been conducted to evaluate the relationship between academic performance and school choice for students in the Charlotte-Mecklenburg Schools (CMS). Between 2001 and 2003, CMS implemented a districtwide open enrollment school choice plan. Researchers were able to analyze two groups of low-income CMS students. One group had won a random lottery for admission to a better school in the district and one had not. The use of a lottery replicates a randomized (or experimental) research design.

Justine Hastings, Thomas Kane, and Douglas Staiger outlined their findings in a quartet of studies published between 2005 and 2007. These researchers found:

- Parents value proximity highly and preferences for schools with higher test scores increase with student income and own academic ability;[96]
- Children of parents whose choices revealed a strong preference for academic quality experienced significant gains in test scores as a result of attending their chosen schools, while children whose parents weighted academic characteristics less heavily experienced academic losses;[97]
- White females experience significant improvements in test scores when randomly placed into their first choice school. They were more likely to choose academically rigorous magnet schools, and had a significant increase in homework hours on self-reported surveys;[98] and
- Losing the school choice lottery caused an increase in voter turnout among whites, while winning the lottery had no effect relative to non-participants.[99]

In a related study, Justine Hastings, Richard Van Weelden, and Jeffrey Weinstein used data from the CMS school choice program to assess claims that low-income parents would be ill equipped to choose the best schools for their children if permitted to make that choice.[100] By simply providing test scores for schools of choice, CMS parents chose higher-performing schools that produced substantial increases in their children's test scores at the end of the first year. In practical terms, a minimal amount of information will help to ensure that parents prioritize academic quality, thereby increasing the likelihood of raising the performance of their children.

Recently, Harvard education professor David Deming built on Hastings, Kane, and Staiger's research on the CMS choice program. In a National Bureau of Economic Research study titled, "School Choice, School Quality and Postsecondary Attainment," Deming, along with co-authors Justine Hastings, Thomas Kane, and Douglas Staiger, evaluated a sample of CMS students to assess the relationship between school choice and college enrollment.[101] Deming and his colleagues concluded that choice recipients from low quality neighborhood school zones were 8.7 percentage points more likely to graduate from high school, 6.6 percentage points more likely to attend a four year college, and 5.7 percentage points more likely to earn a four-year college degree than those not chosen by lottery to participate in the program.

Deming published a follow-up study in the Spring 2012 issue of *Education Next* that examined the relationship between school choice and crime in Charlotte. Deming concluded that high-risk students commit about 50 percent less crime as a result of winning a school choice lottery. Among male high school students at high risk of criminal activity, winning admission to a first-choice school reduced felony arrests from 77 to 43 per 100 students over the study period (2002-2009). Moreover, the attendant social cost of crimes committed decreased by more than 35 percent. Among high-risk middle school students, admittance by lottery to a preferred school reduced the average social cost of crimes committed by 63 percent and reduced the total expected sentence of crimes committed by 31 months or 64 percent. Most importantly, students exhibited lasting changes in behavior. Deming discovered that the impact of winning the school-choice lottery persisted for up to seven years after their initial transfers.[102]

Evidence on charter school performance in North Carolina is mixed. One of the earliest studies of North Carolina charter schools was the 2001 charter school evaluation, "North Carolina Charter School Evaluation Report."[103] Researchers George W. Noblit and Corbett Dickson found that charter schools lost ground over time, that is, charter school students had a lower level of proficiency on state tests than their counterparts did in district schools. The authors also discovered that charter schools had a larger achievement gap between white and minority students. Nevertheless, they observed that differences between charter and district school performance were small. More importantly, at the time of the study, charter school legislation had passed four years prior and the sample was small. Much of what Noblit and Dickson found may be attributed to implementation lag.

As part of a nationwide study of charter schools, "Apples to Apples: An Evaluation of Charter Schools Serving General Student Populations," education researchers Jay P. Greene, Greg Forster, and Marcus A. Winters assessed charter school performance in individual states. They noted that

North Carolina had the weakest results of the five states included in the 2003 study.[104] Although the outcome was disappointing, they pointed out that the results were inconclusive because differences between charter and traditional schools were not statistically significant. In other words, charter school performance in North Carolina was indistinguishable from the performance of district schools.

In a study encompassing nearly all students in elementary charter schools nationwide, Harvard University professor Caroline Hoxby's 2004 study "Achievement In Charter Schools And Regular Public Schools In The United States: Understanding The Differences," concluded that charter students were 5.2 percent more likely to be proficient in reading and were 3.2 percent more likely to be proficient in math on their states' exams.[105] In addition, the longer a charter school was in operation, the greater the advantage the charter school student had over the student in the district school closest to the charter school. Her evaluation of charter schools in North Carolina was less favorable. She acknowledged that North Carolina was the only state in which charter students were statistically significantly less likely to be proficient in both reading and math, a four percent disadvantage in both subjects.[106]

In "Reassessing North Carolina's Charter Schools: A Note on Caroline Hoxby's Findings," Craig M. Newmark, an economics professor at North Carolina State University, pointed out that Hoxby did not account for important differences between the charter and district school student populations in North Carolina.[107] In particular, Hoxby failed to factor in the higher fraction of gifted students in public schools. She also used a sample that included charter, but no district, schools that served at-risk students. When accounting for these differences, Newmark found that there was no statistically significant difference between charter and district school performance in North Carolina.

The most quoted study of charter school performance in North Carolina is Robert Bifulco and Helen F. Ladd's 2004 paper, "The Impacts Of Charter Schools On Student Achievement: Evidence From North Carolina."[108] Bifulco and Ladd concluded that achievement gains in charter schools were smaller than those in district schools, even in charter schools that had been in operation longer. Furthermore, they observed that competition from charter schools did not improve performance at nearby district schools.

A year later, Craig Newmark published a response to the Bifulco and Ladd study. Newmark's study, "Another Look at the Effect of Charter Schools on Student Test Scores in North Carolina," found several shortcomings in their study.[109] According to Newmark, Bifulco and Ladd failed to take into account student characteristics like gifted students, were unwilling to distinguish between charter schools serving at-risk students and regular charter schools, and were reluctant to acknowledge that their statistical model could not account for some of the differences between charter and district schools. Interestingly, Newmark questioned whether charter schools have the same motivation to increase state test scores as their district school counterparts do. As reform-minded schools, charter schools may not emphasize state tests, providing an advantage to public schools that Bifulco and Ladd could not account for in their study.

Finally, the Center for Research on Education Outcomes (CREDO) at Stanford University evaluated charter school performance in 15 states, including North Carolina, and the District of Columbia. In their 2009 study, the researchers found that low-income charter school students in North Carolina did better in reading, but worse in math, than their traditional public school peers. They noted, however, that a cap on the number of charter schools, which North Carolina had at the time, was a major factor in lowering student test scores.[110]

One important study shifts the debate by arguing that charter schools in North Carolina actually improve student performance in nearby district-run public schools. The three university researchers who co-authored the study found that competition from charter schools raised the performance of nearby district schools substantially.[111] In "Does School Choice Increase School Quality?" George M. Holmes, Jeff Desimone, and Nicholas G. Rupp concluded that charter school competition raised the performance of students at district schools who were at or near the cutoff score for grade-level proficiency. The authors concluded that school choice was a more cost-effective alternative than lowering class size in improving North Carolina student achievement. Lowering class size increased student performance by a little over a third of a percentage point, while school choice increased student performance by a full percentage point, which represents about a quarter of the average yearly improvement in student performance.

Appendix B: The Constitutionality of School Choice

North Carolina's Constitution specifies that the public school system must be "general and uniform."[112] This provision does not mean that all schools must be public schools. Instead, this merely establishes a minimum standard for the state, a standard that is not at odds with establishing alternative schools and programs that are not a part of the public school system.

Indeed, the famous *Leandro* court decision declared that every child in North Carolina has the constitutional right to a "sound basic education."[113] The court defined a sound basic education as having sufficient skills, abilities, and knowledge to thrive in post-graduate life. Nothing in the definition of a sound basic education specifies how the state should meet the requirement.

The North Carolina Constitution is one of the few state constitutions that do not contain religious clauses that would prohibit school choice for religious schools. The constitution does not contain an Establishment Clause or a "compelled support" clause (also known as a Blaine Amendment) that restricts the government's ability to support sectarian organizations or churches.

Although the North Carolina Constitution does not contain restrictive religious clauses, a school choice program in North Carolina would still have to comply with religion clauses of the U.S. Constitution. In *Zelman v. Simmons-Harris* (2002), the U.S. Supreme Court ruled that school choice does not violate the First Amendment's establishment clause because parents, not the state, choose the schools their children attend. Therefore, neither the state nor federal constitutions would prohibit a comprehensive school choice program in North Carolina.

Endnotes

1.   Deborah J. Cassidy, "Implementation of NC Pre-K: Presentation to the Joint Legislative Oversight Committee on Health and Human Services," October 11, 2011, http://www.ncleg.net/gascripts/DocumentSites/browseDocSite. asp?nID=144&sFolderName=\Handouts%20and%20Minutes\October%2011,%20 2011. Lisa Hollowell, "NC Pre-K Overview," Fiscal Research Division, North Carolina General Assembly, November 12, 2012, http://www.ncleg.net/gascripts/ DocumentSites/browseDocSite.asp?nID=144&sFolderName=\Handouts%20and%20 Minutes\November%2013,%202012. Lisa Hollowell, "NC Pre-K compared to More at Four Program," Fiscal Research Division, North Carolina General Assembly, October 6, 2011. "NC Child Care Snapshot," NC Division of Child Development and Early Education, North Carolina Department of Health and Human Services, http:// ncchildcare.dhhs.state.nc.us/general/mb_snapshot.asp#Child%20Care%20Highlights.

2.   "Session Law 2011-395: An Act To Allow An Individual Income Tax Credit For Children With Disabilities Who Require Special Education And To Create A Fund For Special Education And Related Services," North Carolina General Assembly, June 20, 2011, http://www.ncleg.net/Sessions/2011/Bills/House/HTML/H344v7.html.

3.   North Carolina General Statutes, Chapter 115C 111.2: Contracts with private service providers, http://www.ncga.state.nc.us/gascripts/Statutes/StatutesTOC. pl?Chapter=0115C

4.   "North Carolina Biennial Tax Expenditure Report: 2011," North Carolina Department of Revenue, http://www.dor.state.nc.us/publications/biennial.html.

5.   U.S. Department of Education, "Table 22: Distribution of Federal Pell Grant Recipients by Recipients State of Legal Residence and Control of Institution, Award Year 2010-11," Federal Pell Grant Program 2010-2011 End of Year Report, www2. ed.gov/finaid/prof/resources/data/pell-data.html.

6.   N.C. Department of Public Instruction (NC DPI), "Highlights of the North Carolina Public School Budget, 2012," p. 29-33, http://www.dpi.state.nc.us/fbs/resources/ data/.

7.   N.C. Division of Non-Public Education (NC NPE), "North Carolina Home School Statistical History," http://www.ncdnpe.org/homeschool2.aspx.

8.   NC DPE, "North Carolina Private K-12 School Statewide Statistical History," http:// www.ncdnpe.org/hhh500.aspx.

9.   David Roland, "School Choice And The North Carolina Constitution," Institute for Justice and the N.C. Education Alliance, April 2006, www.johnlocke.org/acrobat/ policyReports/school_choice-constitution.pdf.

10.   Jeanette Doran, "School Choice Scholarship Programs Would Not Violate the First Amendment of the U.S. Constitution," North Carolina Institute for Constitutional Law, November 6, 2012, http://ncicl.org/article/793.

11.   Herbert J. Walberg and Joseph L. Bast, "Design Guidelines for School Vouchers," in Education and Capitalism: How Overcoming Our Fear of Free Markets and Economics Can Improve America's Schools, Stanford, CA: Hoover Institution Press, 2003, p. 289-315.

12.   Brian Gottlob, "The Fiscal Impact of Tax-Credit Scholarships in Oklahoma," The

Friedman Foundation for Educational Choice, 2011.

13. The studies are available from the Friedman Foundation for Educational Choice website, http://www.edchoice.org/Research/Our-Studies---Reports.aspx.

14. "The Corporate Income Tax Credit Scholarship Program Saves State Dollars," The Florida Legislature, Office of Program Policy Analysis & Government Accountability, Report No. 08-68, December 2008, http://www.oppaga.state.fl.us/Summary.aspx?reportNum=08-68.

15. R. Q. Herzber and C. Fawson, *Estimating Demand and Supply Response to Tuition Tax Credits for Private School Tuition in Utah*, Logan, UT: Utah State University, 2004.

16. David N. Figlio, "Evaluation of the Florida Tax Credit Scholarship Program Participation, Compliance and Test Scores in 2009-10," Florida Department of Education, August 2011, http://www.stepupforstudents.org/OurCause/TheResults.

17. Paul DiPerna, Editor, "The 2012 ABCs of School Choice," The Friedman Foundation for Educational Choice, January 2012, p. 10, http://www.edchoice.org/Foundation-Services/Publications/ABCs-of-School-Choice-3.aspx.

18. *Ibid*, p. 12-13.

19. *Ibid*, p. 14-15.

20. *Ibid*, p. 24-25.

21. *Ibid*, p. 28-30.

22. *Ibid*, p. 32-33.

23. *Ibid*, p. 40-41.

24. "New Hampshire - Corporate Education Tax Credit," The Friedman Foundation for Educational Choice, http://www.edchoice.org/School-Choice/Programs/Corporate-Education-Tax-Credit.aspx.

25. DiPerna, "The 2012 ABCs of School Choice," 64-65.

26. *Ibid*, p. 66-76.

27. *Ibid*, p. 68-69.

28. Adam B. Schaeffer, "Diversity & Choice or Regulation & Monopoly," Cato@Liberty, May 24, 2012, http://www.cato-at-liberty.org/diversity-choice-or-regulation-monopoly/. See also Adam B. Schaeffer, "Market Structure & Barriers to Entry in Education Tax Credit Programs," Cato@Liberty, May 29, 2012, http://www.cato-at-liberty.org/market-structure-barriers-to-entry-in-education-tax-credit-programs/.

29. In Florida, the scholarship can be used at any one of the 1,350 private schools whose participation has been approved by the state.

30. Florida has taken one further step, which is to report learning gains of any school with at least 30 students with test scores for two years.

31. John Kirtley, "School choice movement can't give grenades to opponents," redefinED, May 24, 2012, http://www.redefinedonline.org/2012/05/school-choice-movement-cant-give-grenades-to-opponents. See also John Kirtley, "Program design is crucial for tax credit scholarships," redefinED, May 22, 2012, http://www.redefinedonline.org/2012/05/design-for-school-choice-programs-is-crucial.

32. DiPerna, "The 2012 ABCs of School Choice," 82-83.

33. Schaeffer, "Diversity & Choice or Regulation & Monopoly."

34. North Carolina State Constitution, Article V, Section 2: State and local taxation, http://www.ncleg.net/Legislation/constitution/ncconstitution.html.

35. Adam B. Schaeffer, "The Public Education Tax Credit," Cato Institute Policy Analysis No. 605, December 5, 2007, http://www.cato.org/publications/policy-analysis/public-education-tax-credit.

36. Adam B. Schaeffer, "Policy Implications of Education Tax Credit Percentages," Center for Educational Freedom, Cato Institute.

37. DiPerna, "The 2012 ABCs of School Choice." Malcom Glenn and Michelle Gininger, "School Choice Yearbook, 2011-12," Alliance for School Choice, January 2012, http://www.allianceforschoolchoice.org/yearbook.

38. "The Student-Centered Funding Act," American Legislative Exchange Council (ALEC), www.edchoice.org/Documents/SchoolChoice/Student-Centered-Funding-Act.aspx. "The Great Schools Tax Credit Program Act," American Legislative Exchange Council (ALEC), www.edchoice.org/Documents/SchoolChoice/Great-Schools-Tax-Credit-Program-Act.aspx. Adam B. Schaeffer, "The Education Investment Tax Credit," Center for Educational Freedom, Cato Institute, March 2012, www.cato.org/pdfs/model-tax-credit-legislation-schaeffer-cato.pdf.

39. Kirtley, "Program design is crucial for tax credit scholarships."

40. North Carolina General Statutes, Chapter 115C-549: Standardized testing requirements, http://www.ncga.state.nc.us/gascripts/Statutes/StatutesTOC.pl?Chapter=0115C.

41. North Carolina General Statutes, Chapter 115C 548: Attendance; health and safety regulations, http://www.ncga.state.nc.us/gascripts/Statutes/StatutesTOC.pl?Chapter=0115C.

42. North Carolina General Statutes, Chapter 115C 549: Standardized testing requirement.

43. North Carolina General Statutes, Chapter 115C 550: High school competency testing, http://www.ncga.state.nc.us/gascripts/Statutes/StatutesTOC.pl?Chapter=0115C.

44. North Carolina General Statutes, Chapter 115C 566: Driving eligibility certificates; requirements, http://www.ncga.state.nc.us/gascripts/Statutes/StatutesTOC.pl?Chapter=0115C.

45. Private schools are already required to comply with nondiscrimination policies under federal law with respect to race, color, and national origin (42 USC 1981). In addition, if private schools are recipients of federal funds they are subject to nondiscrimination requirements under 42 USC 2000d (race, color, national origin) and 29 USC 794 (disability).

46. This requirement may pose a barrier to entry, as it favors established schools. On the other hand, it offers proof to the scholarship granting organization that the school is viable financially. If barriers to entry are a concern, other methods of demonstrating financial feasibility may be used.

47. N.C. DPI, "Table 22 - North Carolina Current Expense Expenditures by Source of Funds," Statistical Profile [Online], http://apps.schools.nc.gov/pls/apex/f?p=1:1:1585779640129002.

48. Adding multiple grades each year may be possible in later years.

49. "The Student-Centered Funding Act," American Legislative Exchange Council (ALEC). "The Great Schools Tax Credit Program Act," American Legislative Exchange

Council (ALEC). Schaeffer, "The Education Investment Tax Credit."

50. *Ibid.*

51. "Funding Levels: Empowerment Scholarship Accounts," Arizona Department of Education, http://www.azed.gov/esa/faq.

52. "Empowerment Scholarship Account (ESA) Fund Use," Arizona Department of Education, http://www.azed.gov/esa/faq.

53. Jonathan Butcher, "Preventing Fraud and Abuse in Education Savings Accounts," October 3, 2012, http://goldwaterinstitute.org/blog/preventing-fraud-and-abuse-education-savings-accounts.

54. Matthew Ladner, "The Way of the Future Education Savings Accounts for Every American Family," Friedman Foundation for Educational Choice, October 2012, http://www.edchoice.org/Research/Reports/The-Way-of-the-Future--Education-Savings-Accounts-for-Every-American-Family.aspx.

55. Jonathan Butcher, "Education Savings Accounts: A Path to Give All Children an Effective Education and Prepare Them for Life," Goldwater Institute Policy Report, No . 253, October 30, 2012, http://goldwaterinstitute.org/article/education-savings-accounts-path-give-all-children-effective-education-and-prepare-them-life.

56. "Credits & Deductions for Child Care & Education," Louisiana Department of Revenue, December 2011, http://revenue.louisiana.gov/sections/publications/tg.aspx.

57. "School Expense Tax Deduction," Louisiana Department of Revenue, http://www.revenue.louisiana.gov/sections/individual/schoolexpensededuction.aspx. See also "Individual Income Tax FAQ," Louisiana Department of Revenue, http://www.revenue.louisiana.gov/sections/FAQ/default.aspx?type=GEN&cat=PER#faq-390.

58. "Tax Exemption Budget, FY 2011-12," Louisiana Department of Revenue, http://www.rev.state.la.us/sections/Publications/sp.aspx.

59. "An Introduction to 529 Plans," U.S. Securities and Exchange Commission, http://www.sec.gov/investor/pubs/intro529.htm.

60. "North Carolina's 529 College Savings Plan," North Carolina Department of Revenue, http://www.dornc.com/taxes/individual/college.html.

61. "North Carolina Biennial Tax Expenditure Report: 2011," p. 66.

62. If 529 contributions exceed $13,000, they may be subject to gift taxes. See Department of the Treasury, Internal Revenue Service, "Tax Benefits for Education: For use in preparing 2011 returns," Publication 970, http://www.irs.gov/publications/p970.

63. *Ibid.*

64. "Family Education Savings Account Act," American Legislative Exchange Council (ALEC), www.federationforchildren.org/system/uploads/133/original/The_Education_Savings_Account_Act.pdf?1312816673.

65. Kristopher Nordstrom, "Session 2011 Legislative Fiscal Note of House Bill 41: Tax Fairness in Education," General Assembly of North Carolina, April 13, 2011, p. 6.

66. In 2011, for example, Public Policy Polling, a left-leaning firm, released results from a poll that asked respondents to evaluate various education reforms and proposals. The bottom line is that North Carolinians like charter schools. Overall, 54 percent of North Carolinians supported charter schools. Over 60 percent of Republicans and Independents supported charters, and a plurality of Democrats (45

percent favorable vs. 27 percent unfavorable) were on board. African-Americans were just as likely as white respondents to have a favorable view of charter schools. Urban and suburban areas (area codes 704, 910, and 919), which also have the bulk of North Carolina's charter schools, strongly supported them.

67. The 100-cap remained in place for 15 years. The conditions that led to this kind of stagnation is described in *Post-Punctuation Politics: The Evolution of Charter School Policy in North Carolina* by Wayne D. Lewis, Ph.D. dissertation, North Carolina State University, 2009. As Lewis points out, "Following the passage of charter school policy in North Carolina, traditional public school interests have been able to reassert themselves. Conversely, charter school interests' emergence with the passage of charter school legislation did not result in a new, stable, and enduring policy subsystem. Presently, traditional public school interests not only have influence in state education policy making, but they have regained a position of dominance in education policy making. In fact, traditional public school interests are so dominant and the overall impact of charter school legislation in the state has been so small that future research should address the question of whether the passage of charter school legislation in North Carolina was a true punctuation at all." p. 138-139.

68. North Carolina General Statutes Chapter 115C 238.29F (f): General Requirements, http://www.ncga.state.nc.us/gascripts/Statutes/StatutesTOC.pl?Chapter=0115C.

69. North Carolina State Board of Education (N.C. SBE), "Vision of Public Education in North Carolina: A Great Public Education System for a Great State," http://stateboard.ncpublicschools.gov/front-page/resources/north-carolina-ambassador-resources.

70. N.C. SBE, "Category U: Charter School Administration," N.C. State Board of Education Policy Manual [Online], http://sbepolicy.dpi.state.nc.us.

71. Terry Stoops, "Zero Tolerance for Charter Schools: The State Board of Education should regard all public schools as equals," John Locke Foundation, Spotlight No. 382, February 3, 2010, http://www.carolinajournal.com/issues/display_story.html?id=6068.

72. A budget provision denies charter schools a share of funds from the North Carolina Education Lottery, but the distribution of lottery funds will not be discussed in this chapter.

73. See, for example, Sara Burrows, "Parties Battle Over Charter School Funding, Oversight, Diversity: Charter supporters says Democrat attacks are inaccurate, hypocritical," Carolina Journal Online, March 4, 2011, http://www.carolinajournal.com/issues/display_story.html?id=7482.

74. Alison Consoletti, Editor, "The Essential Guide to Charter School Law — 2012 Charter School Laws Across the States: Full Report," Center for Education Reform (CER), April 2012, http://www.edreform.com/issues/choice-charter-schools/laws-legislation. See also CER, "Charter School Law," http://www.edreform.com/issues/choice-charter-schools/laws-legislation.

75. North Carolina Session Law 2011-164, June 13, 2011, http://www.ncga.state.nc.us/Sessions/2011/Bills/Senate/HTML/S8v8.html.

76. CER, "Charter School Law."

77. See Terry Stoops, "Why UNC Needs Charter Schools: Charter Demonstration

Schools Can Improve Teacher Education," John Locke Foundation, Spotlight No. 333, December 4, 2007.

78. CER, "Charter School Law."

79. Teacher quality is an essential component of a successful charter school. See Cedric L. Stone, "What are the differences between effective and ineffective charter schools in North Carolina?" The University of North Carolina at Charlotte, Ed.D., dissertation, 2010.

80. Celeste K. Carruthers, "Faculty Composition and Student Achievement in Charter Schools," University of Florida, Ph.D. dissertation, 2009.

81. CER, "Charter School Law."

82. Sara Burrows, "Charter School Wins Funding Battle in N.C. Court of Appeals: Charter advocates want legislature to ensure equal funding in the future," Carolina Journal Online, September 29, 2011, http://www.carolinajournal.com/exclusives/display_exclusive.html?id=8298.

83. "The State of Charter School Authorizing 2011," National Association of Charter School Authorizers, January 2012, http://www.qualitycharters.org/publications-resources/annual-authorizer-survey.

84. *Ibid.*

85. Wayne Washington, "State's voters approve charter amendment," *The Atlanta Journal-Constitution*, November 6, 2012, http://www.ajc.com/news/news/charter-school-amendment-heading-toward-passage/nSy2J.

86. DiPerna, "The 2012 ABCs of School Choice," p. 24-25.

87. Jeanne Allen, Alison Consoletti, and Kara Kerwin, "The Essential Guide to Charter School Lawmaking: Model Legislation for States," Center for Education Reform, October 2012, p. 20-21, www.edreform.com/issues/choice-charter-schools/laws-legislation.

88. *Ibid.*

89. For a summary of the studies, see "Gold Standard Studies: Evaluating School Choice Programs," The Friedman Foundation for Educational Choice, http://www.edchoice.org/Research/Gold-Standard-Studies.aspx.

90. "How does school choice affect public schools?" The Friedman Foundation for Educational Choice, http://www.edchoice.org/School-Choice/School-Choice-FAQs/How-does-school-choice-affect-public-schools.aspx.

91. Other studies of school choice in North Carolina focus on other aspects of choice. For example, see Robert Bifulco, Helen Ladd, and Stephen Ross, "Public School Choice and Integration: Evidence from Durham, North Carolina," Social Science Research, Vol. 38, No. 1, March 2009, p. 71–85. For a discussion of who did and did not accept a voucher from the Children's Scholarship Fund, see Joshua Cowen, "Who chooses, who refuses? Learning more from students who decline private school vouchers," *American Journal of Education*, Vol. 117, No. 1, 2004.

92. Jay Greene, "The Effect of School Choice: An Evaluation of the Charlotte Children's Scholarship Fund Program," Manhattan Institute Civic Report No. 12, August 2000. Jay Greene, "Vouchers in Charlotte," *Education Next*, Summer 2001.

93. Joshua Cowen, "School Choice as a Latent Variable: Estimating 'Complier Average Causal Effect' of Vouchers in Charlotte," *Policy Studies Journal*, November

2007.

94. Michael Patrick Willie, "School vouchers: Source/amount of funds and effects on math/reading scores," Georgetown University, M.P.P. thesis, 2010.

95. Comfort O. Okpala, Genniver C. Bell, and Kwami Tuprah, "A Comparative Study of Student Achievement in Traditional Schools and Schools of Choice in North Carolina," *Urban Education,* Vol. 42, 2007.

96. Justine S. Hastings, Thomas J. Kane, and Douglas O. Staiger, "Parental Preferences and School Competition: Evidence From a Public School Choice Program," NBER Working Paper No. 11805, Cambridge, MA: National Bureau of Economic Research, Inc., 2005.

97. Justine S. Hastings, Thomas J. Kane, and Douglas O. Staiger, "Preferences and Heterogeneous Treatment Effects in a Public Choice Lottery," NBER Working Paper No. 12145, Cambridge, MA: National Bureau of Economic Research, Inc., 2006.

98. Justine S. Hastings, Thomas J. Kane, and Douglas O. Staiger, "Gender and Performance: Evidence From School Assignment by Randomized Lottery," *American Economic Review,* Vol. 96, No. 2, 2006.

99. Justine S. Hastings, Thomas J. Kane, Douglas O. Staiger, and Jeffrey M. Weinstein, "The Effects of Randomized School Admissions on Voter Participation," *Journal of Public Economics,* Vol. 91, No. 5/6, 2007.

100. Justine S. Hastings, Richard Van Weelden, and Jeffrey Weinstein, "Preferences, Information, and Parental Choice Behavior in Public School Choice," NBER Working Paper No. 12995, Cambridge, MA: National Bureau of Economic Research, Inc., March 2007.

101. David J. Deming, Justine S. Hastings, Thomas J. Kane, and Douglas O. Staiger, "School Choice, School Quality and Postsecondary Attainment," NBER Working Paper No. 17438, Cambridge, MA: National Bureau of Economic Research, Inc., September 2011. David James Deming, "Long-term impacts of educational interventions," Harvard University, Ph.D. Dissertation, 2010.

102. David J. Deming, "Does School Choice Reduce Crime? Evidence from North Carolina," *Education Next,* Vol. 12, no. 2, Spring 2012. David James Deming, "Long-term impacts of educational interventions," Harvard University, Ph.D. Dissertation, 2010. Deming considered four possible explanations for this -- incapacitation, contagion, skill attainment, and peer effects, but none of them explained the phenomenon to his satisfaction. He found little evidence that incapacitation (occupying youth with long bus rides during high-crime hours) and contagion (removing kids from high-crime neighborhoods) played a significant role in discouraging criminal activity among choice recipients. Rather, Deming's analysis revealed evidence that lottery winners obtained superior skills and knowledge in their higher-quality destination school, possibly enabling them to find employment or take advantage of other opportunities that made criminal activity less appealing. Finally, exposure to crime-prone peers had a small effect on middle school students in the choice group, but overall Deming found little evidence that peers encouraged or discouraged criminal activity.

103. George Noblit and Dickson Corbett, "North Carolina Charter School Evaluation Report," Department of Public Instruction of North Carolina and The University of

North Carolina at Chapel Hill, 2001.

104. Jay P. Greene, Greg Forster, and Marcus A. Winters, "Apples to Apples: An Evaluation of Charter Schools Serving General Student Populations," Manhattan Institute Education Working Paper, July 2003, http://www.manhattan-institute.org/html/ewp_01.htm.

105. Caroline M. Hoxby, "Achievement In Charter Schools And Regular Public Schools In The United States: Understanding The Differences," National Bureau Of Economic Research, December 2004.

106. *Ibid*, p. 14.

107. Craig Newmark, "Reassessing North Carolina's Charter Schools: A Note on Caroline Hoxby's Findings," John Locke Foundation Policy Report, July 18, 2005, http://johnlocke.org/policy_reports/display_story.html?id=58.

108. Robert Bifulco, Robert and Helen F. Ladd, "The Impacts of Charter Schools on Student Achievement: Evidence From North Carolina," Chapel Hill, NC: Terry Sanford Institute of Policy, Working Papers Series SAN04-01, 2004.

109. Craig Newmark, "Another Look at the Effect of Charter Schools on Student Test Scores in North Carolina," John Locke Foundation Policy Report, April 11, 2005, http://johnlocke.org/policy_reports/display_story.html?id=56.

110. "Multiple Choice: Charter School Study in 16 States," Center for Research on Education Outcomes (CREDO), June 2009, http://credo.standford.edu.

111. George M. Holmes, Jeffrey DeSimone, and Nicholas G. Rupp, "Does School Choice Increase School Quality?" NBER Working Paper No. 9683, Cambridge, MA: National Bureau of Economic Research, Inc., May 2003, http://ssrn.com/abstract=406055.

112. North Carolina State Constitution, Article IX, Section 2: Education, http://www.ncleg.net/Legislation/constitution/ncconstitution.html

113. *Hoke County Board of Education v. State*, 599 S.E.2d 365 (N.C. 2004).

◇◇◇◇◇◇◇◇◇◇◇◇◇◇◇◇◇◇◇◇◇

Public School Reform: Improving standards, accountability, personnel, and funding

by Terry Stoops

In his classic essay "Education and the Individual," North Carolina native Richard Weaver argued that the American education system of his day failed to challenge students, to build their character, and to introduce them to the greatest ideas and discoveries of the arts and sciences. "Most Americans take a certain satisfaction in regarding themselves as tough-minded when it comes to successful ways of doing things," Weaver wrote. "But in deciding what is and is not pertinent to educating the individual, far too many of them have been softheads."

The good news is that over the past three decades, the public constituency for fundamental education reform has grown. Most voters now favor instituting a more rigorous curriculum in the public schools, using credible assessments of what students learn, and holding educators accountable for results. As this chapter demonstrates, there are many sound policies that would improve the performance of public schools. What has been lacking in the past is the political will to implement them.

Evidence from unrestricted school choice programs in other countries suggests that most parents will continue to choose to send their children to district-run public schools.[1] As such, ensuring that every child receives a high-quality education requires much more than school choice. It requires rethinking the way that our traditional public school system delivers instruction, employs teachers, and allocates resources.

Section 1. Standards and Testing

In 2012, North Carolina's public schools witnessed the first phase of a massive overhaul of the state's curriculum standards and testing program. The North Carolina Department of Public Instruction (DPI) introduced new curriculum standards for all public school students during the 2012-13 school year. The state-led Accountability and Curriculum Reform Effort completely revised North Carolina's curriculum and testing program. In addition, the NC State Board of Education unanimously approved Common Core State Standards (CCSS) for math and English in June 2010.

Common Core State Standards

Originally, the Common Core State Standards were a product of two independent organizations: the National Governors Association and the Council of Chief State School Officers. While these groups coordinated the standards' development, neither had the financial or political influence to convince states to sign on. As a result, education officials in North Carolina and elsewhere had little incentive to adopt standards created by two Washington organizations. So, in 2010 the federal government joined forces with them and declared that any state officially adopting the common standards would receive "bonus points" toward its application for a piece of the $4.5 billion federal Race to the Top fund. Since then, the U.S. Department of Education has been the leading proponent of national curriculum standards and tests. By doing so, the federal government became involved in matters that traditionally (and constitutionally) have been state and local responsibilities.

Critics of the CCSS outlined five legal, political, and educational arguments against the development of national standards and assessments:

- There is no constitutional or statutory basis for national standards, national assessments, or national curricula.
- There is no consistent evidence that a national curriculum leads to high academic achievement.
- The national standards on which the administration is planning to base a national curriculum are inadequate.
- There is no body of evidence for a "best" design for curriculum sequences in any subject.
- There is no research basis for a single high school curriculum for all students.[2]

A sixth objection could have been, "There is no money." Given continuing fiscal pressures, states such as North Carolina can ill afford to appropriate tens of million of dollars a year for new standards and tests.

Authors of the CCSS have not offered estimates of the cost of the transition to common standards, but independent organizations have. Researchers from the Pioneer Institute, the American Principles Project, and the Pacific Research Institute have estimated that implementation of Common Core State Standards in English and math will cost participating states $15.8 billion over seven years. This total includes the cost of new assessments, professional development, instructional materials, textbooks, and technology. According to the report, North Carolina will need to spend $200 million for professional development, $85 million for textbooks and materials, and $240 million for technology over the next seven years to implement the Common Core standards. That is a total of $525 million or an average of $75 million per year.

A report written by researchers at the Thomas B. Fordham Institute estimated that the cost would be lower, depending on the extent of implementation. Fordham, an outspoken proponent of the CCSS, predicted that North Carolina could save $36 million if the state used a "bare bones" approach. A so-called "balanced implementation," the Fordham Institute's preferred strategy, would require a $40 million investment. Fully implementing the standards would require $302.5 million from the state.

States are not the only ones that will spend millions to implement CCSS. The U.S. Department of Education has invested $360 million into the development of a uniform student assessment system. Currently, two consortia of states are developing tests that align with the CCSS. North Carolina is a member of the SMARTER Balanced Consortia and, presumably, will adopt the tests developed by its 28 member states. The 24 states under the Partnership for Assessment of Readiness for College and Careers (PARCC) are undertaking the same task. Six states are members of both. Education officials from these states will determine which group of assessments will be administered in their states. All states will begin administering common core assessments during the 2014-15 school year.

CCSS will force states to spend tens of millions of dollars and relinquish control of their public school curriculum and testing programs. But there are other troublesome aspects of the CCSS. There is growing evidence that the quality of the standards is low. Although CCSS may exceed existing standards in states such as North Carolina, researchers have identified serious flaws in the design of common standards and tests, including:

- Less emphasis on fiction, literary study, and classical literature;
- Tests that define "college-ready" as reading at a 7th-grade level;
- Failure to provide historical context for selected readings;
- Math standards that would put American students two years behind their counterparts in high-performing nations;
- Placing Algebra I in 9th grade, thereby making it difficult for students to take calculus in high school; and
- Promoting an unproven method of teaching geometry.[3]

A handful of states have resisted pressure to adopt CCSS or participate in the test development process. Five states (Alaska, Minnesota, Nebraska, Texas, and Virginia) have opted out of one or both of the Common Core standards. The Utah State Board of Education voted to withdraw from the Smarter Balanced Assessment Consortium (SBAC). Despite the decision to withdraw, Utah will proceed to implement Common Core math and English standards. North Carolina legislators should reevaluate the adoption of CCSS and participation in SBAC. North Carolinians should insist that our schools use world-class standards, curricula, and tests — nothing less.

Testing

North Carolina's accountability efforts have been a work in progress since the General Assembly approved the state's testing program, the ABCs of Public Education, in 1996. Since its inception, the NC Department of Public Instruction has added and eliminated several tests, changed cut scores, and even discarded results. This *ad hoc*, even haphazard, approach to standards and student assessment is one reason why few North Carolinians have faith in the state's ability to implement a sound academic accountability program.

In the fall of 2012, DPI implemented another series of changes to the state testing program. The READY Accountability Model will introduce new tests, including common core tests, to the state's public school system. Obviously, it is too early to evaluate the quality of these assessments. Nevertheless, READY will have the same major flaw as the ABCs of Public Education — many of the tests will be developed in-house. As in the past, North Carolinians will not be able to compare test results to those of other states.[4]

Despite READY, state education officials have demonstrated a willingness to administer national tests. DPI adopted the WorkKeys assessment and began administering the test to qualified public school students throughout North Carolina in 2012. WorkKeys is a series of tests that evaluate the skills and knowledge of high school students interested in business, manufacturing, allied health, and other highly specialized professions. Based on their WorkKeys scores, students can determine if they have the skills needed for a given job or profession. Those who fall short in attaining the requisite scores in one or more of the three areas can recognize their weaknesses and improve upon them in their remaining years in high school.[5]

In addition, students who meet WorkKeys standards can earn a National Career Readiness Certificate (NCRC). The certificate shows that the individual has met basic requirements for entry into a profession. It is the first step in the process of "stacking" credentials, such as industry-specific certification, formal on-the-job training, and/or a degree from an institution of higher education. High school graduates who have an NCRC may choose to forgo higher education altogether and instead pursue various industry certifications or credentials. In this way, they can acquire the skills and knowledge to be successful in their careers without wasting valuable time and borrowing thousands of dollars to attend community colleges, technical schools, or universities.

WorkKeys or a similar testing program should become a permanent part of North Carolina's testing program, particularly if the state begins to place greater emphasis on career and technical education. Likewise, the state should adopt nationally norm-referenced tests and standards-based tests that gauge college readiness. The assessment selected by the NC State Board of Education, the ACT, does both.[6]

Institutions of higher education commonly use the ACT in the college admissions process. North Carolina is one of nine states to require high school students to take the ACT. Most district and charter school students in the state will be required to take the ACT test in eleventh-grade. In 10th grade, students take a test that is similar to the ACT, called PLAN.[7]

Statewide administration of the ACT gives North Carolinians an opportunity, albeit a limited one, to make annual state-by-state comparisons. The state should give North Carolinians more opportunities to compare student achievement across states. One way to do this would be to adopt norm-referenced tests for all subject areas and tested grades. Norm-referenced test results allow us to compare student performance to all other students taking the test. For example, most norm-referenced tests generate percentile rankings that indicate the relationship between any given score and all others. Examples of norm-referenced tests include the California Achievement Test, Comprehensive Test of Basic Skills, Iowa Test of Basic Skills, Tests of Academic Proficiency, Metropolitan Achievement Test, and Stanford Achievement Test.

In addition, tests developed in conjunction with the CCSS will permit interstate comparisons of student performance. The quality of those assessments remains to be determined. If tests are only as good as the standards that inform them, then the outlook for the common core assessments is not encouraging.

Section 2. Teachers

North Carolina has had a uniform teacher salary schedule for about 100 years.[8] Like most states (and unlike most professions), North Carolina's public schools pay teachers based on a scale that rewards experience and credentials. But a growing number of lawmakers and school officials are working to discard the one-size-fits-all salary schedule and implement comprehensive teacher pay programs that attract and reward excellence.

Teacher credentials and teacher quality

There is no question that high-quality teachers produce high achieving students. The problem is that none of the standards that states traditionally use to identify high quality teachers has a significant effect on student performance. A large body of research shows that advanced degrees, years of experience, education courses, teacher test scores, and certification status do not improve teacher effectiveness.[9] Writer Malcolm Gladwell said it most succinctly, "Teaching should be open to anyone with a pulse and a college degree — and teachers should be judged after they have started their jobs, not before."[10] Until we reach Gladwell's ideal, there are ways to reform the current certification and licensure system.

Unfortunately, North Carolina's teacher certification policies continue to use these criteria to determine who can and cannot teach. These policies guarantee that mediocre but credentialed teachers remain in public schools, while talented but uncertified applicants are excluded from the teaching profession. The goal of North Carolina's public schools should be to recruit the highest-quality teachers for our children, rather than finding teachers who have jumped through a sequence of required hoops.

North Carolina offers an alternative route to state certification called "lateral entry." The lateral-entry process allows qualified but uncertified candidates to earn state certification while teaching in a public school. Lateral-entry teachers must pass a series of tests and successfully complete a course of study prescribed by a college or university (or courses specified by one of the state's three alternative-licensing centers).

North Carolina's alternative-certification process is very similar to traditional certification. In fact, there is only one aspect of the process that is truly "alternative" — lateral-entry teachers complete state certification requirements after they receive a college degree, rather than before. A genuine alternative certification program is one that allows prospective teachers to earn state certification or otherwise qualify to teach in a North Carolina public school without enduring the expensive, time-consuming, and often unproductive sequence of education school coursework. The preponderance of research bears out this point.

Several studies show, for example, that the average lateral-entry teacher struggles in the classroom.[11] Researchers Alisa Chapman and Gary Henry found that both alternative-entry and out-of-state teachers generally performed lower than the average North Carolina public school teacher. Graduates of UNC System universities performed slightly above average. On the other hand, of all types of teachers evaluated in the study, Teach for America teachers were, by far, the most effective novice teachers assessed. The Teach for America (TFA) program recruits top-notch college graduates (most of whom do not have an education degree or state certification) to teach in low-performing and/or low-income schools for two years.

Chapman and Henry's findings about TFA teachers and certification (whether it is traditional or lateral-entry) are not unique. Another study using data from North Carolina evaluated the effectiveness of TFA teachers at the high-school level. Researchers found that inexperienced and unlicensed TFA teachers generally outperformed more experienced and licensed teachers. In fact, they concluded that disadvantaged students in secondary schools would be better off with TFA teachers, especially for the subjects of math and science, than with fully licensed in-field teachers with three or more years of experience.[12]

Experience has a positive effect on student performance during the teacher's first five years in the classroom. Multiple studies of North Carolina teachers confirm that teachers with one or two years of experience produce larger gains in student achievement than teachers with no experience.[13] Of course, few would dispute the claim that teachers with experience tend to outperform those with none. Yet, there is evidence that teacher experience effects flat-line after a handful of years in the profession.

In 2011, UNC-Chapel Hill professors Gary Henry and Kevin Bastian and Georgia State University professor C. Kevin Fortner published a study of teacher retention and attrition in North Carolina.[14] Henry and his associates asked a critical question: Did measures of teacher effectiveness increase because the early-career teachers acquired on-the-job skills or because less effective teachers left the profession?[15]

The researchers examined teachers and test scores from North Carolina public schools and concluded:

1. On average, teachers substantially increase their effectiveness between their first and second years of teaching.
2. For teachers who remain in the profession for at least five years, returns to experience generally flatten after the third year of teaching.
3. Frequently, teachers who leave after their first year are less effective than those who continue teaching into their second or later years.
4. Teachers who leave after their third or fourth year are less effective in their final year of teaching, on average, than teachers who continue teaching into a fifth year.
5. The performance of teachers who leave after three or four years of teaching often drops in the final year of teaching.[16]

As mentioned earlier, North Carolina's teacher pay scale is based on credentials and experience. If teacher effectiveness plateaus after the third year of teaching, then why does the state compensate teachers partly based on experience? The state pays experienced teachers more because they assume that experience continues to make teachers more effective or valuable over the course of their educational careers. If this is not the case, then we should pay teachers differently.

National Board Certification and the state salary schedule

Over 19,000 North Carolina teachers (or 18 percent of the public-school teaching workforce) have earned National Board of Professional Teaching Standards (NBPTS) certification. North Carolina has the largest number of NBPTS-certified teachers of any state in the nation, eclipsing Florida by approximately 5,500 teachers.[17] To encourage teachers to undertake the certification process, the state provides low-interest loans to pay the $2,500 assessment fee and three additional paid release days. The state awards those who successfully complete requirements outlined by the NBPTS a 12 percent raise for 10 years.[18]

Research on NBPTS-certified teachers in North Carolina has shown mixed results. The Cary-based SAS Institute concluded that a NBPTS-certified teacher produced student achievement gains that were comparable to their non-certified colleagues.[19] Later that year, a separate research study examined a sample of NBPTS teachers in North Carolina and concurred with the SAS Institute report.[20] Schools with NBPTS-certified teachers serving as principals performed no better than schools with non-board certified principals.[21] On the other hand, subsequent studies have drawn different conclusions. Two notable studies found that National Board Certification may raise student achievement and produce other positive outcomes for students.[22]

There is even disagreement about turnover among teachers who have NBPTS certification. One study concluded that NBPTS-certified teachers change teaching jobs and work in more affluent schools at higher rates than their non-certified counterparts, while others found that NBPTS-certified teachers are more likely to stay in their teaching positions.[23]

In 2008, the National Research Council published the most comprehensive study of NBPTS certification to date. In an assessment of the full body of research literature, analysts from the Council acknowledged that "even in North Carolina, the findings were not consistent across subjects, grade level, different groupings of teachers, or different choices of statistical models."[24]

Given the conflicting results, the National Board Certification salary schedule should not be maintained in its current form. While a slight pay increase may be warranted for teachers who complete the battery of NBPTS requirements for certification, there is no consistent evidence that the state's 12 percent, 10-year investment is a productive use of taxpayer funds. How could the state salary schedule be changed to make it more productive?

In "Scrap the Sacrosanct Salary Schedule," Duke University professor Jacob Vigdor points out that the current method of paying teachers does not correspond to what we know about the relationship between credentials, experience, and student performance.[25] As pointed out above, there is very little evidence that credentials, such as graduate degrees in education, raise academic achievement. In addition, teachers improve dramatically in their initial years of teaching, but the positive effects of experience fade over time.

Vigdor recommends that states eliminate additional pay for master's degrees because there is little evidence that teachers with graduate degrees outperform those who do not have them. He also suggests that states design a salary schedule that focuses "rewards on the early rungs of the experience ladder," a recommendation supported by a number of research studies.[26] Finally, Vigdor contends that the premium paid to NBPTS-certified teachers is "larger than what evidence would support."[27] He recommends reducing the bonus to 5 percent, rather than the current 12 percent premium.

Performance pay

Performance pay is a popular idea, but few attempts to implement broad performance-pay programs have been successful.[28] Resistance from teacher's unions and other public school advocacy organizations play a role, but poor implementation and "policy churn" are also to blame. In short, performance-pay programs have had a notoriously short shelf-life.[29] Nevertheless, merit pay for teachers shows great promise.[30] Policymakers and elected officials in North Carolina should work toward discontinuing across-the-board pay increases and begin to implement a comprehensive pay program that attracts and rewards teaching excellence.

North Carolina has been considering performance-pay initiatives for over 50 years. The North Carolina Commission for the Study of Teacher Merit Pay and Implementation of a Revised Public School Curriculum published a study of merit or performance pay in 1960.[31] Researchers concluded, as we do today, "The key of a true merit schedule is reward of quality. Devices for extra pay for extra duties which reward quantity of service, not quality, are not merit provisions."[32] Five years later, the NC Department of Public Instruction conducted a four-year, experimental study of merit-pay pilot programs in Gastonia, Martin County, and Rowan County.[33] North Carolina has had a number of performance pay initiatives over the years. Between

1996 and 2009, North Carolina awarded bonuses to teachers in schools that met or exceeded academic growth expectations on state tests. Although an evaluation of the so-called "ABC bonuses" identified some positive aspects of the program, the design of the initiative had significant flaws.[34] Most notably, the program awarded ABC bonuses to entire schools, not individual teachers. That meant that the state awarded bonuses to thousands of poorly performing teachers in good schools and failed to award excellent teachers in struggling schools.

From 2001 to 2004, the NC Department of Public Instruction implemented a performance pay pilot program called the North Carolina Bonus Program. The state awarded bonuses of up to $1,800 to math, science, and special education teachers in low-income or low-performing middle and high schools. An independent evaluation by Duke University researchers indicated that this program yielded impressive results.[35] Encouraged by those results, the 2007 session of the North Carolina General Assembly passed a pilot program for alternative teacher-salary plans.[36] In 2007, the state also launched The Collaborative Project, a three-year state-funded school reform initiative. An evaluation of the program conducted by researchers at UNC-Chapel Hill found that performance incentives "did succeed in rewarding the most effective teachers" that participated in the program.[37] In 2011, state legislators gave each school district the authority to implement a merit-pay plan of their own. In late 2012, the state used federal dollars to award merit bonuses of up to $1,500 for each teacher, administrator, and staff member in low-performing schools that exceeded academic growth expectations.[38]

Various school districts, including Charlotte-Mecklenburg Schools and Guilford County Schools, have developed performance-pay programs.[39] Guilford County's Mission Possible program provides an excellent model of a high-quality, district-based program of merit pay.[40] Starting in 2006, Guilford County Schools offered recruitment and retention bonuses of between $2,500 and $10,000, depending on grade level and position. The school district awards performance bonuses of between $2,500 and $5,000 to teachers who are able to raise student achievement one standard error above the mean on a value-added score.

Results from the Mission Possible program suggest that financial incentives may raise the quality of the workforce in schools that need it the most. On average, high-poverty schools employ less effective teachers.[41] To encourage high-quality teachers to work in "hard to staff" schools, school districts should provide incentive pay of up to $5,000 annually.[42]

In addition, school districts should consider providing an annual $2,500 supplement for those who either 1) score at least 1.25 standard deviations above the mean on the Praxis II exam, a test that teachers must pass in order to obtain state certification, or 2) earn a master's degree in math or science (not education) and teach in those areas.[43] Research indicates that a uniform salary schedule may contribute to turnover of math and science teachers. Thus, a targeted salary supplement for math and science teachers is justified.[44]

More importantly, North Carolina is competing with nearby states for math and science teachers, a number of which offer attractive financial incentives for teachers in high-demand subjects. In Georgia, certified math and science teachers begin on step 5 of the state salary schedule. Thus, their initial pay is significantly higher than incoming teachers in low-demand fields.[45] In 2013, a teacher on step 5 of Georgia's state salary schedule earned $36,617, compared to the state's entry-level salary of $31,586.[46] North Carolina's entry-level salary is $30,800.[47] While there is a small difference between entry-level salaries in the two states, the starting salary of a new math or science teacher would be nearly $6,000 higher in Georgia than in North Carolina.

Performance pay: Design and implementation

Mississippi Gov. Phil Bryant was one of five sitting governors to propose performance pay programs in 2012.[48] To better understand the dynamics of designing and implementing a performance pay initiative, Governor Bryant requested a comprehensive performance pay analysis from the Research and Curriculum Unit (RCU) at Mississippi State University. The RCU report is a comprehensive, research-based analysis of the moving parts of performance-pay programs, including structure, organization alignment design, implementation, payouts, and mitigating risks.

Structure. The first step is identifying and rewarding excellent teachers using reliable measures. The largest weights should belong to test-score data and other quantitative measures of student performance. Alternative measures of teacher performance should be approached with caution. Components may be added to teacher evaluation instruments that "pad" the evaluation with qualitative measures that allow ineffective teachers to remain in the classroom when they do not possess talent or requisite skills. The RCU recommends quantitative and qualitative components for the performance pay system. They suggest utilizing Mississippi's existing teacher-evaluation instrument for the qualitative portion.

Similarly, North Carolina should select parts of the state's new teacher evaluation system to use for a performance pay component. The new evaluation system addresses five areas:

- Teachers demonstrate leadership.
- Teachers establish a respectful environment for a diverse population of students.
- Teachers know the content they teach.
- Teachers facilitate learning for their students.
- Teachers reflect on their practice.

Evaluators rated teachers in each area according to a five-category scale — not demonstrated (lowest), developing, proficient, accomplished, and distinguished (highest). The state will add measures of students' academic growth during the 2012-13 school year.

In order to be eligible for a performance-pay bonus, teachers should be required to achieve a "distinguished" rating in key areas. One possible configuration would extend eligibility only to those who have a "distinguished" rating in content knowledge and instructional abilities. While leadership and an appreciation of diversity are important, they are not reliable indicators of teacher quality. Of course, the self-evaluation lacks objectivity.

For the quantitative portion of the performance pay system, the RCU recommends using a "value-added" algorithm. Mississippi is in the process of developing a value-added system. Unlike Mississippi, however, North Carolina would not be starting from scratch. School and district administrators in our state have used the state's Education Value-Added Assessment System (EVAAS) since 2007. If the state wants to identify and reward the best teachers in the state, EVAAS data is the place to start.

Value-added analysis uses standardized tests to estimate teacher effectiveness. This powerful evaluation method employs advanced statistical techniques to project the future performance of individual students based on their past performance. The difference between the projected and actual performance of students determines the value added or subtracted by the teacher. North Carolina's public schools calculate and record value-added scores for teachers in EVAAS, but state officials have not released the data to the public. Examinations of value-added methodology, including those that use North Carolina's value-added data, generally agree that value-added measures are sound indicators of teacher quality.[49]

Performance pay is a useful application of value-added measures. School districts can compare the value-added scores of teachers regardless of the level of students they teach. This is important because it neutralizes the advantage of teaching classes of advanced students. Value-added measures report the *progress* or *growth* of individual students, which is much different than (and superior to) the current method of reporting proficiency levels or scale scores by school. In this way, teachers who made great progress with low-performing students would be more likely to receive a performance bonus than teachers who made few gains with high-performing kids. Absent a value-added system, a school district would likely reward the latter teacher.

The RCU also recommends that the performance-pay program include both individual and school-wide measures. School-wide measures include graduation rates, proficiency rates on state tests, and the like, particularly for those who teach subjects that are not subject to state testing requirements. But school-wide measures may be misleading. In early 2012, the New York City Department of Education released performance data for the district's 18,000 public school teachers. A preliminary analysis of the data found that high percentages of ineffective teachers were not clustered in schools with a high percentage of low-income and/or low-performing students. Rather, bad and good teachers were evenly distributed across schools. This is one key reason why teacher evaluation must focus primarily on individual performance, not just school-level achievement.[50]

Organization Alignment Design. The RCU recommends that performance-pay initiatives be closely aligned with the state testing program and teacher evaluation system. They also suggest that the state should build flexibility into the system by allowing principals to customize the plan to their school. For example, principals would have the discretion to change the weights given to the qualitative and quantitative components of the evaluation. Principals may also choose to award performance pay to teachers who improve on specific deficiencies identified by their individual evaluations.

Implementation. A sound approach to implementation is one of the most important (and overlooked) aspects of developing a successful performance-pay program. The RCU recommends a two-stage implementation. First, performance pay would be integrated into the teacher evaluation process, so long as funds are available to do so. During this stage, qualitative measures will be the primary source of information for the performance pay program.

The second and more controversial proposal is to delay the use of quantitative measures until at least 2015. The RCU recognizes that states, including Mississippi and North Carolina, plan to implement math and English assessments aligned with the Common Core State Standards in 2014. The 2014-15 school year would serve as the baseline year. Thus, the 2015-16 school year would be the first opportunity to use value-added metrics based on the common core.

To ease implementation, the North Carolina General Assembly should consider creating a dual salary schedule similar to the one adopted by legislators in Florida.[51] Under the Florida plan, current teachers are allowed to remain in an existing salary schedule (that includes a performance-pay component) or opt into a performance-based salary schedule. The state will place all teachers hired after June 30, 2014 in the revised, performance-based, system.

Under the new system, Florida teachers will receive a performance bonus only if they achieve a rating of "highly effective" or "effective" on the state's teacher evaluation instrument. Current teachers have an incentive to opt into the performance-based system. The monetary rewards for teachers who earn the "highly effective" rating exceed salary adjustments provided by the existing schedule. Moreover, the performance-based plan provides bonuses for teaching in low-income schools, low-performing schools, or high-need subject areas.

Payouts. The RCU establishes two principles for payout: 1) only exceptional results should be rewarded and 2) rewards need to be meaningful. As mentioned above, the performance pay tied to the state testing program failed to reward excellence. Under the ABC bonus system, the state awarded bonuses to thousands of poorly performing teachers in good schools. More importantly, it failed to reward excellent teachers in struggling schools.

Mitigating Risks. The RCU offers three recommendations for mitigating risks of implementing a performance-pay program. First, the program requires support from the top. This means that the NC State Board of Education and Department of Public Instruction would have to be fully committed to the program. District superintendents and central office personnel would also have a significant role in implementing a successful initiative. Second, RCU recommends appointing a performance-pay manager who "understands how to embed a new process into an organization." Finally, they recommend that teachers count assessment results as a major test grade, so that teachers are not adversely affected by student apathy toward standardized assessments.

In sum, North Carolina and Mississippi will encounter many of same challenges in their efforts to create statewide performance pay programs. Nevertheless, North Carolina is a year or two ahead of Mississippi in the area of quantitative evaluation of teacher effectiveness, a key element in the design of any performance-pay effort.

The goal of any performance-based compensation system is to ensure that public schools are retaining the best teachers.[52] A study of teacher attrition in North Carolina suggested that high-performing teachers are more likely to leave the teaching profession than their low-performing counterparts. They are also more likely to leave disadvantaged schools.[53]

Tenure

In recent years, state legislators from across the nation have been active in making changes to or eliminating teacher tenure laws. According to the Education Commission of the States, more than a dozen state legislatures made changes to their states' tenure laws in 2011 alone.[54] Idaho adopted the most explicit rejection of tenure laws. Proposed legislation in Idaho mandated, "No new employment contract between a school district and certificated employee shall result in the vesting of tenure, continued expectations of employment or property rights in an employment relationship."[55] Modifications to tenure laws in other states were not as radical.

Most states adopted changes to dismissal laws or strengthened standards required to obtain tenure. For example, in 2011 Tennessee increased the teacher probationary period from three years to five years. In addition, tenure is only granted to a teacher in Tennessee if he achieves a rating of "above expectations" or higher during the previous two years of his employment.[56] During the same year, states such as Delaware and Oklahoma also added teacher ratings to tenure standards. In order to receive tenure in these states, teachers must prove that they are effective. Value-added data may be useful in this regard.[57]

Figure 1: Tenure laws in the United States

State/ Jurisdiction	State made change in policy on teacher tenure due to economy or other factors (2011)	Frequency of evaluations for tenured and non-tenured teachers is the same (2012)	Frequency of evaluations for tenured teachers (2012)	Frequency of evaluations for non-tenured teachers (2012)
Alabama	No	Yes	Annually	Annually
Alaska	No	No	Every other year	Twice a year
Arizona	Yes	No	Annually	Twice a year
Arkansas	No	Yes	Annually	Annually
California	No	No	Every other year	Annually
Colorado	Yes	No	Every three years	Annually
Connecticut	No	Yes	--	--
Delaware	Yes	No	Every other year	Annually
District of Columbia	No	Yes	--	--
Florida	No	No	Annually	Twice a year
Georgia	No	Yes	Annually	Annually
Hawaii	Yes	No	Every five years	Annually
Idaho	No	No	Annually	Twice a year
Illinois	No	Yes	Every other year	Every other year
Indiana	No	Yes	--	--
Iowa	Yes	No	Every three years	Every other year
Kansas	No	No	Every three years	Twice a year
Kentucky	No	No	Every three years	Annually
Louisiana	Yes	Yes	--	--
Maine	No	Yes	--	--
Maryland	Yes	No	Twice every five years	Annually
Massachusetts	No	No	Every other year	Annually
Michigan	Yes	Yes	Annually	Annually
Minnesota	No	No	--	Annually
Mississippi	No	Yes	--	--
Missouri	No	Yes	--	--

State/Jurisdiction	State made change in policy on teacher tenure due to economy or other factors (2011)	Frequency of evaluations for tenured and non-tenured teachers is the same (2012)	Frequency of evaluations for tenured teachers (2012)	Frequency of evaluations for non-tenured teachers (2012)
Montana	No	Yes	--	--
Nebraska	No	No	--	Twice a year
Nevada	Yes	No	Annually	Three times a year
New Hampshire	No	Yes	--	--
New Jersey	No	No	Annually	Three times a year
New Mexico	No	No	Every three years	Annually
New York	Yes	Yes	Annually	Annually
North Carolina	No	Yes	Annually	Annually
North Dakota	No	No	Annually	Twice a year
Ohio	Yes	No	Every two years	Annually
Oklahoma	Yes	No	Annually	Twice a year
Oregon	No	No	--	Annually
Pennsylvania	No	No	Annually	Twice a year
Rhode Island	Yes	Yes	Annually	Annually
South Carolina	No	No	Annually	Twice a year
South Dakota	No	No	Every other year	Annually
Tennessee	Yes	No	Four times per year	Six times per year
Texas	No	Yes	Every five years	Every five years
Utah	No	No	Annually	Twice a year
Vermont	No	Yes	--	--
Virginia	No	No	Every three years	Annually
Washington	Yes	No	Annually	Twice a year
West Virginia	No	No	--	Twice a year
Wisconsin	No	No	Every three years	Annually
Wyoming	No	No	Annually	Twice a year
U.S. Total	15	19	--	--

In addition to Idaho, Florida also largely abandoned the traditional tenure system. The Florida legislature adopted a system that awards annual contracts to teachers hired after the 2010-2011 school year. To receive an annual contract, teachers must be certified and receive a recommendation for contract renewal by a superior. In addition, teachers must meet performance goals. Teachers who receive multiple ratings of "unsatisfactory" or "needs improvement" are not permitted to receive a contract renewal.[58]

The idea of "elite tenure" could be one way to strike a compromise between tenure supporters and opponents.[59] Elite tenure awards tenure status to a small number of highly effective teachers. Louisiana adopted a system by which the teachers rated as 'ineffective' (bottom 10 percent) lose tenure, while teachers rated as 'effective' (top 10 percent) for five out of six years are granted tenure.

Tenure in North Carolina

The NC General Statutes outline the criteria required for teachers to obtain tenure, also called "career status."[60] The law requires teachers to be employed by a North Carolina public school system for four consecutive years. Prior to receiving tenure, probationary teachers are observed and evaluated four times a year by one or more school administrators. Administrators observe and evaluate teachers with career status three times a year.[61]

North Carolina is one of 19 states that require at least annual evaluations for tenured and non-tenured teachers (See Table 1).[62] Most states do not evaluate tenured teachers with the same frequency as non-tenured teachers.

The National Council on Teacher Quality (NCTQ) evaluates state tenure systems by examining four goals. According to the NCTQ, nine states, including North Carolina, earned a rating of "meets a small part of goal." The four goals or standards outlined by the NCTQ include the following:

1. A teacher should be eligible for tenure after a certain number of years of service, but tenure should not be granted automatically at that juncture.
2. Evidence of effectiveness should be the preponderant criterion in tenure decisions.
3. The state should articulate a process, such as a hearing, that local districts must administer in considering the evidence and deciding whether a teacher should receive tenure.

4.   The minimum years of service needed to achieve tenure should allow sufficient data to be accumulated on which to base tenure decisions; five years is the ideal minimum.[63]

NCTQ criticizes North Carolina for failing to base tenure on student performance or teacher effectiveness. They offer three recommendations:

1.   Ensure evidence of effectiveness is the preponderant criterion in tenure decisions. North Carolina should make evidence of effectiveness, rather than years in the classroom, the most significant factor when determining this leap in professional standing.

2.   Articulate a process that local districts must administer when deciding which teachers get tenure. North Carolina should require a clear process, such as a hearing, to ensure that the local district reviews a teacher's performance before making a determination regarding tenure.

3.   Require a longer probationary period. North Carolina should make certain its probationary period allows for a collection of sufficient data that reflect teacher performance.[64]

Policymakers should be sensitive to the ways that policies like tenure create productivity declines among tenured teachers. One study examined absences among a sample of North Carolina teachers and found a significant relationship between increased absenteeism and two variables, tenure and experience.[65] This may lead to subsequent declines in student performance.

Section 3: The Funding System for Education

It is easy for elected officials to adopt the notion that less public school funding is bad and more is good. One left-leaning pollster, Public Policy Polling, asked North Carolinians if their local public schools should receive more funding, less funding or about the same amount. Predictably, two-thirds of respondents thought that schools should receive more funding. But when other pollsters first inform voters how much is currently spent on education and then ask if the amount should rise, support drops off dramatically.[68]

Rather than asking whether the state allocates "enough" resources to provide children a quality education, we should be asking "how" public schools spend their money. Maximizing the return on our $12 billion investment in public schools is one of the most important reasons to rethink North Carolina's funding model for public schools.

Public school advocacy groups often dismiss the "how" because it requires them to concede that educational productivity — the relationship between inputs and outcomes — actually matters. The research on educational productivity, from researchers on both sides of the ideological spectrum, provides compelling evidence that increasing student performance takes much more than reaching some arbitrary amount of spending. It takes strategic investments in exceptional people and proven practices.[69]

The design of North Carolina's funding system

The NC Department of Public Instruction describes North Carolina's school funding system as a "complex and integrated process."[70] The complexity of the system led the NC General Assembly to commission a study of the state's public school funding system in 2009. The goal of the study was to determine if the state should create a new, less complicated, and more productive way of funding our public schools.

The legislature hired Denver-based consulting firm Augenblick, Palaich and Associates (APA) to conduct the study. In September 2010, the Joint Legislative Study Committee on Public School Funding Formulas received the final report, "Recommendations to Strengthen North Carolina's School Funding System."[71] This study explains how North Carolina can work within the parameters of the current system to improve our school funding model.

Other types of funding models, e.g. block funding for school districts or attaching funding to the student, are superior to the fixes outlined by APA. Nevertheless, other types of funding models may not be politically feasible in the short term. For now, legislators should use the APA recommendations to inch closer to funding a public school system that empowers parents and children to make educational choices that are in the best interests of individual families.

North Carolina's school finance system has three basic types of allotments. Position allotments distribute state funds to school districts for teachers, administrators, and other district employees. The state provides dollar allotments for teacher assistants, textbooks, central office administration, and classroom supplies.[72] Categorical allotments are targeted toward a specific purpose or population, such as at-risk students, special needs children, non-instructional support personnel, and transportation.[73] APA researchers could not assemble a list of the actual formulas used to allocate funds because of the complex structure of the state funding system. They observed:

> *Perhaps the largest weakness is the number of allotments used to distribute state support. The fact is that the precise number of allotments is hard to determine because several of them use multiple subformulas. The vast majority of state support is allocated through only a few allotments while numerous other allotments each distribute less than two percent of all state support.*[74]

APA identified two major problems that may undermine the effectiveness of North Carolina's allotment system. First, the allotment structure increased the likelihood that districts received duplicate funding for similar expenses. Researchers found duplication in allotments for at-risk students, for example. Second, the potential for "political decisionmaking" increases as the number of allotments increases.[75]

The 10 recommendations proposed by APA are distinct and listed in order of the ease of implementation. An 11th recommendation incorporates several of the ideas listed into one major overhaul of the funding system.

- **Combine all allotments that are distributed on the basis of total enrollment.** In other words, North Carolina should collapse multiple allotment categories into a single, per-pupil allotment and give school districts the flexibility to use the allotted funds as needed.

- **Modify the Special Education Allotment.** APA proposed a three-tiered system for special needs allotment – mild, moderate, and severe. Funding would be calculated based on the allotment for a mild disability. A moderate disability would receive 2.5-times the amount allocated for a student with a mild disability. A student with a severe disability would receive 5.0-times the amount allocated for a student with a mild disability. For example, all students with a mild disability would receive an additional $1,000. Those with a moderate disability would receive $2,500 more, and the severely disabled child would receive an additional $5,000.

- **Modify the Low Wealth County Allotment.** APA proposes two alternative approaches. The first is creating two distinct allotments that would be based on simple formulas (one based on district wealth and another based on district school tax effort). The second is creating a single formula that would use a power equalizing procedure. According to the authors, " 'Power equalizing' is a procedure that takes into consideration both wealth and tax effort and calculates state aid in such a way that every district receives a different amount based on its particular circumstances, with aid decreasing as wealth increases and increasing as tax effort rises."[76]

- **Modify the At-Risk Student Allotment and the Disadvantaged Student Supplemental Fund Allotment.** APA recommends combining the at-risk and Disadvantaged Student Supplemental Fund allotments and distributing the funds in one of two ways. First, the state could simply allocate funds based on the number of low-performing students in the district. To determine this number, the state would set the performance standard based on student test scores and other outcome-based metrics. Another approach is to establish a proxy for performance, such as the number of students eligible to receive federal Title I funding or the number of students eligible for a free or reduced price lunch.

- **Modify the Small County Allotment.** Researchers for APA recommend that any "small county" allotment focus exclusively on district enrollment, not the population of the county. They argue that the size of the district creates the cost pressure on the county tax base, not vice versa. Therefore, the state should mitigate the cost pressure produced by the school district.

- **Change the way that Lottery funds are distributed.** This is the most controversial of the APA recommendations. They argue that lottery funding for school facilities should be based on the wealth of the district and structured in a way that provides an incentive for districts to support facilities on the local level. To do this, they recommend using the "power equalizing" approach discussed above. While a good short-term solution, there are larger questions about the state's role in funding school facilities. Lottery and corporate income tax funding provide the two sources of state funding for school facilities, but districts receive relatively little funding from these sources. Instead, the state expects local school districts and county commissions to assume the bulk of the expenses to build and maintain school buildings.

There are two problems with using lottery and corporate income tax funding for school facilities. The first is variability. The amount of lottery and corporate income tax funding received by the state is not stable and thus cannot be relied upon as a consistent source of revenue. In addition, Republicans may choose to decrease or eliminate the corporate income tax, likely placing a heavier burden on lottery funding for school facilities unless the legislature establishes an alternative source of revenue.

Perhaps a better approach to allocating lottery revenue is to give school districts the flexibility to use both the school construction and the class size portions of the lottery allotment for any operational or capital expenditure that they see fit. This means that districts would have control of around 75 percent of the lottery revenue distributed in any given year. The remaining 25 percent would continue to go toward prekindergarten programs, need-based college scholarships, and UNC financial aid. To put this in dollar terms, in FY 2011, the lottery allocated $205.4 million for class size reduction, that is, mostly teacher salaries and benefits. During the same year, the lottery distributed $100 million for school construction.[77] Rather than separating funding into two discrete purposes, the NC General Assembly should simply block grant the $305.4 million amount to school districts based on student enrollment.

- **Modify the Teacher Allotment**. APA recommends changing the way that the state calculates the number of state-funded teaching positions allocated to each district. Their alternative method would distribute funding based on a weighted student count. In other words, funding would be determined by student characteristics and risk factors, e.g., disability, English language proficiency, course of study, etc. Special needs students would receive funding based on the severity of their disability or need. Students enrolled in vocational education programs, English Language Learner (ELL) courses, or gifted and talented programs would receive additional state allotments.

- **Modify the Statewide Teacher Salary Schedule.** According to the APA report, a one-size-fits-all salary schedule ignores two cost pressures on school districts in North Carolina: (1) geographic cost differences that reflect differences in prices for consumer goods and (2) the attractiveness of districts to teachers due to factors such as population density. By allowing school districts to determine salaries, they may better respond to local job market conditions.

- **Modify the way the Teacher Allotment salaries are applied.** In addition, APA recommends an alternative approach to the current allotment system. They advocate a formula that multiples the number of eligible teachers by the statewide average salary and is adjusted for factors such as education level, average years of experience, geographic cost, and teacher attractiveness. As they point out, "Under this approach, each district would receive a lump sum of money, which could be used to pay teachers or, in the name of flexibility, anything the district wants."[78]

- **Consider modifying the structure of the Statewide Teacher Salary Schedule.** Like most states, North Carolina has a statewide salary schedule that awards pay based on credentials and years of experience. In most cases, neither of these factors corresponds to teacher effectiveness. APA does not propose a specific reform of the salary schedule, but encourages the state to examine alternatives that will reward teachers based on student performance, teacher evaluation, and other outcomes.

- **Create a "foundation" type formula.** The final recommendation is for the state to consider a "foundation" formula, a system of public school funding used in many other states. A foundation formula sets a base cost and adjusts the amount based on student and district characteristics. Additional state aid would be added to the base. APA points out:

  Additional state aid could still be provided for low wealth school districts, to promote particular programs or services of interest to the state, to provide incentives to districts to generate local funds, for transportation, and for capital purposes. This could be accomplished by adding several "tiers" to the foundation program.[79]

Of course, this kind of large-scale system would supplant the first 10 recommendations, which were designed to modify the existing system.

Conclusion

While lawmakers should feel free to sever North Carolina's ties to the Common Core State Standards, a number of the structural reforms outlined in this chapter address some of North Carolina's most deeply embedded, and in some cases deeply cherished, practices. Indeed, one should not "take a stab" at changing the salary schedule, teacher tenure, or the state funding system. Rather, it will require surgical precision to restore the health of our public schools.

Endnotes

1. Terry Stoops, "Educational Market Share: Despite the growth of school choice, public schools dominate," Policy Report, John Locke Foundation, July 2012, http://johnlocke.org/research/show_story.html?id=245&type=policy%2oreports.

2. "Closing the door on innovation: Why One National Curriculum is Bad for America," May 6, 2011, http://www.k12innovation.com/Manifesto/_V2_Home.html.

3. See Mark Bauerlein and Sandra Stotsky, "How Common Core's ELA Standards Place College Readiness at Risk," Pioneer Institute, White Paper No. 89, September 2012. B.A. Birch, "Does Common Core Provide an International Benchmark?" *Education News*, November 22, 2011, http://www.educationnews.org/education-policy-and-politics/ does-common-core-provide-an-international-benchmark. Emmett McGroarty and Jane Robbins, "Controlling Education From the Top: Why Common Core Is Bad for America," Pioneer Institute and American Principles Project, White Paper No. 87, May 2012. James Stergios, "Myths About National Standards: Myth # 1," *Boston Globe*, November 16, 2011, http://boston.com/community/blogs/ rock_the_schoolhouse/2011/11/myths_about_national_ standards.html. Sandra Stotsky, *The Death and Resurrection of a Coherent Literature Curriculum*, New York: Rowman & Littlefield, 2012. Sandra Stotsky & Ze'ev Wurman, "Common Core's Standards Still Don't Make the Grade," Pioneer Institute, White Paper No. 65, July 2010. Grant Wiggins, "The Common Core Math Standards: They Don't Add Up," *Education Week*, Vol. 31, Issue 5, September 28, 2011, http://www.edweek.org/ew/ articles/2011/09/28/05wiggins.h31.html. Joanne Yatvin, "A Flawed Approach to Reading in the Common-Core Standards," *Education Week*, Vol. 31, Issue 22, February 27, 2012, http://www.edweek.org/ew/articles/2012/02/29/22yatvin.h31.html.

4. North Carolina Department of Public Instruction (NC DPI), READY resources, http://www.dpi.state.nc.us/ready/resources/.

5. NC DPI, "ACT, PLAN, and WorkKeys," http://www.ncpublicschools.org/ accountability/act.

6. "What Kind of Interpretations Can Be Made on the Basis of ACT Scores?" ACT, Inc., 2008, http://www.act.org/research/policymakers/briefs.html.

7. NC DPI, "ACT, PLAN, and WorkKeys."

8. State Superintendent of Public Instruction, "The salary schedule and classification of schools," Raleigh, N.C., 1922.

9. Of course, not all researchers agree that credentials are poor indicators of teacher quality. A group of researchers led by Gary Henry of the University of North Carolina conducted a comprehensive assessment of the relationship between student performance, credentials, and experience. Henry and his colleagues found that students perform better when their teacher 1) has a degree or certification in the field in which they teach and 2) are beyond their first few years of teaching. Master's degrees had no effect on high school performance and a slightly positive effect on the performance of elementary and middle school students. In addition, Duke University professors Charles Clotfelter, Helen Ladd, and Jacob Vigdor agree. Their study, "Teacher Credentials and Student Achievement in High School: A Cross-Subject Analysis with Student Fixed Effects," used data for 10th grade

students in North Carolina to determine if teacher credentials had an effect on student achievement. (Charles Clotfelter, Helen Ladd, and Jacob Vigdor, "Teacher Credentials and Student Achievement in High School A Cross-Subject Analysis with Student Fixed Effects," *The Journal Of Human Resources*, Vol. 45, No. 3, Summer 2010) They concluded that subject-specific certification and licensure appeared to have a reasonably large, positive effect on student achievement. Similar results were found for special needs children in North Carolina. (See Bianca E. Montrosse, "Estimating the Effects of Teacher Certification on the Academic Achievement of Exceptional High School Students in North Carolina," Claremont Graduate University, Ph.D. dissertation, 2009.) Clotfelter and his colleagues warn, however, that the distribution of subject-specific certified teachers was uneven. Low-income children were less likely to be taught by a teacher with multiple years of experience, National Board Certification, or a subject-specific certification than their more affluent peers.

10. Malcolm Gladwell, "Most likely to succeed: How do we hire when we can't tell who's right for the job," *The New Yorker*, December 15, 2008, http://www.newyorker.com/reporting/2008/12/15/081215fa_fact_gladwell.

11. A few studies have also found little difference between traditionally and alternatively licensed teachers. In a study of technology education teachers in North Carolina, for example, one researcher found no statistical difference between these two groups of teachers. (Bradley Davis Bowen, "Measuring Teacher Effectiveness When Comparing Alternatively Licensed and Traditionally Licensed High School Technology Education Teachers in North Carolina," North Carolina State University, Ph.D. dissertation, 2011.)

12. Zeyu Xu, Jane Hannaway, and Colin Taylor, "Making a Difference?: The Effects of Teach for America in High School," *Journal of Policy Analysis and Management*, Vol. 30, No. 3, 2011.

13. Charles T. Clotfelter, Helen F. Ladd, and Jacob L. Vigdor, "How and Why Do Teacher Credentials Matter for Student Achievement?" CALDER Working Paper 2, Washington, DC: The Urban Institute, 2007. Charles T. Clotfelter, Helen F. Ladd, and Jacob L. Vigdor, "Teacher Credentials and Student Achievement in High School: A Cross-Subject Analysis with Student Fixed Effects." CALDER Working Paper 11, Washington, DC: The Urban Institute, 2007. Helen F. Ladd, "Value-Added Modeling of Teacher Credentials: Policy Implications." Paper presented at the second annual CALDER research conference, "The Ins and Outs of Value-Added Measures in Education: What Research Says," Washington, D.C., November 21, 2008, http://www.caldercenter.org/upload/Sunny_Ladd_presentation.pdf. Douglas N. Harris and Tim R. Sass, "Teacher Training, Teacher Quality, and Student Achievement." CALDER Working Paper 3, Washington, DC: The Urban Institute, 2007.

14. Gary T. Henry, Kevin C. Bastian, and C. Kevin Fortner, "Stayers and Leavers: Early-Career Teacher Effectiveness and Attrition," *Educational Researcher* Vol. 40, No. 6, August/September 2011. For another perspective on attrition, see C. Kirabo Jackson, "Match Quality, Worker Productivity, and Worker Mobility: Direct Evidence From Teachers," NBER Working Paper No. 15990, Cambridge, MA: National Bureau of Economic Research, Inc., May 2010. Jackson argues that teacher performance

relies on the compatibility of the teacher and school. Using data from North Carolina, he found that teacher effectiveness increases after a teacher moves to a different school. Jackson argues that "match quality" has just as important an affect on student achievement as "teacher quality." In addition, teachers are likely to stay at their schools when "match quality" is high. His study suggests that these decreases in turnover do not occur as a result of compensation but have to do more with psychological factors such as satisfaction and validation.

15. Henry, Bastian, and Fortner, "Stayers and Leavers: Early-Career Teacher Effectiveness and Attrition."

16. *Ibid.*, p. 271-2.

17. "NBCTs by State 2010-2011," National Board for Professional Teaching Standards, http://www.nbpts.org/resources/nbct_directory/nbcts_by_state.

18. "State Information: North Carolina," National Board for Professional Teaching Standards, http://www.nbpts.org/resources/state_local_information/NC.

19. William Sanders, James Ashton, and S. Paul Wright, "Comparison of the Effects of NBPTS-Certified Teachers with Other Teachers on the Rate of Student Academic Progress Institution," SAS Institute, 2005.

20. Wendy McColskey, James H. Stronge, Thomas J. Ward, Pamela D. Tucker, Barbara Howard, Karla Lewis, and Jennifer L. Hindman, "A Comparison of National Board Certified Teachers and non-National Board Certified Teachers: Is there a difference in teacher effectiveness and student achievement?" National Board for Professional Teaching Standards, June 2005.

21. Amy Talbert Bailey, "Leadership Skills Of North Carolina Principals With Certification From The National Board Of Professional Teaching Standards," University of North Carolina at Charlotte, Ed.D. dissertation, 2010.

22. Lloyd Bond, Richard Jaeger, Tracy Smith, and John Hattie, "The Certification System of the National Board of Professional Teaching Standards: A Construct and Consequential Validity Study," Center for Educational Research and Evaluation, University of North Carolina, Greensboro, September 2000. Daniel Goldhaber and Emily Anthony, "Can teacher quality be effectively assessed?" Urban Institute, 2004, http://www.urban.org/UploadedPDF/410958_NBPTSOutcomes.pdf.

23. Milton D. Hakel, Judith Anderson Koenig, and Stuart W. Elliott, Editors, "Assessing Accomplished Teaching: Advanced-Level Certification Programs," Committee on Evaluation of Teacher Certification by the National Board for Professional Teaching Standards, National Research Council, 2008. Daniel C. Humphrey, Julia E. Koppich, and Heather J. Hough., "Sharing the wealth: National Board Certified Teachers and the schools that need them most," *Education Policy Analysis Archives*, Vol. 13, 2005. Daniel Goldhaber and Michael Hansen, "National Board Certification and teacher career path: Does NBPTS Certification influence how long teachers remain in the profession and where they teach?" *Education Finance and Policy*, Vol. 4, No. 3 Summer 2009.

24. Milton D. Hakel, Judith Anderson Koenig, and Stuart W. Elliott, Editors, "Committee on Evaluation of Teacher Certification by the National Board for Professional Teaching Standards," National Research Council, 2008.

25. Jacob Vigdor, "Scrap the Sacrosanct Salary Schedule," *Education Next*, Vol. 8,

No. 4, Fall 2008, http://educationnext.org/scrap-the-sacrosanct-salary-schedule.
26. Charles T. Clotfelter, Helen F. Ladd, and Jacob L. Vigdor, "How and Why do Teacher Credentials Matter for Student Achievement?" NBER Working Paper No. 12828, Cambridge, MA: National Bureau of Economic Research, Inc., January 2007. Charles T. Clotfelter, Helen F. Ladd, and Jacob L. Vigdor, "Teacher Credentials and Student Achievement: Longitudinal Analysis with Student Fixed Effects," *Economics of Education Review* Vol. 26, No. 6, December 2007. Gary T. Henry, Kevin C. Bastian, and C. Kevin Fortner, "Gains in novice teacher effectiveness: On-the-job development or less effective teachers leaving?" Carolina Institute for Public Policy, 2011. Dan Goldhaber, "Teachers matter, but effective teacher quality policies are elusive," in *Handbook of Research in Education Finance and Policy*, ed. Helen F. Ladd and Edward B. Fiske, New York: Routledge, 2008. Matthew Wiswall, "The Dynamics of Teacher Quality" Social Science Research Network, January 2011. Charles T. Clotfelter, Helen F. Ladd, and Jacob Vigdor, "Teacher credentials and student achievement: Longitudinal analysis with student fixed effects." *Economics of Education Review* Vol. 26, 2007. Lauren Akers, Sarah Cordes, Mary Kingston, Jackson Miller, and Caleb Varner, "Making North Carolina's Teacher Salary Schedule More Effective: Report to the North Carolina General Assembly's Fiscal Research Division," Terry Sanford Institute of Public Policy, Duke University, May 1, 2009.
27. Jacob Vigdor, "Scrap the Sacrosanct Salary Schedule."
28. For an example of the limitations of research on merit pay, see Charles Clotfelter, Elizabeth Glennie, Helen Ladd, and Jacob Vigdor, "Would Higher Salaries Keep Teachers in High-Poverty Schools? Evidence From a Policy Intervention in North Carolina," National Bureau of Economic Research, Working Paper 12285, June 2006. The authors concluded, "The fact that the [merit pay] program appears to have reduced departure rates of teachers from the schools serving disadvantaged and low-performing students means that the program could potentially have raised student achievement *had it remained in operation for a longer period of time.*" p. 20, emphasis mine.
29. Donald B. Gratz, *The Peril and Promise of Performance Pay: Making Education Compensation Work*, New York: R&L Education, 2009, p. 63.
30. A growing body of research has found a significant relationship between teacher working conditions and student achievement. See Susan J. Rosenholtz, *Teachers' Workplace: The Social Organization of Schools*, New York: Longman, 1989. Joan Talbert, Milbrey Wallin McLaughlin, and Brian Rowan, "Understanding Context Effects on Secondary School Teaching." *Teachers College Record*, Vol. 95, No. 1, 1993. Anthony S. Bryk and Barbara Schneider, *Trust in Schools: A Core Resource for Improvement.* New York: Russell Sage Foundation, 2002. Richard M. Ingersoll, *Who Controls Teachers' Work?: Power and Accountability in America's Schools*, Cambridge: Harvard University Press, 2003. Susanna Loeb and Linda Darling-Hammond, "How Teaching Conditions Predict Teacher Turnover in California Schools," *Peabody Journal of Education*, Vol. 80, No. 3, 2005. Carrie R. Leana and Fritz K. Pil, "Social Capital and Organizational Performance: Evidence from Urban Public Schools," *Organization Science*, Vol. 17, No. 3, May-June 2006. Eric Hanushek, and Steven G. Rivkin, "Pay, Working Conditions and Teaching Quality," *The Future of Children*, The Brookings

Institution Vol. 17, No. 1, Spring 2007.

31. Commission for the Study of Teacher Merit Pay and Implementation of a Revised Public School Curriculum, North Carolina General Assembly, "Report Of The Commission For The Study Of Teacher Merit Pay And Implementation Of A Revised Public School Curriculum: To the Honorable Luther H. Hodges, Governor of the State of North Carolina," 1960, http://www.ncleg.net/library/Collections/studies/year1966.html.

32. *Ibid.*

33. North Carolina Department of Public Instruction, "The North Carolina Teacher Merit Pay Study: A Four-Year Experimental Study in Three Pilot Centers, Gastonia, Martin County, Rowan County: A Report to the 1965 General Assembly," 1965, http://www.ncleg.net/library/Collections/studies/year1966.html

34. Jacob L.Vigdor, "Teacher Salary Bonuses in North Carolina," National Center on Performance Incentives, 2008, http://www.performanceincentives.org/data/files/directory/ConferencePapersNews/Vigdor1.pdf. See also Thomas Ahn and Jacob Vigdor, "Making Teacher Incentives Work: Lessons from North Carolina's Teacher Bonus Program. Education Outlook. No 5.," American Enterprise Institute for Public Policy Research, June 2011. Cassandra M. Guarino, Abigail B. Brown, Adam E., Wyse, "Can Districts Keep Good Teachers in the Schools that Need Them Most?" *Economics of Education Review*, Vol. 30, No. 5, October 2011.

35. Clotfelter, Glennie, Ladd, and Vigdor, "Would Higher Salaries Keep Teachers in High-Poverty Schools?" p. 20.

36. "North Carolina General Assembly, Session Law 2007-453, HB 966: An act directing the state board of education to establish a pilot program authorizing the implementation of alternative teacher salary plans," August 1, 2007, http://www.ncga.state.nc.us/Sessions/2007/Bills/House/HTML/H966v6.html. See also, Dorothy Hines and Kayla Mathis, "Regional Specific Incentives for Teacher Recruitment and Retention," North Carolina Department of Public Instruction, July 2007, http://www.ncpublicschools.org/intern-research/reports/?&print=true.

37. Charles L. Thompson, Gary T. Henry, David C. Kershaw, Adrienne Smith, Rebecca A. Zulli, "Evaluation of The Pilot Phase of The Collaborative Project (2007-08 through 2009-10)," The Carolina Institute for Public Policy, UNC Chapel Hill, April, 2011, p. ii.

38. NC DPI, "Bonuses Will Go To Teachers For Significant Growth In Low-Achieving Schools," November 6, 2012, http://www.dpi.state.nc.us/newsroom/news/2012-13/20121106-01.

39. Sylvester Ngoma, "Improving Teacher Effectiveness: An Examination of a Pay for Performance Plan for Boosting Student Academic Achievement in Charlotte-Mecklenburg Schools," April 15, 2011, http://www.eric.ed.gov/ERICWebPortal/detail?accno=ED518815. Rachel Curtis, "Putting the Pieces in Place: Charlotte-Mecklenburg Public Schools' Teacher Evaluation System," Aspen Institute, March 2012. Susan Moore Johnson, John P. Papay, "Expecting Too Much of Performance Pay," *School Administrator*, Vol. 67, No. 3, March 2010.

40. See Terry Stoops, "Performance Pay for Teachers: Increasing Student Achievement in Schools with Critical Needs," John Locke Foundation Policy Report, September 2008, http://johnlocke.org/policy_reports/display_story.html?id=175.

See also Holli Gottschall Bayonas, et al. "Guilford County Schools Mission Possible Program, Year 1 (2006-07) External Evaluation Report," SERVE Center, University of North Carolina at Greensboro, April 2, 2008.

41. Tim R. Sass, Jane Hannaway, Zeyu Xu, David Figlio, and Li Feng, "Value Added of Teachers in High Poverty Schools and Lower Poverty Schools," Andrew Young School of Policy Studies Research Paper Series Working Paper 12-07, January 2012. Zeyu Xu, Jane Hannaway, and Colin Taylor, "Making a Difference? The Effects of Teach For America in High School," *Journal of Policy Analysis and Management*, Vol. 30, No. 3, Summer 2011.

42. Glennie, Elizabeth, and Justin Wheeler, "Can Pay Incentives Improve the Recruitment and Retention of Teachers in America's Hard-To-Staff Schools? A Research Summary." *Policy Matters*, Center for Child and Family Policy, Duke University, Summer 2007, http://www.eric.ed.gov/ERICDocs/data/ericdocs2sql/content_storage_01/0000019b/80/37/0f/2d.pdf. Clotfelter, et al, "Would Higher Salaries Keep Teachers in High-Poverty Schools?"

43. Lauren Akers et al., "Making North Carolina's Teacher Salary Schedule More Effective."

44. Richard J. Murnane and Randall J. Olsen, "The Effects of Salaries and Opportunity Costs on Length of Stay in Teaching: Evidence from North Carolina," *The Journal of Human Resources*, Vol. 25, No. 1, Winter, 1990.

45. Georgia General Assembly, "House Bill 280: Quality Basic Education Act," April 22, 2009, http://www1.legis.ga.gov/legis/2009_10/sum/hb280.htm.

46. Georgia Department of Education, "State Salary Schedule: 2013," http://www.doe.k12.ga.us/Finance-and-Business-Operations/Budget-Services/Pages/default.aspx.

47. NC DPI, "2012-2013 Salary Schedules," http://www.ncpublicschools.org/fbs/finance/salary.

48. Chris Christie (NJ), Dannell Malloy (CT), and Dennis Daugaard (SD) were the others.

49. There is a significant body of scholarly work on value-added programs. See Lars Lefgren and David Sims, "Using Subject Test Scores Efficiently to Predict Teacher Value-Added," *Educational Evaluation and Policy Analysis*, Vol. 34, No. 1, March 2012. Sass, et al., *Value Added of Teachers in High-Poverty Schools and Lower Poverty Schools*. Roderick A. Rose, Gary T. Henry, Douglas L. Lauen, "Comparing Value Added Models for Estimating Teacher Effectiveness," Carolina Institute for Public Policy, February 2012. Raj Chetty, John N. Friedman, and Jonah E. Rockoff, "The Long-Term Impacts of Teachers: Teacher Value-Added and Student Outcomes in Adulthood," NBER Working Paper No. 17699, Cambridge, MA: National Bureau of Economic Research, Inc., 2011, http://obs.rc.fas.harvard.edu/chetty/value_added.pdf. Goldhaber, Dan, Hyung-Jai Choi, and Lauren Cramer, "A Descriptive Analysis of the Distribution of NBPTS-Certified Teachers in North Carolina," *Economics of Education Review* Vol. 26, No. 2, 2007. Jesse Rothstein, "Teacher Quality In Educational Production: Tracking, Decay, And Student Achievement" *The Quarterly Journal of Economics*, February 2010. For a response to Rothsetin's concerns, see Josh Kinsler, "Assessing Rothstein's Critique of Teacher Value-Added Models," University of Rochester, December 14, 2011, http://www.econ.rochester.edu/

people/Kinsler/kinsler_value_added.pdf and Eric A. Hanushek and Steven G. Rivkin, "Generalizations about Using Value-Added Measures of Teacher Quality," *American Economic Review*, Vol. 100, No. 2, May 2010. Dan Goldhaber, "Everyone's Doing It, but What Does Teacher Testing Tell Us about Teacher Effectiveness?" *Journal of Human Resources*, Vol. 42, 2007. Charles Clotfelter, Helen F. Ladd, and Jacob L. Vigdor, "Teacher–Student Matching and the Assessment of Teacher Effectiveness," *Journal of Human Resources*, Vol. 41, 2006.

50. Dylan Scott, "NYC Releases Teacher Performance Data," *Governing*, February 24, 2012, http://www.governing.com/news/local/gov-nyc-releases-teacher-performance-data.html.

51. Florida Legislature, "Chapter 2011-1: Education Personnel," http://laws.flrules.org/node/5656.

52. Charles Clotfelter and his colleagues find that the state accountability system may play a role in driving high performing teachers away from low-performing schools. See Charles Clotfelter, Helen Ladd, Jacob Vigdor, and Roger Aliaga Diaz, "Do School Accountability Systems Make It More Difficult for Low Performing Schools to Attract and Retain High Quality Teachers?" *Journal of Policy Analysis and Management*, Vol. 23, No. 2, 2004.

53. Daniel Goldhaber, "Teacher Career Paths, Teacher Quality, and Persistence in the Classroom: Are Public Schools Keeping Their Best?" *Journal of Policy Analysis and Management*, Vol. 30, No. 1, 2011.

54. Kathy Christie and Jennifer Dounay Zinth, "Teacher Tenure or Continuing Contract Laws," Education Commission of the States, August 2011, http://www.ecs.org/html/Document.asp?chouseid=9493.

55. *Ibid.*

56. Asenith Dixon, "Focus on Teacher Reform Legislation in SREB States: Tenure, Dismissal and Performance Pay Policies" Southern Regional Education Board (SREB), November 2011, http://www.sreb.org/cgi-bin/MySQLdb?VIEW=/public/docs/view_one.txt&docid=1733.

57. Dan Goldhaber and Michael Hanson, "Assuming the Potential of Using Value-Added Estimates of Teacher Job Performance for Making Tenure Decisions," National Center for Analysis of Longitudinal Data in Education Research (CALDER), Working Paper 31, February 2010.

58. *Ibid.*

59. Public Impact, "Seizing Opportunity at the Top: Reaching Every Student with Excellent Teachers, A Policymakers Checklist," 2012, www.opporunityculture.org.

60. Central office and school-based administrators are not eligible for career status. Teachers, media coordinators, guidance counselors, and certain types of professional staff may be granted career status.

61. North Carolina General Statutes, "Chapter 115C 325: System of employment for public school teachers," http://www.ncga.state.nc.us/gascripts/Statutes/StatutesTOC.pl?Chapter=0115C. The local school board votes on the decision to grant career status to a teacher. If they refuse to grant career status, he or she may not teach beyond that term. Superintendents must give notice to the career status teacher that he or she will be dismissed, and the teacher has the right to a hearing.

The local school board makes the final decision.

62. Editorial Projects in Education, "Research Center: Custom Table Builder," *Education Week*, http://www.edweek.org/rc/2007/06/07/edcounts.html?intc=thed.

63. National Council on Teacher Quality, "2011 State Teacher Policy Yearbook: North Carolina," January 2012, http://www.nctq.org/stpy11/reports.jsp.

64. *Ibid.*

65. Michael Hansen, "Career concerns incentives and teacher effort," University of Washington Working Paper and and Center on Reinventing Public Education, November 2008, http://ftp.utdallas.edu/research/tsp-erc/pdf/seminar_hansen_teacher_effort.pdf.

66. Charles T. Clotfelter, Helen F. Ladd, and Jacob L. Vigdor, "Are Teacher Absences Worth Worrying About in the U.S.?" NBER Working Paper No. 13648, Cambridge, MA: National Bureau of Economic Research, Inc., 2007.

67. Jay P. Greene, "Education Myths: What Special Interest Groups Want You to Believe About Our Schools--And Why It Isn't So," New York: Rowman & Littlefield Publishers, 2006, p. 8.

68. See North Carolina Policy Watch, "Carolina Issues Poll – April 2012," April 9, 2012, http://www.ncpolicywatch.com/2012/04/09/carolina-issues-poll-april-2012; and William Howell, Martin West and Paul E. Peterson, "Reform Agenda Gains Strength," *EducationNext*, Vol. 13, No. 1, Winter 2013, http://educationnext.org/reform-agenda-gains-strength/.

69. For examples, see United States Department of Education, "Increasing Educational Productivity: Innovative Approaches & Best Practices," http://www.ed.gov/oii-news/increasing-educational-productivity. Ulrich Boser, "Return on Educational Investment: A District-by-District Evaluation of U.S. Educational Productivity," Center for American Progress, January 19, 2011, http://www.americanprogress.org/issues/education/report/2011/01/19/8902/return-on-educational-investment. Marguerite Roza, Dan Goldhaber, and Paul T. Hill, "The Productivity Imperative: Getting More Benefits from School Costs in an Era of Tight Budgets," January 2009, http://www.crpe.org/publications/productivity-imperative-getting-more-benefits-school-costs-era-tight-budgets.

70. NC DPI, "Highlights of the North Carolina Public School Budget, 2012," p. 1, http://www.dpi.state.nc.us/fbs/resources/data.

71. "Recommendations to Strengthen North Carolina's School Funding System," Augenblick, Palaich and Associates, September 2010, www.ncleg.net/documentsites/committees/JLSCPSFF/APA%20Final%20Report/APA_PSFFFinalReport_ExecSummary.pdf.

72. Researchers have evaluated one of those allotments, the Disadvantaged Student Supplemental Fund or DSSF. The DSSF was established in 2004 to provide additional funding to better serve low-income students, but studies of the DSSF allotment have not yielded positive findings. The 2007 Disadvantaged Student Supplemental Fund (DSSF) Pilot Evaluation identified "serious issues that may present obstacles for moving greater numbers of North Carolina students into academic proficiency, even with the substantial funding increases." Gary T. Henry, Charles L. Thompson, Dana K. Rickman, C. Kevin Fortner, and Kelley M. Dean, "First Report Of The

Evaluation Of The Disadvantaged Student Supplement Fund (DSSF)," April 2007, soe.unc.edu/fac_research/spotlight/2007/dssf.pdf. A follow-up report concluded that the DSSF produced statistically insignificant achievement gains for middle school students in DSSF pilot districts. Researcher Gary Henry and his colleagues wrote, "For both reading and mathematics achievement, at the end of three years of the DSSF program, academically disadvantaged DSSF students scores were statistically equivalent to those of academically disadvantaged students in the other districts." Gary T. Henry, Charles L. Thompson, C. Kevin Fortner, and Rebecca A. Zulli, "The Impact of the Disadvantaged Student Supplemental Fund on Middle School Student Performance in Pilot Districts," University of North Carolina, Carolina Institute for Public Policy, April 2009, publicpolicy.unc.edu/research/The_Impact_of_the_DSSF_on_Middle_School_Student_Performance_in_Pilot_Districts.pdf. See also Gary T. Henry, C. Kevin Fortner and Charles L. Thompson, "Targeted Funding for Educationally Disadvantaged Students: A Regression Discontinuity Estimate of the Impact on High School Student Achievement," *Educational Evaluation and Policy Analysis*, Vol. 32, No. 2, June 2010. Gary T. Henry, Charles L. Thompson, C. Kevin Fortner, Dana K. Rickman, and Rebecca A. Zulli, "The Impact of the Disadvantaged Student Supplemental Fund on High School Student Performance in Pilot Districts," University of North Carolina at Chapel Hill Carolina Institute for Public Policy, 2008.

73. NC DPI, "Highlights of the North Carolina Public School Budget, 2012," p. 1.

74. Recommendations to Strengthen North Carolina's School Funding System," p. 103-104.

75. *Ibid.*, p. 104.

76. *Ibid.*, p. 107-108.

77. North Carolina Education Lottery, "FY '11 Beneficiary Brochure," June 30, 2012, http://www.nc-educationlottery.org/beneficiary.aspx.

78. "Recommendations to Strengthen North Carolina's School Funding System," p. 111.

79. *Ibid.*, p. 113.

∞∞∞∞∞∞∞∞∞∞∞∞∞∞∞

The Next Steps on Regulatory Reform

by Jon Sanders

As the longtime editor of The Wall Street Journal, *Raleigh native Vermont Royster wrote frequently about the increasing role that government regulation played in the day-to-day operation of business. While supportive of rules that ensured public safety and protected consumers from fraud, Royster was suspicious of arrogant regulators who, assuming superior information, sought to substitute their own judgment for that of willing buyers and sellers. "One of the most persistent delusions to cloud our minds," Royster once wrote, "is the belief that there exists a solution if only we were clever enough to find it." In reality, he said, the "right" solution as imposed by government regulation might not prove to be so obviously right in retrospect.*

Royster made this point not to deny the necessity of government regulation but to argue that the power be employed judiciously and efficiently, and only when demonstrable benefits clearly exceed costs. In this chapter, Jon Sanders applies the same philosophy to regulatory reform in our state.

The regulatory climate in North Carolina has improved over the past couple of years. The General Assembly overrode Gov. Bev Perdue's veto of the Regulatory Reform Act (RRA) of 2011, reducing state agencies' cumbersome rules and regulations on private business.[1] Legislators also passed other reforms, including medical liability reform (vetoed and overridden), tort reform for citizens and businesses, workers' compensation reform, and the Regulatory Reform Act of 2012. Perdue had signed an executive order in 2010 bringing regulatory review to the executive and Cabinet agencies under her control, reforming the rulemaking process while helping reduce the costs of regulation.[2]

Those were steps in the right direction, but the journey to a freer, less-burdensome regulatory environment is far from over. North Carolina's regulatory process is still internally biased toward increasing regulation, a bias that is imposing significant burdens on business and hampering economic recovery. A state's economic climate is helped by good rules that give a clear picture of the legal framework for conducting business in the many enterprises within the state. But the economic climate is harmed when rules appear arbitrary, multiply and compound, persist after practical obsolescence, and work more to help the regulating agencies than to benefit consumers and businesses.

Note that such concerns are as old as the very founding of the nation to which the State of North Carolina belongs. Two of the charges laid against King George III in the Declaration of Independence were that "He has erected a multitude of New Offices, and sent hither swarms of Officers to harass our people and eat out their substance" and that "He has combined with others to subject us to a jurisdiction foreign to our constitution, and unacknowledged by our laws; giving his Assent to their Acts of pretended Legislation."[3]

That acknowledgment is not to equate state agencies with British authoritarian excesses; instead, it is to illustrate the danger of giving unelected, unaccountable officials broad lawmaking powers. In North Carolina as elsewhere, robust economic growth is a happy by-product of free people able reasonably to dictate their own affairs under a government that guards personal and property rights, enforces contracts, sets proper legal boundaries, and otherwise leaves market choices to individuals. The regulatory environment in such a society would be suspicious of changing rules until they were proven prudent, reasonable, and necessary.

For North Carolina it would mean making a few key reforms, which are spelled out in this chapter. The principles underlying these reforms are: opening the rulemaking process to the public, setting up procedures by which to identify beneficial rules and discard the rest, establishing guidelines for selecting regulations only when they are necessary, and limiting regulations' negative impact.

The Guiding Principle: Transparency

The linchpin to all the reforms proposed here is accountability. The health of a free society governed by representative democracy absolutely requires the elected representatives of the people to govern in the open, not huddled behind closed doors nor hidden in the cloaks of unelected bureaucracy. We the people are the ultimate authority. As John Locke wrote in his *Second Treatise of Civil Government*:

> *The legislative cannot transfer the power of making laws to any other hands: for it being but a delegated power from the people, they who have it cannot pass it over to others. The people alone can appoint the form of the common-wealth, which is by constituting the legislative, and appointing in whose hands that shall be. And when the people have said, We will submit to rules, and be governed by laws made by such men, and in such forms, no body else can say other men shall make laws for them; nor can the people be bound by any laws, but such as are enacted by those whom they have chosen, and authorized to make laws for them.*[4]

"Openness will strengthen our democracy and promote efficiency and effectiveness in government." Even President Barack Obama has spoken for open, transparent government.[5] As a candidate in 2008, he advocated transparency, and one of his first acts upon taking office was to issue a memorandum pledging "an unprecedented level of openness in Government." Although Obama's follow-through on that score has been highly disappointing,[6] his memo emphasizes transparency's importance.

For example, "Government should be transparent," Obama stated, because "[t]ransparency promotes accountability and provides information for citizens about what their Government is doing," noting shortly afterward that "[p]ublic engagement enhances the Government's effectiveness and improves the quality of its decisions."[7]

North Carolina's leaders need to open government to this public accountability and engagement by opening its books and opening its processes. Technological advances make these goals easier than ever to accomplish — and make it inexcusable not to do so.

Implement Financial Transparency

Government receives its revenue from citizens by coercion, through taxation, with the consent of the governed. The cause of good government insists that this awesome power not be abused nor those revenues wasted. Informed taxpayers can also be sources of cost-saving ideas to elected officials, if they know, for example, of better ways or better vendors to provide government services.[8] Transparency in the following areas would check potential waste and abuse and invite knowledgeable, cost-saving, and efficiency-creating input from taxpayers:

- Have the state controller and each state agency publish detailed spending online, including budgets, contracts, salaries, and check registers.
- Use a format that is structured, searchable, and exportable — not a scanned pdf image whose data would have to be reentered by hand.
- Require frequent updates of the data; e.g., once a month or more often.[9]

Offer More Process Transparency

Good government benefits when taxpayers are well informed not just of spending decisions, but also of pending decisions; or put another way, when taxpayers can monitor and possibly contribute to the decision-making process over budget bills, other legislation, and state regulations. The General Assembly does a good job, for example, of advertising meetings beforehand, and the most recent General Assembly placed the budget online five days before the first House vote and six days before the first Senate vote. Transparency in the processes of state government would include:

- Changing legislative rules to require budget bills to be posted online for at least 72 hours before the first vote.
- Requiring each budget bill to include a five-year forecast (fiscal note) of its impact on spending and taxes.
- Advertising all committee meetings (and posting meeting agendas) well beforehand.
- Archiving meeting debates, minutes, presentations, and documents.
- Including stated objectives and outcome measures for state programs, and holding those programs accountable to them.

- Requiring all state agencies to develop and publicize explicit, measurable, outcome-based mission and vision statements, so that the agencies may be held accountable to them.
- Making agency web sites more user-friendly.
- Publicizing proposed regulations more effectively.
- Advertising public hearings over regulations.

The Goal: Establishing Good Regulations, Eliminating the Rest

Regulations are rules established by state agencies and commissions, under authority delegated them by the legislative branch, for implementing or interpreting enacted legislation. The idea is for the legislature to delegate a narrowly tailored authority to the agency to devise good rules, faithfully interpreting legislation based upon the agency's subject-area expertise. Those rules carry the full force of law, and those regulated can face fines and even jail for violating them. Note that this great power is vested in bureaucrats who are not directly accountable to voters. It is an overly closed system to those affected by its mandates. Any lack of direct accountability is open to potential abuse. The risk here is the existence of *de facto* state law being crafted without the consent of the governed. The need for strict oversight is paramount. Current state protections are insufficient.

Strengthen the Rules Review Commission

The Rules Review Commission (RRC) is a 10-member commission appointed by House and Senate leaders. Established under the Administrative Procedure Act (APA), the commission is tasked with approving regulations before they become finalized. The commission cannot evaluate the merits of a regulation; its general duties include ensuring the regulating agency properly followed procedures in developing the rule, had statutory authority to devise the rule, and produced a clear rule.[10]

Beyond the RRC, there is a way — a very difficult way — for a pending rule to be delayed and potentially blocked under the APA. If the public objects to the rule, and 10 objections to it are filed with the RRC, the rule's implementation will be delayed, during which time the General Assembly can produce legislation disapproving it. Such legislation must pass both houses and be signed by the governor, however.

(Continued on page 150)

Where transparency is lacking: North Carolina auto insurance

If transparency promotes good government through accountability, what does opacity do? Consider North Carolina's byzantine, government-controlled automobile insurance system.

A hidden tax averaging 6 percent is attached to every auto insurance policy written in North Carolina. The tax supports the government-mandated Reinsurance Facility, a high-risk insurance pool for risky drivers. The facility is the largest residual insurance market among the states, but most North Carolina drivers have never even heard of it. The tax to fund it is *hidden by state law* — insurers are forbidden by law to disclose the tax on statements.[11]

The high-risk pool uses the tax to subsidize the policies of risky drivers, whose rates are capped by state regulations. State law also guarantees insurers a profit — meaning there is no market risk to private insurers to write policies in North Carolina. The harm is sloughed off to consumers. Insurers are allowed to deposit any driver into the high-risk pool whose risk factors would make insuring them unprofitable, owing to the cap. Safe drivers across the state unwittingly pick up the difference between the capped rate and the actual amount the risky driver should pay. As a consequence of such a system, North Carolina's residual market is a monster compared with the residual markets in other states. Several private insurers dump all or nearly all of their customers in the pool. Where most states' residual markets comprise hundredths of a percent of drivers, North Carolina's engulfs nearly one-fourth of drivers. Drivers in North Carolina make up over three-fourths (78 percent) of the national residual market across the United States.[12]

Nevertheless, this massive pool remains hidden to N.C. drivers. Drivers who, unbeknownst to them, have been dumped into the Reinsurance Facility still receive statements from their private insurance companies, still do business with their agents, and still call the private insurance companies' 800 numbers with questions. The Facility covers their liability instead of the insurance companies, and the drivers are none the wiser.

Since insurers in North Carolina are guaranteed a profit but cannot write policies fully covering risky drivers, they compensate by charging higher prices on safe drivers (the usual structure would have risky drivers subsidize good drivers). *The best drivers in North Carolina do not get the best insurance rates.* Roughly three-quarters of the state's drivers pay their own rates plus portions of risky drivers' rates.

Rate-setting in North Carolina is also a tangled mess of bureaucracy. Five different entities have a say: the North Carolina Rate Bureau, the insurance commissioner, the court system, the Reinsurance Facility, and private insurers. Furthermore, the Rate Bureau is the only one in the nation that goes so far as to set a rate plan for all auto insurance. The prospect of significant paperwork has stifled companies from offering innovative products in North Carolina that are available in other states. Unlike their peers in other states, customers in North Carolina generally cannot find rate quotes online. They cannot even take advantage of such popular features as seeing competitors' rate quotes side-by-side.[13]

Research published by the John Locke Foundation addressing North Carolina's auto insurance system proposes the following reforms:[14]

- End the Rate Bureau's role in setting insurance rates. In so doing, require insurers to file rate plans at their own expense and increase staffing at the Insurance Department to process paperwork.
- Abolish the insurance industry's profit guarantee.
- Over time, require "clean risk" drivers in the Reinsurance Facility to pay their own way — disclosing the hidden tax in good drivers' insurance rates that subsidizes them and phasing it out. Make the "clean risk" drivers pay an increasingly higher share of their actual insurance surcharge until they pay their full way.
- Allow drivers to leave the Reinsurance Facility for lower-cost or otherwise more attractive insurance packages.
- Redesign the Reinsurance Facility as a true market of last resort.
- Establish a "flex band" for smaller changes in insurance. After getting the Rate Bureau out of rate-setting (or abolishing it altogether), set up a flex band allowing insurers to make slight adjustments to rates without needing much paperwork. The flex band would allow insurers to adjust rates within a set percentage spread; most flex-band states allow a range of between 5 and 15 percent.
- Encourage insurance product innovation by expanding insurers' ability to use a wide range of data.

(Continued from page 147)

A 2010 John Locke Foundation study of the rules-review process showed how rare it is for a regulation to be blocked. Of the 6,510 permanent rules introduced between 2004-05 and 2008-09, only 218 (about 3 percent) were subject to legislative review, which saw only 28 bills introduced in the legislature to disapprove them (i.e., about seven out of every eight rules subject to legislative review are ignored and allowed to go into effect). Just seven of those bills passed. In other words, only about one-tenth of one percent of regulations were ultimately blocked.[15]

That study also showed how the RRC's authority to review a regulation to determine if it is "within the authority delegated to the agency by the General Assembly" is practically limited.[16] Agencies have challenged unfavorable rulings by the RRC over statutory authority and won. Courts have favored expansive readings of statutes, and conversely, the legislature has often produced broad statutory language open to interpretation. Agencies will naturally seek the broadest expansions of their own power.[17]

The cause of proper oversight requires that the General Assembly amend the APA so that the RRC reviews a regulation to ensure it is "*clearly* within the authority delegated to the agency by the General Assembly," defining that *clear statutory authority exists when no reasonable argument could be made that denies statutory authority.* Such an amendment would also mandate rejection of a regulation when a reasonable argument could be made that denies statutory authority for the rule.

Furthermore, the General Assembly should amend the APA to stipulate that the RRC may approve regulations only if they align with the intent of the legislature upon first delegating authority to the agency. State agencies are not the proper vehicles for deciding and dictating major matters of policy. The North Carolina Supreme Court has recognized the propriety of the General Assembly delegating "a limited portion of its legislative powers" to agencies tasked to deal with intricacies the legislature could not effectively handle directly, but it noted that "such transfers of power [delegation] should be closely monitored to insure that decision-making by the agency is not arbitrary and unreasoned and that the agency is not asked to make important policy choices which might just as easily be made by elected representatives in the legislature."[18] The amended APA would therefore allow the RRC to approve a regulation only after the agency proved that, at the passage of the statute, legislators believed (a) the agency was better positioned than they to handle the specific subject matter of the regulation and (b) they had given the agency the authority to issue the regulation.[19]

The General Assembly should also address the issue of statutory authority from within. In drafting bills, legislators should establish clear boundaries around what agencies may do to implement the bills' provisions. They should also challenge draft legislation that is overly broad in delegated authority. Those reforms cannot be made via legislation, however, but require internal monitoring.

Strengthen cost/benefit analysis and oversight of all proposed regulations

The legislature, again building on the governor's reforms for Cabinet agencies, brought a good measure of cost/benefit analysis to state agencies in the Regulatory Reform Act of 2011.[20] Reforms included requiring:

- Each agency to quantify (monetize) costs and benefits of a proposed rule.
- Opportunity costs to be included.
- A description of all who would be affected by the proposed rule and what costs it would impose upon them.
- An agency proposing a rule with substantial economic impact to assess the baseline condition prior to the rule, project the expected condition after the rule, and compare the two.
- An agency proposing a rule with substantial economic impact to consider at least two alternatives and explain why the alternatives were rejected.

Those reforms provide a solid foundation, but they are incomplete. For example, at present the law leaves it to the discretion of the agency to determine whether its proposed rule would have substantial economic impact — and therefore would be subject to greater scrutiny by the Office of State Budget and Management (OSBM). Future reform should give OSBM greater oversight over proposed regulations, including determining whether a rule would have substantial economic impact.

It is also not enough to require costs and benefits to be merely quantified. Those data should be actionable. In other words, where agencies find the costs of a proposed rule to exceed its benefits, they should be mandated by law to reject the rule.

A rejection requirement must not, however, work conversely as an *adoption requirement* if benefits are found to exceed costs. Other reforms in this chapter stress the importance of adopting good, narrowly tailored rules only when adopting a rule is absolutely necessary.

Also under a rejection requirement, agencies would be tempted to overstress benefits to tilt the scales toward adoption. A benefit must be an actual, quantifiable societal good. It cannot, for example, be a proxy for a good, the presence of which presumes the presence of the good. For example, if the Environmental Management Commission proposed a new regulation of carbon dioxide (CO_2) emissions to address man-made global warming, the commission might consider the reduction of CO_2 emissions to be a benefit, but that would be because it is thought that reducing CO_2 emissions would reduce global warming. The actual benefit, however, would be a reduction in global warming. To estimate that benefit, the agency would have to calculate the likely impact on the world's temperatures of lower CO_2 emissions from just the State of North Carolina. Since that would effectively be zero,[21] the proxy of CO_2 emissions reduced would be easier to manipulate and monetize as a benefit.

However quantified, benefits are not comparable with rights. North Carolina recognizes as inalienable an individual's rights to life, liberty, the enjoyment of the fruits of his own labor, the pursuit of happiness, etc.[22] Rules that would have the state usurp individuals' rights for a social benefit should be rejected out of hand.

Along those lines, rules that would force changes in individual behavior — e.g., prevent people from making some consumer choices they otherwise would make, or so alter production costs that significantly different prices drive consumers to alternatives — must not count the result of the new, artificial choice as a "benefit." If people wanted those things and the benefits they supposedly bring, they would be choosing them without government action. Because they don't, they have already essentially conducted private cost/benefit analyses finding in favor of their choices *before* the intrusive rule change. Forcing them to switch leaves them worse off, not better.

An extreme example of the fallacy of the compulsory "private benefit" came in propaganda supporting North Carolina's notorious forced-sterilization program.[23] A 1950 pamphlet entitled "You Wouldn't Expect ..." published by the Human Betterment League of North Carolina to promote "sterilization of the mentally unfit at state expense" concluded with the following private benefits to the sterilized (which at least were not explicitly monetized):

> **Protect** *handicapped men and women so that those in need of this protection [i.e., sterilization] may get it without expense to themselves.*
> **Save** *helpless children from mental affliction and unwholesome surroundings. (Emphasis in original.)*[24]

The Obama administration has been particularly notorious for quantifying such "private benefits" in justifying excessive regulation, for example, crediting "reduced fuel consumption and shorter refueling times" as the bulk of the benefits of new fuel-economy standards. As *The Economist* noted, "values placed on such private benefits are highly suspect. If consumers were really better off with more efficient cars or appliances, they would buy them without a prod from government."[25]

In considering alternatives to rules with substantial economic impact, the agency should include *making no change* as one of the alternatives to quantify (unless, of course, new federal or state legislation or a court order requires a change). Agencies should be required to choose the least burdensome alternative.[26]

In sum, legislators should build upon the good foundation of cost/benefit analysis provided in RRA 2011 by making the analysis a potential deal-breaker for a proposed rule. In so doing, however, they must draft carefully so as not to erect a false front, a veneer by which agencies lacking proper oversight quantify as benefits things that are not actual benefits (proxies), choices that would not have been willingly made ("private benefits"), or the consolation prizes for individual rights curtailed. Transparency and good government need an open rule-making process with honest accounting.

Enact stronger periodic review of existing rules and regulations

Among other things, Gov. Perdue's executive order on regulatory reform established the Rules Modification and Improvement Program (RMIP) within OSBM to require annual review of rules issued by Cabinet agencies and their associated boards and commissions. The order aimed to weed out rules that had become outdated, unnecessary, unduly burdensome, vague, or otherwise inconsistent with clear, well-developed, and efficient rule-making. The program involved OSBM inviting public comment and suggestions on those agencies' existing rules and requirements, then reviewing the merits of the reform suggestions and following through on those deemed meritorious.[27] Within months the governor credited RMIP with culling 900 outdated, excessive, unnecessary rules.[28]

Following through with that idea, RRA 2011 expanded RMIP to apply to all state agencies. It also required each state agency "to conduct an annual review of its rules to identify existing rules that are unnecessary, unduly burdensome, or inconsistent" with its reform of the rulemaking process.[29]

Such review was welcome but insufficient. The review, though annual and applying at least topically to all agency rules, relies more on public input (and knowledge of the RMIP process) and offers a passive approach to reform. The U.S. Small Business Administration (SBA) recommends reviewing rules every five years after their first publication.[30] That periodic review would follow the same scrutiny given proposed new rules, with the burden placed on agencies to justify the rules' continued existence. It should also take into account whether technological or economic changes or other factors render the regulations unnecessary or highlight a need for changing them.

Periodic review would benefit from two other rule-making reforms discussed above. The same thorough cost/benefit analysis in rule-making should also apply during review of current rules. Also, having agencies list stated objectives and outcome measures for their rules would allow a second level of scrutiny to be applied, as the agencies would be required to check whether the rules are meeting those objectives and outcomes.

Case Study: Intrusive occupational licensing

Perhaps nothing illustrates the perils of abusive bureaucracy operating beyond legislative intent to the detriment of individual freedom, let alone economic growth, better than North Carolina's hyperactive occupational licensing system. It has made national news recently thanks to the North Carolina Board of Dietetics/Nutrition's vendetta against a blogger, Steve Cooksey.

Hospitalized with Type II diabetes in 2009, the same disease that killed his grandmother, Cooksey turned to exercise and a carbohydrate-limiting, high-protein "Paleo" diet. He lost 78 pounds, got off the insulin, and then got into blogging about his experiences, freely answering readers' questions about controlling diabetes through diet and also offering paid life-coaching services to readers adopting the Paleo lifestyle, which drew the licensing board's ire. In January 2012, the board told Cooksey that, free or not, he could not offer personal dieting advice without a license and that even his private e-mail messages and telephone conversations amounted to unlicensed and illegal dietetic assessment and advice. The board gave Cooksey 19 pages' worth of his own writings with passages marked with red pen to explain what he was not allowed to say.

Threatened with a misdemeanor conviction, jail time, and thousands of dollars in fines, Cooksey discontinued his life-coaching and advice column. Then he sued the state for violating his speech rights (the suit is ongoing).[31]

Essentially, an occupational license is a grant of permission from the government to an individual to enter a certain field of work — which requires a de facto prohibition against someone working in a profession he chooses until he secures state approval. Though North Carolina's Constitution, Article I, Section 1 recognizes a right of all persons to "the enjoyment of the fruits of their own labor,"[32] the state licenses more occupations than most other states. Just crossing the border from North into South Carolina reduces the

Figure 1: Number of Licensed Job Categories, North Carolina and Nearby States[33]

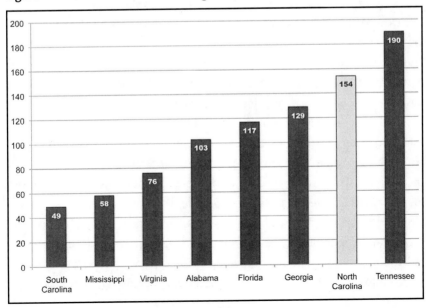

155

number of occupations requiring state licensure by over two-thirds (105 occupations).[34]

Such an infringement on liberty and individual rights should have a strong justification to exist. Supposedly, occupational licensing is rooted in the state's interest to protect its citizens from fraudulent or negligent providers and ensures safety and quality of services provided. For example, the Dietetics/Nutrition Act of 1991 that established the Board of Dietetics/Nutrition included this stated purpose:

> It is the purpose of this Article to safeguard the public health, safety and welfare and to protect the public from being harmed by unqualified persons by providing for the licensure and regulation of persons engaged in the practice of dietetics/nutrition and by the establishment of educational standards for those persons.[34]

Similar language is to be found in other legislation establishing state licensing boards. But as University of Minnesota Professor Morris Kleiner found in surveying research literature on occupational licensing, "The most generally held view on the economics of occupational licensing is that it restricts the supply of labor to the occupation and thereby drives up the price of labor as well as of services rendered."[35] So those whom occupational licensing really protects are those already in the regulated industry.

Occupational licensing protects current practitioners by placing hurdles in the way of prospective entrants, effectively blocking would-be competitors. Those hurdles include imposing licensing costs and fees, mandating certain amounts of pricey, time-consuming academic instruction, and requiring passage of a qualifying exam or exams, which also includes exam fees.

With the supply of competitors limited, established members of the profession reap higher earnings — and their customers face higher costs, driving some to take risks in seeking substitutes or doing the work themselves. The earnings premium of occupational licensing is why most members in a licensed profession favor it, and why the General Assembly in 2011 saw music therapists, herbalists, personal trainers, makers of orthotic shoes, landscapers, locksmiths, property managers, X-ray technicians, and radiation therapists attempt to secure new licensing laws in their fields.[37] Since 2000, North Carolina has added licensing boards for respiratory care professionals,[38] locksmiths,[39] interpreters and transliterators,[40] on-site wastewater contractors and inspectors,[41] and irrigation contractors.[42]

Licensing boards — of which North Carolina has more than 50 — tend to feature incumbent practitioners with a glaring conflict of interest, and those with "public" members tend to see them defer to the incumbent practitioners, anyway. They also tend to seek to expand their scope, further restricting competition in price and quality.[43] Worse, they also tend to fight off innovation — new dieting advice, for example, or African hair-braiding techniques learned in immigrants' girlhoods that now supposedly require 300 hours' worth of costly cosmetology training.[44]

As far as protecting consumers, the best-available evidence finds that punishing confirmed bad actors after the fact is just as effective as seeking to block them from entry, without imposing the additional negative effects of raising costs on consumers, restricting opportunities, and discouraging new entrants and new ideas. Reforming North Carolina's costly licensing structure would entail abolishing some licensing boards outright and reforming and merging others. (To give just a few examples, there are separate boards for landscape architects and landscape contractors, separate boards for professional counselors, occupational therapists, and pastoral counselors, separate boards for barbers and cosmetics, and separate boards for physical therapists, recreational therapists, and athletic trainers.) Those reforms would lead to more job opportunities, bring competitive pricing for consumers, welcome young entrepreneurs, and encourage innovation.

The Hippocratic Approach: New Rules Only When Necessary

The Hippocratic Oath, a founding statement of medical ethics, contains the principle of nonmaleficence[45] popularized in the phrase "First, do no harm." A more common expression of the same principle is "If it ain't broke, don't fix it." Under either conception, the principle would be an important addition to the reforms started by leaders of both political parties of the state's broken rulemaking process.

Enact REINS in N.C.

Last year the U.S. Congress considered a bill that addressed at the federal level the problem discussed here at the state level: major rules carrying the force of law made by unelected executive-branch bureaucracies. H.R. 10, the Regulations from the Executive In Need of Scrutiny Act of 2011 (REINS), would require Congress to approve any proposed rule that would have a major impact on the economy; cause significant cost or price increases on consumers; or significantly harm competition, employment, productivity, and other healthy economic activities. A joint resolution approving the regulation would have to pass both chambers and be signed by the president for the rule to take effect. Also, if no vote on the regulation took place within 70 session days, the regulation would not take effect. The REINS Act passed the House, 241-184, but languished in the Senate.[46]

REINS's distinction between major and nonmajor rules is important. Good-government advocates would blanch at requiring legislative approval of small matters that are properly within the scope of the executive branch. As cited above, the N.C. Supreme Court found the legislature's delegation of "a limited portion" of its powers to be proper so long as state agencies are not "asked to make important policy choices."[47] Major policy changes are the province of the legislature, whose members are directly accountable to voters. As noted above, current law uses the deliberative process of the legislature to dissuade *blocking* new regulations. The REINS approach would use the process to *allow* only those deeply impactful rules that can obtain majority support from elected, accountable representatives of the people.

The purpose of the REINS Act is instructive for North Carolina's leaders:

The purpose of this Act is to increase accountability for and transparency in the federal regulatory process. Section 1 of article I of the United States Constitution grants all legislative powers to Congress. Over time, Congress has excessively delegated its constitutional charge while failing to conduct appropriate oversight and retain accountability for the content of the laws it passes. By requiring a vote in Congress, the REINS Act will result in more carefully drafted and detailed legislation, an improved regulatory process, and a legislative branch that is truly accountable to the American people for the laws imposed upon them.[48]

The idea behind REINS is not new. It was proposed in October 1983 in a lecture at Georgetown University Law Center by Stephen Breyer, then a federal appellate judge, later appointed to the U.S. Supreme Court by

President Bill Clinton. Breyer offered a qualified analysis "suggesting that Congress condition the exercise of a delegated legislative power on the enactment of a confirmatory statute, passed by both houses and signed by the President. It would be perfectly in keeping with the Constitution's language, Mr. Breyer noted, while simulating the function of the traditional legislative veto."[49]

Adopting the REINS principle in North Carolina would require legislation that would do the following:[50]

- Define a "major rule" according to its projected (by the Office of State Management and Budget directly, or indirectly upon approving the agency's fiscal note for the rule) negative annual economic impact, imposition of significant cost and price increases on consumers, or other nontrivial negative economic impacts, such as on market competition, employment, productivity, investment, and technological or other innovations. (RRA 2011 defined a rule as having "substantial economic impact" if it had "an aggregate financial impact on all persons affected" of at least $500,000;[51] the REINS Act, surveying a national economic impact, counted as "major" any rule with an averse economic impact of $100 million or more.)
- Require the General Assembly to consider a vote to approve any major rule proposed by a state agency.
- Mandate that without a vote of approval from both chambers of the legislature and the governor's signature within a set period of time (e.g., 70–90 days), the proposed major rule would die.
- Stipulate that the vote in the General Assembly is not a vote to enact the major rule as state law but instead is a grant of legislative authority to the agency to proceed with the proposed major rule under the regulatory process.

A REINS approach to regulation in North Carolina would not only require that major changes in state rules be approved by elected representatives directly accountable to the voters. It would also, by virtue of that fact, offer two key improvements in future state regulations. Legislators, knowing they would face votes over proposed regulations and could no longer rely on unelected bureaucrats to make major policy decisions, would have new incentives to write clearer, more narrowly focused bills. The bureaucrats, knowing they would face defeat by legislative action or inaction if they overstepped their bounds, would have new incentives to write better, more circumspect rules clearly within their statutory authority.[52]

Apply the No-More-Stringent Standard to All Agencies

Occasionally the purviews of federal and state agencies overlap, creating the potential for two separate standards imposed in an area under regulation. Redundancy is only part of the problem. Bearing in mind that regulation involves compliance costs to industry and deadweight loss to the economy, it is no trivial matter for a state agency to impose a stricter standard than federal regulators. Not only do those additional costs harm job creation and economic growth, but also they incentivize businesses that can to set up shop in other states without the stricter standards. Most important is the issue of accountability: if North Carolina is to have a stricter regulation than that imposed by federal regulators, then it should be elected representatives of the people (legislators), not agency bureaucrats, who make that decision.

Many states have laws prohibiting agencies from expanding state rules beyond the scope of federal regulations in, for example, environmental policy. Such laws are known as "no more stringent" laws. North Carolina used them from the 1970s to the 1990s for several environmental areas.[53]

RRA 2011 addressed the lack of "no more stringent" laws in environmental policy. Among other things, it decreed that environmental agencies "may not adopt a rule for the protection of the environment or natural resources that imposes a more restrictive standard, limitation, or requirement than those imposed by federal law or rule," unless expressly required by state or federal legislation, by court order, or by a "serious and unforeseen threat to the public health, safety, or welfare."[54] A bill that passed the Senate but not the House in the 2011 session would have prohibited state agencies from "adopt[ing], implement[ing], or enforc[ing] a rule that regulates greenhouse gas emissions or that limits human activity for the purpose of reducing greenhouse gas emissions if the rule is not required by a federal regulation or law or is more stringent than a corresponding federal regulation or law."[55]

While "no more stringent" laws forbid state agencies from adopting, on their own initiative, stricter regulations than their federal counterparts, they place no restriction at all on the legislature voting to enact stricter standards. Again, the issue is accountability: making a major, structural change to the

Arbitrarily imposing a stricter standard: Mercury emissions in NC

In 2005, the U.S. Environmental Protection Agency developed regulations that forced coal-fired power plants to reduce mercury emissions by 70 percent.

The stated reason for the regulation was to reduce a form of mercury, methylmercury, found in fish, which it was feared made them unhealthy for human consumption — a concern that was entirely speculative, there not having been one known instance of methylmercury poisoning from fish consumption.

Furthermore, what problem there was might not even be addressed by reducing power-plant mercury emissions, since they account for only 1 percent of all mercury emissions in the world, whereas two-thirds are from natural sources (such as volcanic eruptions) and re-emitted sources (past man-made emissions re-emitted into the atmosphere). As it was, this sweeping, major new dictate was the first of its kind not just in the United States, but in the world, and would have significant negative effects on prices for ratepayers.[56]

Nevertheless, it wasn't sweeping enough for environmental activists in North Carolina.[57] Pressuring the Environmental Management Commission (EMC), they succeeded in obtaining even tighter standards. On November 9, 2006, the EMC announced new rules to cut mercury emissions by coal-fired power plants in North Carolina by 88 percent. Power plants that failed to reduce emissions according to the state's stricter standard (and faster timetable) would be shut down.[58]

The federal EPA regulations represented a significant change that would already have had adverse impacts on North Carolina ratepayers and utilities without any proven justification. Unfortunately, state regulators made the problem even worse, also without any additional reason to justify it.

Such a major new policy, eclipsing federal regulations and having the force of law, was not deliberated upon by elected representatives accountable to voting constituents, but was instead issued forth as executive edict by unaccountable bureaucrats in conjunction with narrow special interests.[59]

the General Assembly should extend "no more stringent" laws to all state agencies, not just ones dealing with the environment.

Furthermore, "no more stringent" laws should apply not just to future rulemaking, but also to current regulations as well, either explicitly or through the strengthened periodic review discussed above.

Final Protections: Lessening Regulations' Negative Impact

Along with establishing a transparent process for crafting regulations and ensuring that current and existing regulations are necessary and good, North Carolina's leaders should acknowledge that regulations have differing impacts on regulated parties and work to smooth those differences out.

Extend Reform in the Administrative Appeals Process

RRA 2011 included a very important reform to bring fairness to the regulatory process, at least when the regulating body is a state environmental agency. This reform involved the way in which disputes between a regulated party and the regulating agency are resolved. If an agency levied a fine against an individual for an alleged rule violation, the individual could file a complaint with the Office of Administrative Hearings (OAH), which is a quasi-judicial agency of the executive branch that was established by the legislature. An administrative law judge (ALJ) would hear the complaint and issue a ruling.

If the ALJ's ruling went against the individual, he could appeal (at a great expense of time and attorney's fees) to the Superior Court. Prior to RRA 2011, if the ruling went against the agency, the agency could simply overrule the decision. The process resulted in a stacked deck against individuals; a study of the process found that, in 2010, the overwhelming majority of OAH hearings favored the agency, and of the rest, the agency overruled the ALJ's decisions in 88 percent of the cases.[60] This setup is of questionable constitutionality, as it risks depriving citizens of their due process rights.[61]

RRA 2011 partially ended that constitutionally questionable appeals practice, but only as it pertained to state environmental agencies. Now, rather than overturn any unfavorable ALJ ruling, those agencies have the same appeals process as the regulated parties; i.e., challenge the decision in Superior Court. Other state agencies, however, can still overrule any unfavorable ALJ decision.

Legislative leaders should take the simple but necessary step of expanding RRA 2011's reform of the administrative appeals process to apply to all state agencies, not just the environmental agencies.

Adopt Regulatory Flexibility for Small Businesses

State leaders should also be sensitive to the greater impact regulations have on small businesses. These businesses, defined as having fewer than 500 employees, comprise 98 percent of the employers in North Carolina, according to the SBA. They employ nearly half (47 percent) of the state's private-sector workforce. Especially important in this context, they represented 82 percent of net new private-sector jobs from 2005–08.[62]

Nevertheless, small businesses have greater struggles than larger firms in handling the cost of regulation. Unlike big firms, small businesses generally lack their own compliance and legal staffs which can help them navigate state and federal regulations. Those regulations impose significant deadweight costs on businesses; a 2010 study conducted for the SBA tallied the annual cost just for federal regulations to exceed $1.75 trillion in 2008.[63]

The National Federation of Independent Businesses is currently warning of a "tidal wave" of over four thousand impending new federal regulations that would increase federal regulatory costs by $515 billion across the nation and negatively affect $107 billion of North Carolina's gross domestic product.[64]

The SBA study estimated that the costs to small businesses to comply with federal regulations was 36 percent higher than the costs faced by larger firms.[65] This finding concerns the costs of complying only with federal regulations, however, not regulations imposed at the state and local levels. Furthermore, at the federal level small businesses have a tool that helps keep that cost disparity down: small business flexibility analysis.

Originally passed by the U.S. Congress in 1980 under the Regulatory Flexibility Act and strengthened in 1996 under the Small Business Regulatory Enforcement Fairness Act, flexibility analysis required federal agencies to "consider the impact of their regulatory proposals on small entities, analyze equally effective alternatives, and make their analyses available for public comment."

The tool helps balance a perceived need for regulatory intervention by accounting for the disproportionate compliance costs faced by small businesses. As the SBA put it, "Congress intended that agencies consider impacts on small businesses to ensure that, in their efforts to fulfill their public responsibilities, their regulatory proposals did not have unintended anticompetitive impacts and that agencies explored less burdensome alternatives that were equally effective in resolving agency objectives."[66]

A 2005 report by the SBA estimated that small business flexibility analysis resulted in $17.1 billion's worth of savings in regulatory costs. Rather than being consigned to deadweight loss, those savings are reinvested into helping the businesses (and by extension, the economy) grow.[67]

Again, those savings are realized at the federal level, not the state level. Many states across the nation have adopted small business flexibility analysis, however, but not North Carolina. That means that small businesses in North Carolina, responsible for roughly four of every five new private-sector jobs created in the state, are still struggling with a disproportionate regulatory burden preventing more investment, job creation, and other productive uses of the foregone savings.

Surveys of business leaders in North Carolina show regulatory costs ranking second only to taxes in terms of causing harm to the state's economic competitiveness.[68] Meanwhile, the regulators have been very active, adding over 2,300 new pages to the North Carolina Register every year.[69] Four out of five North Carolina business leaders considered the state's regulations unjustifiable based on costs and benefits.[70]

State-based regulatory flexibility analysis would help small businesses in North Carolina manage their regulatory burden by offering less stringent compliance and reporting requirements, less onerous scheduling or reporting deadlines, use of performance standards rather than design or operational standards, and exemption from some or all requirements of particular regulations. Such flexibility takes into account small businesses' needs with respect not only to financial resources, but also to the scarce resource of time. It would also help small businesses in North Carolina by extending to them protections afforded their peers in most other states in the union.

How would a regulatory flexibility analysis bill be worded? The SBA offers a four-page model bill,[71] the main part including the following:

a. *Prior to the adoption of any proposed regulation on and after [bill adoption date] each agency shall prepare a regulatory flexibility analysis in which the agency shall, where consistent with health, safety,* environmental, and economic welfare consider utilizing regulatory methods that will accomplish the objectives of applicable statutes while minimizing adverse impact on small businesses. The agency shall consider, without limitation, each of the following methods of reducing the impact of the proposed regulation on small businesses:

1. The establishment of less stringent compliance or reporting requirements for small businesses;

2. The establishment of less stringent schedules or deadlines for compliance or reporting requirements for small businesses;

3. The consolidation or simplification of compliance or reporting requirements for small businesses;

4. The establishment of performance standards for small businesses to replace design or operational standards required in the proposed regulation; and

5. The exemption of small businesses from all or any part of the requirements contained in the proposed regulation.

b. Prior to the adoption of any proposed regulation that may have an adverse impact on small businesses, each agency shall notify the [Department of Economic and Community Development or similar state department or council that exists to review regulations] of its intent to adopt the proposed regulation. The [Department of Economic and Community Development or similar state department or council that exists to review regulations] shall advise and assist agencies in complying with the provisions of this section.

Adopting regulatory flexibility analysis in North Carolina would add a smart protection for small businesses that should pay economic dividends statewide.

Conclusion

The past few years have seen leaders in North Carolina commit themselves to reforming the state's regulatory process. They have made good progress, but the journey is incomplete. The final phase requires restoring transparency and accountability to the rulemaking process and putting the ultimate authority for major policy matters back in the legislature's hands. It needs a process that imposes only those rules that are absolutely necessary, and it needs additional protections for individuals and owners of small businesses who feel the effects of regulation more keenly. As North Carolina struggles to emerge from years of a down economy, freeing the job creators from unnecessary, burdensome rules and rulemakers would help quicken the recovery and set the state on a more productive path in the future.

Endnotes

1. S.L. 2011-398, (S.B. 781), www.ncga.state.nc.us/Sessions/2011/Bills/Senate/HTML/S781v6.html.

2. Daren Bakst, "Perdue's Regulatory Executive Order: A step in the right direction," John Locke Foundation Spotlight No. 401, October 27, 2010, johnlocke.org/research/show/spotlights/252.

3. *Declaration of Independence*, July 4, 1776, ushistory.org/declaration/document/index.htm.

4. John Locke, "Of the Extent of the Legislative Power," *Second Treatise of Civil Government*, 1690, www.constitution.org/jl/2ndtr11.htm.

5. President Barack Obama, "Transparency and Open Government," Memorandum for the Heads of Executive Departments and Agencies, www.whitehouse.gov/the_press_office/TransparencyandOpenGovernment.

6. See, e.g., Kim Strassel, "Obama's Empty Transparency Rhetoric," *The Wall Street Journal*, May 4, 2011, online.wsj.com/article/SB100014240527487038492045763032728131163318.html; Jim Harper, "The Promise That Keeps on Breaking," Cato Institute *TechKnowledge* No. 124, April 13, 2009, cato.org/publications/techknowledge/promise-keeps-breaking.

7. Obama, "Transparency and Open Government."

8. Examples and more discussion of financial transparency can be found in Joseph Coletti, "Trust But Verify: Open government is better government," John Locke Foundation Policy Report, December 2009, johnlocke.org/research/show/policyreports/205.

9. Examples of how the states handle the various kinds of transparency may be found at the NIC website transparent-gov.com; a menu on the right lists "Types of Transparency Services," which include state checkbooks, open books, campaign finance and lobbying disclosure, federal stimulus tracking, budget allocation tools, and consumer protection links. Under each subcategory, a "See services…" link provides links to the government web sites of the particular states offering that transparency type (e.g., under "State checkbooks" the links include web sites for Alabama, Alaska, Georgia, Kansas, Kentucky, Missouri, Nebraska, Rhode Island, South Carolina, and Virginia). North Carolina's portal for listing contracts and grants online, NCOpenBook.gov, is included under "Open books."

10. Daren Bakst, "Regulating the Regulators: Seven Reforms for Sensible Regulatory Policy in North Carolina," John Locke Foundation Policy Report, February 2010, johnlocke.org/research/show/policy%20reports/207.

11. Eli Lehrer, "North Carolina's Unfair Auto Insurance System," John Locke Foundation Policy Report, July 2008, johnlocke.org/research/show/policyreports/173. Eli Lehrer, "North Carolina's Auto Insurance System: Still Unfair, Still in Need of Improvements," John Locke Foundation Policy Report, April 2011, johnlocke.org/research/show/policy reports/226.

12. Lehrer reports.

13. Lehrer reports.

14. Lehrer reports.

15. Bakst, "Regulating the Regulators," Figure 1.

16. Bakst, "Regulating the Regulators," the quoted matter is from N.C. Gen. Stat. § 150B-21.9(a).

17. Bakst, "Regulating the Regulators."

18. Adams v. North Carolina Department of Natural and Economic Resources (N.C. DENR), 295 N.C.683 (1978).

19. For a fuller discussion of this proposal and the rationale behind it, see Bakst, "Regulating the Regulators," p. 7.

20. S.L. 2011-398. Also see Bakst, "Perdue's Regulatory Executive Order."

21. On that score, see Roy Cordato, "The Science Is Settled: North Carolina Can Have No Impact on Climate Change," John Locke Foundation Spotlight No. 304, December 10, 2006, johnlocke.org/research/show/spotlights/151.

22. North Carolina State Constitution, Article I, Section 1, www.ncga.state.nc.us/Legislation/constitution/article1.html.

23. For background, see Daren Bakst, "North Carolina's Forced-Sterilization Program: A Case for Compensating the Living Victims," John Locke Foundation Policy Report, July 2011, johnlocke.org/research/show/policy%20reports/233.

24. Human Betterment League of North Carolina, "You Wouldn't Expect …," 1950, available online via North Carolina Digital Collections, digital.ncdcr.gov/cdm4/document.php?CISOROOT=/p249901coll37&CISOPTR=14974&REC=1.

25. "The rule of more: Rule-making is being made to look more beneficial under Barack Obama," *The Economist*, February 18, 2012, www.economist.com/node/21547772.

26. Executive orders by presidents Ronald Reagan and Jimmy Carter both acknowledge this principle; see Bakst, "Regulating the Regulators," p. 7.

27. N.C. Exec. Order No. 2010-70, "Rules Modification and Improvement Program," Office of Governor Bev Perdue, October 21, 2010, www.governor.state.nc.us/NewsItems/ExecutiveOrderDetail.aspx?newsItemID=1518.

28. "Gov. Perdue Announces Regulatory Review Results," press release, Office of Governor Bev Perdue, February 8, 2011, www.governor.nc.gov/NewsItems/PressReleaseDetail.aspx?newsItemID=1652.

29. S.L. 2011-398.

30. "Small Business Regulatory Flexibility Model Legislation Initiative," U.S. Small Business Administration (SBA): Office of Advocacy, September 2005, gopher.sbaonline.sba.gov/advo/laws/law_modelrpt.pdf.

31. See, e.g., Sara Burrows, "State Threatens to Shut Down Nutrition Blogger," *Carolina Journal Online*, April 23, 2012, www.carolinajournal.com/articles/display_story.html?id=8992; Sara Burrows, "Paleo Diet Blogger Sues State for Violating Free Speech," *Carolina Journal Online*, May 31, 2012, www.carolinajournal.com/articles/display_story.html?id=9127; "Caveman Blogger Fights for Free Speech and Internet Freedom," Institute for Justice Litigation Backgrounder, ij.org/north-carolina-speech-backgrounder; Sara Burrows, "Paleo Diet Blogger Loses Round One of Free Speech Case," *Carolina Journal Online*, October 11, 2012, www.carolinajournal.com/exclusives/display_exclusive.html?id=9575.

32. North Carolina State Constitution, Article I, Section 1.

33. Byron Schlomach, "Six Reforms to Occupational Licensing Laws to Increase Jobs and Lower Costs," Goldwater Institute Policy Report No. 247, July 10, 2012, goldwaterinstitute.org/article/six-reforms-occupational-licensing-laws-increase-jobs-and-lower-costs.

34. Schlomach, "Six Reforms to Occupational Licensing Laws."

35. SL 1991-668 (H564), www.ncga.state.nc.us/Sessions/1991/Bills/House/HTML/H564v4.html.

36. Morris M. Kleiner, "Occupational Licensing," *The Journal of Economic Perspectives*, Vol. 14, No. 4, Autumn 2000, pp. 189–202, web.missouri.edu/~podgurskym/Econ_4345/syl_articles/kleiner.pdf.

37. Sara Burrows, "Proposed Occupational Licensing Laws Target Entrepreneurs," *Carolina Journal Online*, June 22, 2011, www.carolinajournal.com/articles/display_story.html?id=7927.

38. SL 2000-162 (H1340), www.ncga.state.nc.us/Sessions/1999/Bills/House/HTML/H1340v6.html.

39. SL 2001-369 (H942), www.ncga.state.nc.us/Sessions/2001/Bills/House/HTML/H942v8.html.

40. SL 2002-182 (H1313), www.ncga.state.nc.us/Sessions/2001/Bills/House/HTML/H1313v5.html.

41. SL2006-82 (H688), www.ncga.state.nc.us/Sessions/2005/Bills/House/HTML/H688v6.html.

42. SL2008-177 (H2353), www.ncga.state.nc.us/Sessions/2007/Bills/House/HTML/H2353v6.html.

43. Adam B. Summers, "Occupational Licensing: Ranking the States and Exploring the Alternatives," Reason Foundation Policy Study No. 361, August 2007, reason.org/news/show/1002854.html.

44. Sara Burrows, "African Hair Braiders Say New Regulations Threaten Craft," *Carolina Journal Online*, May 26, 2010, www.carolinajournal.com/articles/display_story.html?id=6455.

45. See, e.g., Hippocrates, "The Oath," *The Internet Classics Archive*, classics.mit.edu/Hippocrates/hippooath.html, and "Nonmaleficence," *The Medical Dictionary*, FreeDictionary.com, medical-dictionary.thefreedictionary.com/nonmaleficence;

46. H.R. 10, "Regulations From the Executive in Need of Scrutiny Act of 2011," The Library of Congress, thomas.loc.gov/cgi-bin/bdquery/z?d112:h.r.10:.

47. *Adams v. N.C., DENR.*

48. H.R. 10, Section 2.

49. "The Congressional Accountability Act," *The Wall Street Journal*, January 14, 2011, online.wsj.com/article/SB10001424052970203525404576049703586223080.htm. Also see Paul M. Barrett, "REINS Act: Hogtie the Executive Branch!" *Bloomberg Businessweek*, March 24, 2011, www.businessweek.com/magazine/content/11_14/b4222010097754.htm.

50. Ron Arnold, "Reining in Regulation by Delegation: A Guide to the REINS Act," *National Policy Analysis* No. 623, National Center for Public Policy Research, May 2011, www.nationalcenter.org/NPA623.html.

51. S.L. 2011-398.

52. See, e.g., the discussion of REINS in Phil Kerpen, "The REINS Act ends unchecked bureaucratic power," *The Hill's Congress Blog*, December 2, 2011, thehill.com/blogs/congress-blog/politics/196821-the-reins-act-ends-unchecked-bureaucratic-power.

53. See discussion in Reform Seven in Bakst, "Regulating the Regulators."

54. S.L. 2011-398. Along similar lines, RRA 2011 also required state agencies to review their own policies and programs in order to prevent redundant and overlapping regulations.

55. S.B. 308, "State Regulation of Greenhouse Gas Emissions," 2011, www.ncga.state.nc.us/Sessions/2011/Bills/Senate/HTML/S308v2.html.

56. Daren Bakst, "Fish Tales About Mercury: Why regulation of mercury is all cost and no benefit," John Locke Foundation Spotlight No. 300, November 8, 2006, johnlocke.org/acrobat/spotlights/spotlight_300-mercuryregs.pdf, and Bakst, "Regulating the Regulators."

57. Some of whom also turned their argument ex terrori tactics upon Daren Bakst for his research cited supra; see, e.g., Daren Bakst, "Mercury Myths," *The Locker Room* blog, John Locke Foundation, November 14, 2006, johnlocke.org/lockerroom/lockerroom.html?id=10707, and Jon Sanders, "Fishy argumentation — or, Daren, you ignorant slut!", *The Locker Room* blog, John Locke Foundation, November 24, 2006, johnlocke.org/lockerroom/lockerroom.html?id=10822.

58. "Commission Adopts Rules for Curbing Mercury Emissions," press release, N.C. DENR, Division of Air Quality, November 9, 2006, daq.state.nc.us/news/pr/2006/hg_rule_11092006.shtml.

59. This quotation from Bakst, "Regulating the Regulators," describes the cynical political calculus at work: "Why environmental groups prefer that the legislature not make major policy decisions is not hard to understand. Those groups can 'capture' relevant agencies and commissions. It is much easier to influence a small number of unelected individuals, who often have close connections to these environmental groups, than to convince a large number of legislators, who are also beholden to voters. Also, because of the nature of the legislative process, it is difficult to get laws passed."

60. Sara Burrows, "Bill Cutting Red Tape Earns Red Ink," *Carolina Journal Online*, June 11, 2011, www.carolinajournal.com/exclusives/display_exclusive.html?id=7997.

61. See, e.g., this passage from Research Division staff attorney Karen Cochrane Brown's July 7, 2011, brief to House Speaker Thom Tillis and Senate President Pro Tempore Phil Berger, "Re: Constitutionality of SB 781": "Statistics over a number of years dramatically demonstrate that when the ALJ rules against an agency in a contested case, which only happens in a relatively small percentage of cases, the agency simply rejects the ALJ's decision and substitutes its own decision. Agencies argue that they must retain the power to do this in order to preserve the integrity of their policies, about which they are the undisputed experts. However, it is important to remember that when agencies administer their policies in a manner that deprives a citizen of a property interest or prejudices individual rights, it must do so in a manner that satisfies the requirements of due process contained in the State and federal Constitutions [see *Goldberg v. Kelly*, 297 U.S. 254 (1970)]. Maintaining the integrity of administrative policies simply is not a constitutionally recognized value

and certainly cannot ever justify the denial of due process."

62. "Small Business Profile: North Carolina," U.S. SBA: Office of Advocacy, January 2012, http://www.sba.gov/sites/default/files/nc11_0.pdf.

63. Nicole V. Crain and W. Mark Crain, "The Impact of Regulatory Costs on Small Firms," U.S. SBA: Office of Advocacy, September 2010, archive.sba.gov/advo/research/rs371tot.pdf.

64. "The Impact of Regulations on North Carolina," Small Businesses for Sensible Regulations, a project of the National Federation of Independent Business, www.sensibleregulations.org/local-stories/north-carolina, accessed October 24, 2012.

65. Crain and Crain, "The Impact of Regulatory Costs on Small Firms."

66. "Small Business Regulatory Flexibility Model Legislation Initiative," U.S. SBA: Office of Advocacy, September 2005, gopher.sbaonline.sba.gov/advo/laws/law_modelrpt.pdf.

67. "Small Business Regulatory Flexibility Model Legislation Initiative."

68. See, e.g., John Hood and Don Carrington, "Warning Signs: A Survey of North Carolina Business Leaders on Competitiveness, Taxes, and Reform," John Locke Foundation Policy Report, April 2002, johnlocke.org/research/show/policy%20reports/24. John Hood and Chad Adams, "Climate Change: A Survey of North Carolina Business Leaders on Competitiveness, Taxes, and Reform," John Locke Foundation Policy Report, May 2004, johnlocke.org/acrobat/policyReports/business_survey_report_2004.pdf. John Hood and Chad Adams, "Unsteady Ground: A Survey of North Carolina Business Leaders on Competitiveness, Taxes, and Reform," John Locke Foundation Policy Report, November 2005, johnlocke.org/research/show/policy%20reports/63.

69. North Carolina Register, Rules Division, Office of Administrative Hearings, www.oah.state.nc.us/rules/register.

70. Hood and Adams, "Unsteady Ground: A Survey of North Carolina Business Leaders."

71. "Small Business Regulatory Flexibility Model Legislation Initiative," pp. 5–8.

Chapter Six

<><><><><><><><><><><><><><><>

The Patient Protection and Affordable Care Act: How should North Carolina respond to Obamacare?

by Sean Riley

In an article describing the problems associated with the implementation of President Obama's health care plan, economist Thomas Sowell observed that many of its provisions were attempts to address problems such as high insurance costs and low access to care that were themselves the result of government action. "Too many political 'solutions' are solutions to problems created by previous political 'solutions,'" Sowell wrote, "and will be followed by new problems created by their current 'solutions.' There is no free lunch. In the case of health insurance, there is not even an inexpensive lunch."

In this chapter, JLF adjunct policy analyst Sean Riley* discusses the many challenges posed to North Carolina policymakers by the new law — and what they should do about them.

Requiring a controversial Supreme Court decision to determine the constitutionality of its major components, the purported policy solutions in the 2010 Patient Protection and Affordable Care Act[1] (PPACA, often referred to as Obamacare) amount to little more than illusions. These illusions, unfortunately, have served to successfully distract policymakers from addressing the real problems facing health care. There is no question that health care reform in the United States is necessary, that costs are rising, and that access and quality should be expanded. But

* The views expressed in this article are those of the author and do not necessarily represent the views of, and should not be attributed to, the staff, members, or board of the American Legislative Exchange Council (ALEC).

the legislation enacted by President Obama and the Democratic Congress of 2010 fails to address these problems.

Means and Ends

The stated goals of PPACA are to provide better access to care, more affordable coverage, stronger consumer rights and protections, and stronger Medicare[2] — all goals shared by most policymakers interested in meaningful health care reform. But contrary to charges by proponents, the concerns with the law are not with its stated goals. They are instead concerns with the means to achieve them.

First, to increase access to care, the law forces individuals to buy insurance, forces employers to offer insurance, and forced states to expand Medicaid until the Supreme Court struck that provision down as coercive. Now optional, Medicaid expansion shifts people above the poverty level into state-administered public insurance at an estimated cost of $642 billion through 2022.[3] Instead of providing sought-after flexibility, the law additionally blocks states from making changes to their Medicaid programs in the short term, enticing states to pursue increased funding instead. Unfortunately, even if all three strategies were successful, and all states expanded Medicaid, the law would fail to cover nearly half of the 53 million currently uninsured Americans.[4]

Second, to make coverage more affordable, the law imposes federal mandates on what insurance policies must cover and transfers more than $1 trillion in new taxes and penalties to provide subsidies to Americans at up to 400 percent of the federal poverty level. Of course, these subsidies only *offset* costs rather than reduce them.[5] In the process, PPACA usurps state control of health insurance regulation, increasing insurance costs for those not eligible for subsidies, and sets a dangerous precedent for federal control moving forward.

Third, to strengthen consumer rights and protections, the law imposes **guaranteed issue** and **community rating** on insurance providers. Guaranteed issue requires insurers to provide coverage for those with pre-existing conditions. Community rating requires insurers to charge the same rates to individuals regardless of health status. The net effect of these regulations will mirror state-level experiments doing the same, resulting in higher premiums for mostly young and healthy taxpayers to offset the increased costs of providing coverage for those with severe medical needs.[6] Providers will have little choice but to spread costs among all consumers, placing upward pressure on already-rising insurance premiums under the law.

Finally, to strengthen Medicare's financial position, the law cuts some $716 billion from Medicare over 10 years through reductions to hospital services, home health, Medicare Advantage, and Disproportionate Share Hospital (DSH) payments. Though the Congressional Budget Office has estimated these cuts may serve to strengthen Medicare overall, it found that Medicare remains on an unsustainable trajectory despite the cuts.

Putting it all together, the law's provisions fail to address health care costs and quality of care, instead opting for more spending, taxes, and regulation. Rather than serve as a formula for true reform, the law exacerbates the underlying problems in health care leading to increased costs and ultimately reducing access to quality care.

Addressing Popular Provisions

Nonetheless, several provisions within the law are more or less popular with the public, such as requiring insurance companies to cover adults up to age 26 on their parents' plans and those with pre-existing conditions, and preventing insurance companies from charging premiums based on an individual's health status. But even these policies are misguided at the federal level.

If a state wants to force insurance companies to allow adults up to age 26 to remain on their parents' plans, it has been within their ability to do so, and many states extended coverage beyond age 18 prior to PPACA. While this does decrease the number of uninsured, it does nothing to increase affordable access. The costs associated with these regulations are passed on to all consumers through higher premiums, actually limiting access.[7]

And there **is** a serious problem to be addressed for Americans with pre-existing conditions. But this is largely a symptom of a broken system where insurance is tethered to a job and where losing a job often means losing coverage. Meanwhile, there have certainly been instances of unscrupulous insurance practices, including people being dropped from rolls at times when they need care the most. But these problems can be addressed without forcing everyone to buy insurance, mandating what must be covered, or providing subsidies while ignoring cost drivers.

So while the merits of several of the popular provisions have been debated, two things are clear. First, none of these provisions required thousands of pages of federal law and regulation. Each of these issues has been or could be addressed at the state level. Second, these provisions necessarily drive up costs for all other participants in the insurance market.

The Path Forward for States

The negative impacts of PPACA are clear. All told, the latest Congressional Budget Office estimate places PPACA spending at $1.683 trillion through 2022, with even higher projections moving forward once the law is fully implemented.[8] For private insurance, the law's transition of insurance regulation away from the states to the federal government will ultimately drive up costs. And for public insurance, the law's attempt simply to double down on a Medicaid system that itself is in need of reform will aggravate existing problems.[9]

Fortunately a path forward exists for states. The twin pillars of PPACA representing $1.659 of the law's $1.683 trillion in new spending — health insurance exchanges through which subsidies flow and Medicaid expansion — have placed states in a position of considerable leverage. Whereas the federal government assumed all states would immediately create exchanges (supposed marketplaces for consumers to shop for health plans, imposing federal insurance regulations and distributing subsidies), it is clear that many will hold the federal government responsible for implementing the law it narrowly passed. Meanwhile, where PPACA originally threatened to withdraw all Medicaid funding if states did not accept expansion, the Supreme Court has ruled that states can refuse, free from threats to existing funding.

In essence, policymakers now find themselves at a critical decision point with respect to these two central components. One path would see states voluntarily establish exchanges and expand Medicaid, serving as agents of the federal government and becoming further beholden to federal largesse and regulations. The other would see states opt out of state-based exchanges and Medicaid expansion, serving as stewards of real health reform and requiring the federal government to take responsibility for deeply flawed policies passed against the will of the public.

But there should be no illusions harbored by policymakers that refusing expansion and exchanges will solve the health care crisis. This path would stem the tide of an overreaching federal government threatening the foundations of federalism. But while that would represent a significant achievement and is a critical step, more is required. Indeed the health care landscape that existed prior to PPACA paved the way for federal overreach, and the harsh reality is that states have been largely complicit in stifling competition and innovation. Any real solution requires policymakers to think critically about the long-term consequences of health policies at the state level. Focusing on an approach that promotes competition, reduces mandates, and provides increased access will be essential — as will vigilance in fighting entrenched interests content with preserving the status quo.

Health Exchanges

Perhaps the most widely discussed aspect of the law with direct implications for state decision making comes in the area of establishing state health insurance exchanges. While Gov. Bev Perdue previously signaled that North Carolina would enter into a partnership with the federal government,[10] Gov. Pat McCrory has indicated he'll work with the legislature to determine the best course of action going forward.[11] Fundamentally, exchanges under PPACA are a way for the federal, not state, government to implement insurance regulations and distribute over $1 trillion in spending through subsidies by 2022,[12] hardly a market approach. While repeatedly touted by PPACA proponents as simple websites to allow consumers to compare plans, exchanges represent much more and carry significant logistical concerns. Many questions remain as to how exchanges will operate, whether they will be financially viable, whether Washington will be able to handle the task of establishing them in states that refuse, and whether they will actually foster competition and reduce costs under the weight of regulatory burdens.

States thus far have taken varying approaches. While PPACA allows states to establish exchanges, providing millions of dollars in planning grants, states are under no obligation to do so. In fact, the federal government lacks the authority to require states to do so. Instead, states have a choice, with the federal government saying it will step in and create exchanges in states that choose not to. Even then, states are permitted under the law to take control of federally established exchanges at a later date, and several states are preserving that option.

For plan year 2014, the first year in which exchanges are to be operational, more than half the states have signaled that they will let the federal government take ownership of implementation. Reasons vary, but many have cited the absence of critical information from HHS relating to exchange operation and function. More than half of sitting governors in 2012 requested additional information from HHS relating to exchanges on multiple occasions only to be met with silence.[13] These critical questions included:

- When will final regulations be promulgated?
- When will final rules relating to actuarial ratings be released?
- When will details of a federal partnership be released?
- What costs will be associated with collecting and transmitting data?
- Will Congress be able to defund exchange funding for federal exchanges?
- Can states refuse to increase taxes to pay for the cost of operation after federal funding expires in 2015?
- Will exchange subsidies be reduced in 2018?
- When will multi-state plans be available?
- How will high-risk pools be financed?[14]

Exchange Costs

Of course there is another critical question facing the states: how much will an exchange cost to operate if a state volunteers to implement? Fortunately, while HHS has been largely silent on the cost of federally established exchanges or how they will be funded, state estimates exist. While general estimates have pegged costs at anywhere between $10 and $100 million annually,[15] a 2011 Milliman, Inc. report to the North Carolina Department of Insurance estimated costs of roughly $25 million to the state,

Figure 1: Estimated Costs to Operate a State-Created Exchange

	2014	2015	2016
Direct Labor and Related Costs	8,411,018	9,157,513	9,639,917
Salary Driven Costs	512,250	557,713	587,093
Other Direct Costs	14,836,482	15,263,462	16,483,138
Total Annual Expenses	23,759,750	24,978,688	26,710,148

One study estimates that a state-created exchange would cost North Carolina roughly $25 million annually to operate.
Source: North Carolina Health Benefit Exchange Study, Milliman Report for the North Carolina Department of Insurance, 2011

with costs of $24.9 and $26.7 million in 2015 and 2016, respectively.[16] Total costs are comprised of labor and salary costs, equipment, maintenance, and navigator grants. Though exchange costs would be fully funded through 2014 by the federal government, the law requires that state established exchanges be self-funded by January 1, 2015.[17]

Again, Gov. Perdue previously signaled that North Carolina would be entering into a federal partnership exchange. A federal partnership is a third option, created by fiat by HHS in July 2011 when it became apparent that many states would not volunteer to build exchanges and implement the law.[18] Guidance was released in May 2012 on how federally-established exchanges, called federally-facilitated exchanges (FFE), would operate, and how states could function as partners with an FFE.[19]

The guidance was telling. Whereas proponents of state-established exchanges have argued that states must implement or face a government takeover, the guidance instead revealed overtures from the federal government that states would retain their traditional state role regardless of exchange form. But, of course, the real government takeover has already occurred, and took place when PPACA was signed into law. That is, the traditional role of states in setting minimums for insurance requirements has been seized by the federal government, which under the law now prescribes essential health benefits (EHB), the minimum level coverage each American must buy if he is to have any insurance at all. Under the partnership model, federal regulators offered the states the limited option of administering plan management functions and consumer assistance functions, including data collection and review of health plans — essentially an administrative role.[20]

State "Control"

The range of state control in a state-established exchange is not much different, and is ultimately a matter of form rather than function. The control a state could exercise if it created an exchange includes: whether the exchange would be structured as a governmental agency or nonprofit, whether the state would enter into a regional exchange, and whether the exchange would establish a 50-employee limit for businesses seeking coverage through 2015.[21] While employee limits might be of initial concern, federal exchanges will adopt state definitions of the small group market and North Carolina already defines small group as between 1 and 50. If providing exchange services to larger employers is a concern, there is nothing preventing states from establishing their own independent exchanges.

In reality, exchange functions are prescribed by PPACA under section 1311, regardless of form, and include plan certification based on federal guidelines, operation of a hotline and website, provision of information for consumers, establishment of a navigator program, presentation of satisfaction surveys, publication of administrative costs, and consultation with stakeholders.[22] Thus, a state must adhere to federal regulation even if establishing a "state" exchange under PPACA.

Yet there are two material areas where states refusing to implement are foregoing some modicum of control. First, states will be unable to control whether an exchange will operate under a clearinghouse model that accepts all plans meeting federal requirements, or operate as an active purchaser, limiting consumer choices as to which plans can be sold (though these also must adhere to federal requirements). Second, states will be relinquishing the ability to increase mandates on plans within an exchange.[23] Tellingly, **neither of these powers would actually allow a state to make its exchange freer and more competitive.** Guidance indicates that federal exchanges will allow all qualifying plans to compete, at least in the first year, meaning states would only have the ability to restrict access by limiting competition and increasing mandates, both antithetical to free-market principles.

To be sure, a health insurance exchange under PPACA, regardless of state or federal creation, will carry with it some of the traditional benefits of proposals for free-market exchanges. Allowing consumers to easily shop for and compare plans and pool together will presumably result in some marginal reduction in health insurance costs. However, unlike a free-market exchange, these reductions will be offset by price increases. Because exchange plans must adhere to federal insurance mandates and guidelines, regardless of form, consumers will face higher premiums.

Exchange Subsidies

Again, the primary function of exchanges will be to distribute over $1 trillion in new subsidies paid for through $1 trillion in new taxes and penalties levied against individuals and businesses. Subsidies made available through exchanges take two forms, premium credits and cost-sharing subsidies. Under PPACA, several benefit plans will be established within exchanges

Figure 2: Income Thresholds to Qualify for Subsidies Under PPACA

Persons in Household	Annual Income as Percentage of Federal Poverty Level (FPL)						
	100%	133%	150%	200%	250%	300%	400%
1	11,170	14,856	16,755	22,340	27,925	33,510	44,680
2	15,130	20,123	22,695	30,260	37,825	45,390	60,520
3	19,090	25,390	28,635	38,180	47,725	57,270	76,360
4	23,050	30,657	34,575	46,100	57,625	69,150	92,200
5	27,010	35,923	40,515	54,020	67,525	81,030	108,040
6	30,970	41,190	46,455	61,940	77,425	92,910	123,880
7	34,930	46,457	52,395	69,860	87,325	104,790	139,720
8	38,890	51,724	58,335	77,780	97,225	116,670	155,560

The average North Carolina family will qualify for government subisides under the law, including those earning $20,000 more than the average household income.
Source: 2012 Poverty Guidelines for the 48 Contiguous States and the District of Columbia, HHS

ranging from bronze to gold to catastrophic coverage. The first category of subsidies, premium credits, will be made available to individuals and families at up to 400 percent of the federal poverty line (FPL) based on a sliding income scale and tied to the cost of a silver tier plan.[24] For those between 100 and 133 percent of FPL, individuals and families will receive credits to cover the cost of a silver plan exceeding 2 percent of income. Income thresholds rise to 9.5 percent for those between 300 and 400 percent of FPL. The second category, cost-sharing subsidies, will reduce out-of-pocket limits for individuals and families based on a sliding scale, including those earning up to 400 percent of FPL. The two categories combined make up a majority of the law's spending.

The primary concerns with these new subsidies are two-fold. First, they simply offset costs for health care through reallocating taxes, rather than reducing costs or making health care more affordable. It's akin to saying you'll reduce the price of a car by simply taking money from one person and giving it to the purchaser. The actual price of the car is the same, at least for the moment, with the price likely to increase once the market recognizes that car purchasing is being widely subsidized. Second, as a result of the subsidies made available through exchanges to those at up to 400 percent of FPL, more and more individuals and families run the risk of becoming dependent on government, including those who didn't need help in the first place. For example, a single childless adult making up to $44,680 a year, which is nearly the median household income in North Carolina of $45,570, will qualify for premium credits and cost-sharing subsidies under the law. Not only will the average North Carolina family now qualify for government subsidies for health care, but on a pro-rata basis households earning $20,000 more than the median North Carolina household (2.49 persons) will have a new entitlement.[25] This goes beyond preserving a safety net and providing access, and places incentives on a culture of dependency.

Additional Concerns

There is yet another significant dynamic in making the decision whether or not to establish a state exchange. Several outstanding lawsuits challenging the law are making their way through the courts, with more likely to come as provisions take effect, including litigation currently under way challenging IRS rules relating to subsidies being made available in federal exchanges.[26] Again, over half the spending in PPACA comes directly from subsidies being made available to those at up to 400 percent of FPL. Two scholars, Michael Cannon with the Cato Institute and Jonathan Adler with the Case-Western Reserve University School of Law, have outlined arguments in the *Health Matrix: Journal of Law and Medicine* that subsidies are only available in state-established exchanges based on a textual reading of PPACA.[27] These arguments have been proffered in the amended lawsuit by Oklahoma's Attorney General challenging PPACA, currently making its way through the courts.

The implications of this legal argument are substantial. If it is the case that subsidies are only available through state-established exchanges, states opposed to PPACA could block half of the law's spending by refusing to create exchanges. Additionally, due to the manner in which penalties against employers and individuals are triggered for failing to buy insurance, employers and many individuals could be exempt from mandates and penalties. While this would be a considerable victory for individuals, the consequences for employers would be strikingly larger. If employers are exempt from mandates to provide coverage for employees, states refusing to establish exchanges would stand at a considerable advantage in attracting businesses compared to states where employers are mandated to provide coverage. Thus, in addition to freeing employers from burdensome regulations and mandates that drive up costs, North Carolina would potentially be in a position to attract employers from other states by refusing to create an exchange.

Of course, there are arguments against the position Cannon and Adler and the Oklahoma Attorney General have posited, including the IRS's ability to interpret statutes, and the argument that Congress intended subsidies to apply to a federal exchange despite the language of the statute. However, the issue is not settled, and respected health scholars have noted that this litigation could undermine PPACA in its entirety if accepted by the courts.[28,29]

Decision on Exchanges

While refusing to endorse PPACA by disclaiming any state involvement may represent the best path, North Carolina should maintain its course in participating in an FFE partnership if the only alternative is a state exchange. If it is the case that a state-established exchange is in the best interest of North Carolinians, the state has the ability under the law to take "control" of the exchange at a later time under the same rules that would allow it to establish an exchange now. In the short-term, the benefits of establishing a state exchange are nominal. The risks, on the other hand, in cost and political capital with constituents, are clear. North Carolina would be responsible for the costs of exchange operation and accountable for any exchange failures if the state is unable to meet consumer expectations. Meanwhile, any

Figure 3: National Health Expenditures, Historical and Projected

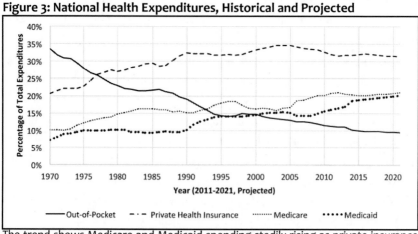

The trend shows Medicare and Medicaid spending stedily rising as private insurance spending flattens and as out-of-pocket spending falls.
Source: Centers for Medicare & Medicaid Services, Historical and Projected National Health Expenditures

guidelines may be changed moving forward now that the precedent has been set for the federal government to dictate insurance regulation in the states.[30] Moreover, current and forthcoming legal challenges to PPACA may prove some states have erred in serving as the test subjects in implementing state exchanges. But even if current and upcoming legal challenges fail, significant information is still missing from HHS as to the benefits of a state exchange. Instead there is cause for North Carolina to approach a state exchange with caution as uncertainties are mitigated moving ahead.

Medicaid Expansion

When Medicaid was first established, it was intended to cover health care for "low-income children deprived of parental support, their caretaker relatives, the elderly, the blind, and individuals with disabilities."[31] While originally foisted upon the states as an all or nothing command, the US Supreme Court found PPACA's mandate that states expand their Medicaid populations — to cover those at up to 133 percent of FPL, including childless adults, at the threat of losing all Medicaid funding — to be overly coercive and unconstitutional. Instead, states have been given the option to expand their Medicaid populations under the law without being punished for deciding against pursuing a questionable course.

Making the decision difficult is how generous the federal government is proposing to be with taxpayer dollars, offering the states 100 percent of costs in the first years of expansion. But the problems plaguing Medicaid have never really been due to a lack of money, but a lack of flexibility in tailoring the program to meet the specific needs of a state. Opting out of Medicaid expansion, and instead focusing on reforming the underlying problems within Medicaid, would be in North Carolina's best interest.

Medicaid Overview

The legislative histories of both Medicare and Medicaid are complex, and have been subject to numerous changes over their nearly 50-year histories.[32] The Medicaid program, created by Title XIX of the federal Social Security Act in 1965 along with Medicare, is essentially a joint state and federal public insurance entitlement, providing medical assistance for low-income families and individuals. While Medicare is a wholly federally funded program covering Americans over the age of 65, Medicaid is aimed towards low-income populations and is administered at the state level with funding from both the states and the federal government.

The financing mechanism in Medicaid generally operates through a federal match known as the Federal Medical Assistance Percentage (FMAP). States receive a minimum 50 percent match, with poorer states receiving a higher FMAP. At an FMAP of 50 percent, a state would receive $1 from the federal government for every $1 the state spends on its Medicaid population. North Carolina's FMAP has historically been around 65 percent.[33] According to the Kaiser Family Foundation, the federal share of overall Medicaid spending was 57 percent in FY 2010.[34]

But even before PPACA, Medicaid rolls throughout the country faced substantial pressure as a consequence of the broader economic impacts resulting from the financial crisis. As a result of the influx of people moving into Medicaid, the federal government stepped in with an enhanced FMAP to assist states in carrying the extra burden of a newly expanded Medicaid population. Rather than leave states to reform their Medicaid programs to meet new economic challenges, the federal government simply shifted more money into a system that was unsustainable.

The broader incentives under the current FMAP relationship are such that states are under pressure to expand their Medicaid populations in order to receive more and more federal money. As the John Locke Foundation's May 2011 policy report pointed out, North Carolina could receive an extra

Figure 4: Trends in Program Spending as a Share of the State Budget

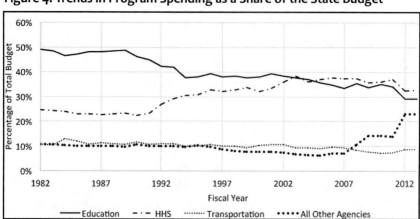

Health spending represents the highest expenditure in North Carolina's budget, placing pressure on education and other spending.
Source: North Carolina Office of State Budget and Management, Historical Budget Data

$1.75 in federal support for every new dollar policymakers are willing to spend on Medicaid.[35] Unfortunately for taxpayers at the state and federal levels, Medicaid expenditures appear to be on a one-way street. While the enhanced match may seem attractive when increasing spending, reducing spending becomes significantly more difficult. The May 2011 report showed that a cut of $2.75 to Medicaid would be required in order to reduce state spending by $1.[36] Politically, the incentives will always be present to increase rather than reduce state expenditures.

So even before PPACA, state expenditures were on a course to reach record levels, placing pressures on other areas within North Carolina's budget. And the trend will continue without real reform. Unfortunately, PPACA does not address any of the underlying problems within Medicaid, but drastically compounds them by using more federal dollars as a tool to entice states into expanding their programs even further.

Expansion under PPACA

While the law's stated goal of reducing the number of uninsured has garnered much attention related to the individual mandate, nearly half of the projected reduction in the number of uninsured Americans under the law comes from simply shifting more individuals into state Medicaid programs. Rather than providing policies to bring down costs, expand competition, and increase access, PPACA essentially doubles down on Medicaid by expanding eligibility to those at up to 133 percent of FPL, including childless adults. And the federal match for covering these new populations? As currently written, PPACA will provide 100 percent of costs for newly eligible Medicaid recipients in years 2014, 2015, and 2016, 95 percent in 2017, 94 percent in 2018, 93 percent in 2019, and 90 percent in subsequent years, assuming continued support from Congress — though that remains in serious doubt.[37]

The law, however, doesn't just expand Medicaid, but places additional burdens on states through what is called maintenance of effort (MOE). Under MOE provisions in PPACA, states are prohibited from adjusting their current eligibility standards in Medicaid and CHIP.[38] In other words, PPACA removes the already limited amount of state flexibility within Medicaid, and blocks states from adjusting eligibility until January 1, 2014 in Medicaid, and September 30, 2019 in CHIP.[39] And so the cycle of state dependency on the federal government continues, but now instead of allowing states to reform their Medicaid programs to meet new challenges, the law explicitly blocks states from doing so.

Expansion Costs

A critical question to ask, beyond how much money states can get, is how Medicaid expansion would impact North Carolina. According to the NC Department of Health and Human Services, Medicaid served roughly 1.7 million people in 2010-2011, including low- and middle-income children and pregnant women.[40,41] The program had an overall budget of $13.6 billion, including over $2.4 billion in state appropriations. As the John Locke Foundation has previously noted, Medicaid expansion in North Carolina would mean adding roughly 600,000 to Medicaid rolls at a combined state and federal annual cost of $4 billion dollars in the short run.[42] The Kaiser Family Foundation estimated North Carolina would pay between $1 and $1.7 billion through 2019, and roughly $3.075 billion through 2022.[43,44] The Heritage Foundation estimated state costs would exceed $1 billion through 2020. The Division of Medical Assistance estimates that the cost to the state will be approximately $830,000 from FY 2014-2019,[45] with a total cost to North Carolina and federal taxpayers exceeding $16 billion over the same time period.[46]

So what would North Carolina get for a billion dollars in state spending and $16 billion in combined state and federal spending?

A report from the Cecil G. Sheps Center for Health Services Research at the University of North Carolina at Chapel Hill estimated 536,000 uninsured nonelderly adults would qualify under PPACA expansion in 2014, though only 382,000 would be newly eligible.[47] An additional 213,000 uninsured children, who are currently eligible but not enrolled, would likely enroll according to the report.[48] The Division of Medical Assistance's official estimates are that 525,000 Medicaid beneficiaries would likely be enrolled in 2014, 79 percent (or 412,000) of whom would be newly eligible, with the remainder coming from those currently eligible but not enrolled.[49] Total enrollment would exceed 2.2 million, representing more than 20 percent of North Carolina's population. New enrollment would be expected to grow marginally each year, with 2019 enrollment for new enrollees at just under 560,000.

The distinction between newly eligible and currently eligible but not enrolled is important. It lends itself to what is known as the "woodwork effect," where those currently eligible, but not receiving benefits, come forward for what they perceive as a new program.[50] Some estimates place the number of North Carolinians currently uninsured but Medicaid-eligible at somewhere between 3 and 4 percent of the state's population, or between 25 and 30 percent of those currently eligible.[51,52] Significantly, the new match under PPACA expansion would only apply to those newly eligible, not those currently eligible but not enrolled. The Kaiser Family Foundation's cost estimates of between $1 and $1.7 billion dollars through 2019 partially reflect the range of costs due to more currently eligible enrollees seeking coverage as a result of expansion efforts.

Federal Budget Concerns

Again, as currently written, PPACA will provide between 93 and 100 percent of costs for expansion through 2019 and 90 percent in all subsequent years.[53] But Washington's ability to service these payments in light of last year's debt talks surrounding the "fiscal cliff" should not be taken for granted. The case for sustaining payments for childless adults and those explicitly above the federal poverty level is weaker than sustaining payments for the truly vulnerable in the broader program. In fact, the administration's proposed budget for FY 2013 included a Medicaid cut to the states of $3.4 billion starting in 2017, with cuts totaling $17.9 billion by 2022.[54]

Under that proposal, the reimbursement rates for newly eligible beneficiaries promised to states under PPACA would be rewritten and instead combined with existing FMAP rates creating a "single blended matching rate" starting in 2017.[55] Projections by the Heritage Foundation based on current population and spending data found that, under this blended rate, costs to North Carolina would rise from a baseline of roughly $891 million in years 2014-2022 to more than $2.85 billion over the same period. Even a 10 percent reduction in the federal match would see North Carolina paying over $2.2 billion over the period for the expanded population.[56] Additional cuts in that proposed budget would bring total cuts in Medicaid funding to $50.9 billion by 2022.[57] While some may argue the proposal was just a proposal, it shouldn't be taken lightly. Previous signals from the Obama administration indicated even more drastic cuts to Medicaid, totaling $100 billion over 10 years.[58] Meanwhile, the fiscal uncertainty moving forward for the broader economy brings additional doubt as to the sustainability of Medicaid payments currently promised under PPACA.

Reimbursement Concerns

Further uncertainties exist surrounding physician reimbursement. PPACA requires all state Medicaid programs to reimburse certain primary care physicians in 2013 and 2014 "at rates no less than the Medicare rates in effect in those calendar years" in fee for service and managed care.[59] The rate will apply to family medicine, general internal medicine, and pediatric medicine practitioners and related specialists. States will receive 100 percent federal matching funds to cover any difference in 2013 and 2014, but will be left to cover the difference thereafter or reduce reimbursements if new federal funding is not authorized. Not only will reducing payments at that point be politically difficult, but other health providers will likely seek reimbursement increases in line with those received by primary care physicians.

Intersection with Exchanges

Another critical area that states must consider is the intersection between federal subsidies made available through health exchanges and Medicaid expansion. As several have pointed out, including former CBO Director Douglas Holtz-Eakin, there is significant incentive for states to forego expansion.[60] One reason is that those between 100 and 138 percent of FPL will receive subsidies through an exchange at no cost to the state if states do not expand. If states expand Medicaid, however, they will be required to share the Medicaid costs for those within the expanded group.[61] While there is an argument that states should expand regardless in order to cover childless adults below 100 percent of FPL, North Carolina had not seen fit to cover this population prior to PPACA.

Additional Concerns

As alluded to by the North Carolina Institute of Medicine, there are likely to be still more fiscal implications beyond the various estimates for North Carolina. While some have argued that "crowding out" — that is shifting those to Medicaid who already have private insurance — is not a significant market threat,[62] administrative costs necessarily will arise.[63,64] Estimates figure that states will be footing an additional 2.48 percent in spending for administrative costs even after a federal match.[65,66] There is also the very real possibility of additional costs to the states to make up for cuts imposed by

PPACA,[67] including $36 billion in reduced Medicare and Medicaid payments to hospitals receiving Disproportionate Share Hospital (DSH) payments.[68] While the reduction in DSH payments is supposed to be balanced by the reduction in the number of uninsured, it's unclear that even Medicaid expansion would cover the cuts. This uncertainty arises because PPACA will still leave more than half of those currently uninsured without coverage; the Congressional Budget Office's revised report following the Supreme Court decision found that roughly 30 million people will still be uninsured by 2022.[69] Demands for increased state spending to make up for PPACA's DSH cuts should be expected; otherwise some hospitals will be forced to close their doors.

Decision on Expansion

With the Supreme Court's June 2012 decision on the constitutionality of Medicaid expansion under PPACA, North Carolina has been returned the power to decide whether or not expansion makes sense for the state. While the initial outlay of federal spending appears attractive to many, there is very significant cause for concern.

What is the population that North Carolina will be covering under Medicaid expansion, and why has North Carolina not previously extended the program to cover these individuals? Additionally, individuals will not be gaining access to insurance *per se*, but instead access to Medicaid, a program rife with problems. Is that the best path forward? Other questions surround how expansion will impact the existing Medicaid population and program, and what impact that will have on patients. But before answering these questions, policymakers should consider why Medicaid hasn't yet been reformed in North Carolina and why North Carolina's Medicaid program ranks among the most expensive in the Southeast.[70]

While opting out of Medicaid expansion at this point would be in North Carolina's best interest, rejecting the expansion of a broken system is not enough. Pursuing waivers and block grants, reforming long-term care, and reigning in optional services should be the first steps in Medicaid reform in North Carolina. Medicaid should be preserved, not as a mechanism for reliance on government assistance, but as a true safety net. Moving away from dependency towards encouraging patient control over health care decisions is essential for a fiscally viable Medicaid program that serves to protect the most vulnerable, as the program was originally intended.

Additional Steps North Carolina Can Take

Rejecting exchanges and Medicaid expansion is not enough. It is incumbent upon policymakers to seek solutions to the underlying problems that paved the way for a federal takeover of health care in the first place. Health care costs are increasing year over year, with medical inflation outpacing general inflation. Premiums are rising, and in the absence of affordable care at the state level protecting the most vulnerable, there will always be calls for federal solutions.

Fundamentally, health care delivery in the United States needs to move away from the current system where patients are unaware of the true costs. Beyond the financial, there are numerous examples of the human costs in a system that pushes families to become dependent on government for answers, only to leave them helpless when a doctor can't be found. While the short-term benefits in the form of subsidies and tax credits have the allure of seemingly being "free," they come with a price. Example upon example in Medicaid and Medicare highlight the political convenience of shifting costs from one group to another, but the consequences of this approach are stark. Once individuals become dependent on the government, it is no longer the patient or the doctor that is in control, but government.

Pursue Flexibility

Health policies that support a true safety net for the genuinely vulnerable should not be abandoned, and reforming Medicaid at the state-level is crucial. North Carolina taxpayers send money to Washington, and then Washington returns it with strings attached. Pursuing flexibility within Medicaid via waivers or block grants should be the cornerstone of state health reform. Beyond flexibility, states need to be on guard against fraud and abuse. Policymakers in North Carolina are to be commended for steps they've taken in implementing innovative technologies to ferret out fraud within Medicaid. But reforming public insurance is only one side of the coin, and opportunities for reforms in private insurance and outside of insurance abound.

Expand Access

Unfortunately, under the guise of regulation, care that would otherwise be given, even freely, is relegated to bureaucracies. A prime example is in the area of licensure for medical professionals, where special interests seek to preserve the status quo rather increase access. Onerous licensure requirements for medical professionals in the name of patient safety are restricting access. Care that could otherwise be provided by advanced registered nurses or other providers is restricted, and patients suffer. Additionally, most states, including North Carolina, forbid volunteer medical professionals from surrounding states to provide charity care. States like Tennessee and Illinois have recognized the absurdity of continuing policies that deem no care to be better than charity care, and both of those states have passed legislation allowing out-of-state volunteers to provide care in their states. If expanding access is the goal, expanding access to health professionals should be implicit.

Expanding access to providers isn't the only area where states can implement positive reforms. As the John Locke Foundation has pointed out, access for North Carolinians is currently being hampered by state Certificate of Need (CON) laws requiring government approval to expand facilities or even update equipment.[71] This scheme ultimately limits the very mechanism that best serves consumers — competition — and should be looked to as an area for immediate reform.

Increase Consumer Choice

Health policies that promote competition between insurance providers are likewise essential. What we have now is an overregulated system where only the entrenched interests can compete. Contrary to popular perception that large businesses disfavor regulation, it is only the largest providers that are able to bear the costs of regulation. This has an absolute negative impact on competition and fosters a system where regulations masquerading as patient protections serve as barriers for innovation and patient choice.

Similarly, reducing the number of mandated benefits should be a first step in allowing individuals and businesses greater choice in shopping for health plans. Restricting choice by mandating consumers pay for benefits they don't want or need is an end run around addressing patients with specific health requirements. Freeing people to shop for plans, rather than requiring them to indirectly subsidize those with particular health conditions, will not only bring down costs, but will allow policymakers to focus on real solutions for helping those vulnerable groups. If reducing mandates is not feasible due to special interests, allowing consumers to shop for plans in other states with fewer mandates is an option. Alternatively, states like Georgia have passed legislation allowing its insurers to sell plans with reduced mandates made available in other states.

Competition doesn't just benefit patients when it occurs between insurance providers, but also when states compete to provide the best services. While the benefits of relaxed medical licensure requirements, removal of barriers to facility expansion, and reduced mandates may not be immediately felt, they create conditions more suitable for markets to work.

Protect Against Future Encroachment

At the same time, states can pursue defensive measures to protect the freedom of patients and consumers. While PPACA's individual mandate has been upheld at the federal level, states can enact measures that would protect individuals and businesses from overzealous state policymakers seeking to enact single-payer systems or mandates like those seen in Vermont and Massachusetts, respectively. Health Care Freedom Acts, measures protecting the rights of individuals to pay directly for health care without being required to rely on insurance, have passed in some 17 states, and legislation has previously been submitted in North Carolina. While these measures will not directly protect individuals from federal mandates, they not only signal to Washington where states stand, but ensure that state-level mandates to buy insurance aren't imposed in the future.

Conclusion

The mechanisms within PPACA amount to federal control of health insurance regulation, a role traditionally held by the states, using the states themselves as an extension of Washington bureaucracy. This is as true in exchanges as it has been in Medicaid. The strongest strategy for blunting the federal government's attack on federalism begins with holding the federal government accountable for the laws it passes. Refusing to build state exchanges and refusing to expand Medicaid places the responsibility of the law in the hands of those who support it, and represents a first step in moving towards real health care reform. Indeed, leveraging these dual powers may give states the opportunity to achieve the flexibility that the law promised in the first place but failed to deliver.

While efforts from committed policymakers will likely continue at the federal level, efforts at the state level in the short and near term will become even more crucial. If the goal is truly to increase access to quality health care while doing what's possible to reduce costs, there is a solution — competitive markets. Pursuing free-market policies gives rise to innovations that cannot be created by bureaucrats. The multitude of problems facing the nation simply cannot be solved through PPACA or any other government fiat coming from Washington.

The federal government is capable of shifting money and costs, increasing regulations, and picking winners and losers in the short term. Their power to manipulate the health care market has never been in question. Where government has and will continue to fall short is in effectively allocating resources. While there is strong agreement that a safety net is necessary for a free and prosperous nation, the responsibility ultimately lies with the people and the states to determine the best path forward.

Under any policy proposal, all citizens should remain free. They should be free to choose a health plan that best suits their needs, free from government mandates that force them to buy services they don't want, and free to pursue their own goals. At their core, free-market health policies should promote competition and foster innovation. These forces are taken for granted, but it is only through markets and competition that innovation arises. At the end of the day, policymakers, analysts, and experts can push prescriptive policies, but the policies that get government out of the way will have the most meaningful impact on providing the most for the most.

While PPACA was written such that consumers and patients may not be free to choose, lawmakers now find themselves at a crucial juncture. Will they choose to continue down a path where the federal government provides "generous" taxpayer funded benefits only to curb them later when the fiscal shortsightedness becomes apparent? Or will they choose to pursue a health care system where individuals, consumers, patients, and doctors are able to provide quality care to more people at lower costs?

Endnotes

1. Patient Protection and Affordable Care Act (P.L. 111-148), as amended by the Health Care and Education Reconciliation Act (P.L. 111-152); housedocs.house.gov/energycommerce/ppacacon.pdf

2. whitehouse.gov/healthreform/healthcare-overview#healthcare-menu

3. cbo.gov/sites/default/files/cbofiles/attachments/43472-07-24-2012-CoverageEstimates.pdf

4. *ibid.*

5. *ibid.*

6. www.cahi.org/cahi_contents/resources/pdf/destroyinginsmrkts05.pdf

7. prescriptions.blogs.nytimes.com/2011/11/23/young-adults-coverage-may-cost-parents-even-more

8. cbo.gov/sites/default/files/cbofiles/attachments/43472-07-24-2012-CoverageEstimates.pdf

9. johnlocke.org/acrobat/policyReports/NCMedicaidReform.pdf

10. governor.state.nc.us/NewsItems/PressReleaseDetail.aspx?newsItemid=2674

11. carolinajournal.com/exclusives/display_exclusive.html?id=9729

12. cbo.gov/sites/default/files/cbofiles/attachments/43472-07-24-2012-CoverageEstimates.pdf

13. rgppc.com/rga-letter-pressing-hhs-for-answers

14. *ibid.*

15. cato.org/publications/commentary/obamAffordable Care Actre-is-still-vulnerable

16. nciom.org/wp-content/uploads/2010/10/NCDOI-Health-Benefit-Exchanges-Report-Version-37_2012-12-9.pdf

17. cciio.cms.gov/resources/files/guidance_to_states_on_exchanges.html

18. healthcare.gov/news/factsheets/2011/09/exchanges09192011a.html

19. cciio.cms.gov/resources/files/FFE_Guidance_FINAL_VERSION_051612.pdf

20. *ibid.*

21. healthcare.gov/law/resources/regulations/guidance-to-states-on-exchanges.html

22. *ibid.*

23. *ibid.*

24. kff.org/healthreform/upload/8061.pdf

25. quickfacts.census.gov/qfd/states/37000.html

26. healthcarelawsuits.org

27. papers.ssrn.com/sol3/papers.cfm?abstract_id=2106789

28. healthblog.ncpa.org/this-could-be-a-fatal-blow-to-obamAffordable Care Actre

29. politico.com/news/stories/1112/84203.html

30. capsules.kaiserhealthnews.org/wp-content/uploads/2012/11/HHS-Letter-to-RGA-11-15-12-.pdf.pdf

31. cms.gov/Research-Statistics-Data-and-Systems/Research/HealthCareFinancingReview/downloads/05-06Winpg1.pdf

32. kff.org/medicaid/medicaid_timeline.cfm

33. aspe.hhs.gov/health/fmap12.shtml

34. kff.org/medicaid/upload/7334-04.pdf

35. johnlocke.org/acrobat/policyReports/NCMedicaidReform.pdf

36. *ibid.*

37. gpo.gov/fdsys/pkg/PLAW-111publ152/pdf/PLAW-111publ152.pdf, Sec. 1201 (1)(b)
38. cbpp.org/files/4-7-10health3.pdf
39. *ibid.*
40. ncdhhs.gov/dma/whoweare.htm
41. kff.org/medicaid/upload/7993-02.pdf
42. johnlocke.org/acrobat/policyReports/NCMedicaidReform.pdf
43. kff.org/healthreform/upload/medicaid-coverage-and-spending-in-health-reform-national-and-state-by-state-results-for-adults-at-or-below-133-fpl.pdf
44. kff.org/medicaid/upload/8384_ES.pdf
45. nciom.org/wp-content/uploads/2012/05/Ch.3-Medicaid.pdf
46. *ibid.*
47. *ibid.*
48. *ibid.*
49. *ibid.*
50. nejm.org/doi/full/10.1056/NEJMp1104948
51. *ibid.*
52. nejm.org/doi/full/10.1056/NEJMp1010866
53. gpo.gov/fdsys/pkg/PLAW-111publ152/pdf/PLAW-111publ152.pdf, Sec. 1201 (1)(b)
54. whitehouse.gov/sites/default/files/omb/budget/fy2013/assets/ccs.pdf
55. *ibid.*
56. heritage.org/research/reports/2012/08/medicaid-expansion-will-become-more-costly-to-states
57. whitehouse.gov/sites/default/files/omb/budget/fy2013/assets/ccs.pdf
58. whitehouse.gov/the-press-office/2011/04/13/fact-sheet-presidents-framework-shared-prosperity-and-shared-fiscal-resp
59. medicaid.gov/Federal-Policy-Guidance/downloads/CIB-11-02-12.pdf
60. americanactionforum.org/topic/american-action-forum-analysis-finds-supreme-court%E2%80%99s-ruling-medicaid-will-add-hundreds-billion
61. forbes.com/sites/aroy/2012/06/28/why-the-supreme-court-decision-on-obamAffordable Care Actre-may-dramatically-increase-the-deficit
62. cbpp.org/cms/index.cfm?fa=view&id=3218
63. nejm.org/doi/full/10.1056/NEJMp1104948
64. heritage.org/research/reports/2012/09/state-lawmakers-guide-to-evaluating-medicaid-expansion-projections#_ednref2
65. heritage.org/research/reports/2012/09/state-lawmakers-guide-to-evaluating-medicaid-expansion-projections
66. aging.senate.gov/crs/medicaid3.pdf (estimates made prior to the Affordable Care Act).
67. heritage.org/research/reports/2012/09/state-lawmakers-guide-to-evaluating-medicaid-expansion-projections
68. cbo.gov/sites/default/files/cbofiles/ftpdocs/120xx/doc12033/12-23-selectedhealthcarepublications.pdf
69. cbo.gov/sites/default/files/cbofiles/attachments/43472-07-24-2012-CoverageEstimates.pdf
70. johnlocke.org/research/show/spotlights/260
71. johnlocke.org/acrobat/policyReports/con_laws-macon_no.1.pdf

◇◇◇◇◇◇◇◇◇◇◇◇◇◇◇◇◇◇◇◇◇

North Carolina 6.0:
A new operating system for state government

by John Hood

The people of North Carolina are conservative. I know this term has taken on a specific ideological meaning in modern politics – and, in fact, I do believe that most North Carolinians embrace conservative ideas on taxes, spending, and other policy matters. But for the purposes of this chapter, I'm using the term "conservative" in its non-ideological sense. What I mean is that, when it comes to changing how their state government looks, feels, and operates, Tar Heel voters have often been skeptical. "The people of North Carolina have treated their constitution with conservatism and respect," wrote John Sanders, director of the University of North Carolina's Institute of Government, in an influential 1989 essay. "The fact that we have adopted only three constitutions in two centuries of existence as a state is the chief evidence of that attitude." In other states, Sanders pointed out, constitutional conventions and voter referendums have approved many more constitutions since the founding of the United States – 10 or more separate state constitutions in a few cases.[1]

Judging by how poorly some of these states have been governed over the years, I think that the natural skepticism of North Carolinians has often served us well. When it comes to changing the basic structure and process of government, the burden of proof *ought* to be placed squarely on those advocating the change. But to be skeptical is not the same as to be cynical or impractical. History has shown that when there is a clear case for changing state government, North Carolina leaders embrace the change – as do voters.

I would submit that we find ourselves in just such a situation in 2013. Past generations of North Carolinians prided themselves on the success of their traditional institutions of government, as evidenced by the fact that the cost of state government was low, the value of state services was high, and the growth of the state's economy was strong.

Unfortunately, none of these conditions applies today. State government has grown in size, scope, and cost, without a commensurate increase in the quantity and quality of state services. North Carolina's economy has performed poorly by regional and national standards since the mid-1990s, and during the first decade of the 21st century posted its first real decline in inflation-adjusted, per-capita income in modern times.[2] During the 2012 election cycle, most North Carolinians told pollsters they thought their state was on the wrong track – and they were right.[3] Nearly two decades of economic stagnation, fractious politics, and high-level corruption has convinced many diehard North Carolina natives that fundamental reform of state government is needed. If you add to their ranks the large numbers of citizens who lack such deep roots in the state – a staggering 49 percent of North Carolina voters who turned out on Election Day 2012 were born somewhere else, and nearly 20 percent had arrived just within the past decade[4] – the potential base of public support for fundamental reform grows still broader.

In this chapter, I will argue that while the basic architecture of North Carolina's government is sound, policymakers and voters ought to consider making some major changes. Put in Information Age terms, we need to redesign the state of North Carolina's operating system. That means simplifying the state's organizational chart, clarifying the lines of accountability from public officials to the voting public, and restoring important constitutional checks on the expenditure of public funds.

While Dr. Sanders is certainly correct that North Carolina has formally ratified only three distinct state constitutions – in 1776, 1868, and 1971 – we have actually adopted five different operating systems over the course of our history, including the colonial period before 1776 and substantial changes to the state constitution in 1835. In the decades between these periods, voters approved other significant amendments to the state constitution, but often as a follow-up or corrective to the major revisions previously implemented or discussed. In a sense, then, what I will argue for in this chapter is a sixth major rewrite of state government's operating system – a North Carolina 6.0, so to speak.

First, I'll describe how our state government currently operates and how it compares to that of other states. Then I'll explain how it got that way. Finally, I'll propose a set of ideas for bringing North Carolina state government into the 21st century, relying heavily on practices or policies already in place in other states.

Our Current Operating System

As of the 2012-13 fiscal year, the state government of North Carolina costs about $52 billion a year to operate in federal, state, and local funds. This includes a General Fund financed with income taxes, sales taxes, and other state taxes and fees ($20 billion), plus federal funds, the Highway Fund and Highway Trust Fund financed with vehicle and fuel taxes, and other programs financed by user fees or dedicated taxes. State government's major operations include public education (accounting for more than half the General Fund and about 30 percent of the total state budget), public assistance and health care (a quarter of the General Fund and a third of the total budget), public safety (11 percent of the General Fund), and transportation (nearly 10 percent of the total budget). The state's legislative, executive, and judicial branches all have indispensable roles to play in carrying out these functions. Like the federal system and those of other states, North Carolina's government relies on checks and balances among these three branches to deter corruption and abuse of power, ensure adequate deliberation and consensus before major policy changes are adopted, and protect individual rights. All political power, however, begins with the people themselves, who not only determine the outcomes of periodic elections but also vote on major issuances of bonded debt as well as constitutional safeguards to protect their long-term interests against the short-run interests of politicians.

Under the current state constitution as amended by the voters, North Carolina elects a House of Representatives with 120 members, a Senate with 50 members, a chief justice and six associate justices of the Supreme Court, 15 judges on the Court of Appeals, and ten members of the executive Council of State: governor, lieutenant governor, secretary of state, state treasurer, state auditor, attorney general, state superintendent of public instruction, agriculture commissioner, insurance commissioner, and labor commissioner.

Legislators serve an unlimited number of two-year terms. Appellate judges serve an unlimited number of eight-year terms. All Council of State executives except the governor serve an unlimited number of four-year terms. The governor can serve two four-year terms in a row, but must then relinquish the job for at least a term before seeking it again.

In 2012, some 4.5 million North Carolinians cast ballots for federal, state, and local offices. Nearly all of them (99 percent) made a selection in the presidential race. Almost as many voted for governor (98 percent). But participation in other statewide races was significantly lower. About 230,000 voters, on average, declined to vote for Council of State officers other than governor. More than a million voters, or nearly a quarter of the electorate, declined to indicate a preference for state Supreme Court or Court of Appeals.

In addition to elected state officials, the ranks of state officeholders include a large number of appointed department heads and managers, governing boards, regulators, commissions, and licensing boards. Here are the most significant:

- **The Governor's Cabinet,** which consists of eight core members. They are the secretaries of Administration, Commerce, Cultural Resources, Environment & Natural Resources, Health & Human Services, Public Safety, Revenue, and Transportation. Outgoing Gov. Beverly Perdue also considered the state's personnel director, chief information officer, and State Board of Education chairman to be members of her Cabinet.

- **The State Board of Education,** with 13 voting members. They include 11 members appointed by the governor to eight-year terms, plus the lieutenant governor and state treasurer as ex-officio members. The state superintendent of public instruction serves as secretary of the board. Eight of the 11 members appointed by the governor represent specific regions of the state, while three are at-large members, including the appointed chairman. The appointive eight-year terms are staggered so that two to three slots open up every two years.

- **The State Board of Community Colleges,** with 21 members. They include 10 members appointed by the governor, four members selected by the House, and four members selected by the Senate, plus the lieutenant governor, state treasurer, and president of the community college system's student government association.

Those last three serve as ex-officio members. The members selected by the governor and legislature serve six-year terms, staggered so that roughly a third come up for reelection every two years. The governor's 10 appointments must include one member from each of the state's six community college regions, plus four at-large members. Each of the system's 58 campuses has its own board of trustees with members appointed by the governor, local school boards, and county commissions.

- **The University of North Carolina Board of Governors,** with 32 voting members. They include 16 members elected by the House and 16 members elected by the Senate. These members serve four-year terms, staggered in such a way that the House and Senate each get to elect eight new members to the UNC board every two years. In addition to these voting members, the UNC system's student government association president serves as a non-voting member, as do some emeritus members (e.g., former state governors and UNC board chairs). Each of the UNC system's main campuses also has its own board of 12 voting trustees (eight selected by the UNC Board of Governors, four by the governor) plus a student-body president as a non-voting member.
- **The North Carolina Board of Transportation,** with 19 voting members appointed by the governor to four-year terms, staggered so that approximately half of the slots become vacant every two years. Five members fill at-large seats while each of the others represents one of the state's 14 regional transportation divisions. The governor's secretary of transportation serves as a 20th, non-voting member of the board.

Some Comparison Shopping

Compared to most state governments in the union, North Carolina has a weak and diffused executive branch; a powerful but often unwieldy legislative branch; a judicial branch with a problematic selection process; and a set of administrative agencies with overlapping jurisdictions, inadequate public oversight, and insufficient benefits to the general public. This last "branch" of state government, the regulators and licensing boards, may in a technical sense be part of the executive branch, but in reality they often make, rather than simply execute, policy (a legislative function) and adjudicate, rather than simply initiate or defend against, cases (a judicial function).

Some of these observations are more easily quantifiable than others. When it comes to the institutional power of North Carolina's governors, for example, statistics are readily available. In most states, executive branch authority is more concentrated in the hands of the governor. While almost every state elects a lieutenant governor, and most states elect their top legal officer (attorney general) and top money-manager (state treasurer or state comptroller), most states do not also elect their state schools superintendent, agriculture commissioner, labor commissioner, and insurance commissioner. The offices of secretary of state and state auditor are special cases. While 31 states elect separate secretaries of state, as North Carolina does, six states combine the offices of lieutenant governor and secretary of state and the remaining states either allow governors or legislatures to select the secretary of state or assign the office's duties to other appointed agency heads. As for the auditing function, 23 states have separately elected auditors, two states combine its duties with that of an elected state comptroller, and the remaining states select auditors through legislative or gubernatorial appointment or assign the office's duties to other appointed agency heads.

Thad Beyle, a political scientist at the University of North Carolina at Chapel Hill, maintains a widely cited rating system for the institutional powers of state governors.[5] Last updated in 2007, the system employs six categories with numerical ratings ranging from 1 (least power) to 5 (most power). The number of executive-branch officials elected separately from the governor is one such category in Beyle's system. The others include 1) the extent to which governors can be reelected to subsequent terms; 2) the extent to which governors appoint agency heads for public education, transportation, health care, welfare, corrections, and utilities regulation; 3) the extent of the veto power that governors enjoy; 4) the extent of other gubernatorial authority over the formation and implementation of state budgets; and 5) the extent to which a governor of one party faces partisan opposition in the state legislature.

I actually don't see this last category as similar to the others – it reflects not the design of state government but the shifting preferences of voters – so I recalculated Beyle's 2007 institutional-power ratings without it. I came up with an average rating of 17.7 for the nation's state governors. New York's governor has the largest amount of institutional power, at 21.5, with Alaska, Maryland, Massachusetts, New Jersey, and West Virginia not far behind at 20.5. By this measure, the weakest governor in the country was Vermont's, at 13, followed by our own chief executive here in North Carolina, at 13.5. Oklahoma, South Carolina, and South Dakota also have relatively weak governors, at 14.

North Carolina's lowest score was, indeed, in the area of separately elected executives. We also scored low in veto power. While North Carolina's governor can only veto bills in their entirety, most state governors can veto parts of bills, a power known as line-item veto. Some governors can go beyond that to mandate lower spending levels for particular sections of budget bills, a power known as item-reduction veto.

Similar comparisons of the formal powers of other state officials, such as legislative leaders and appellate judges, are hard to come by. The closest I was able to find was a 2001 ranking of state speakers of the house by political scientist Richard Clucas. Focusing on their institutional powers over committees, legislation, and other matters, Clucas generated a state-by-state rating with an average of 17.7. North Carolina's speaker received a rating of 20, considerably higher than the national average and the ratings in each of our neighboring states.[6]

When it comes to the operation of state legislatures as a whole, there are several national comparisons that should be of interest to North Carolina reformers. One concerns the amount of time state lawmakers spend in session. According to the National Conference of State Legislatures (NCSL), 39 states limit the length of their legislative sessions – either directly, by constitution or statute, or indirectly, by such means as cutting pay or expense reimbursements when sessions run long. North Carolina is one of the 11 states that impose no direct or indirect session limit.[7]

However, after Republicans took control of the North Carolina legislature in 2010, they chose to follow a voluntary policy of reducing the amount of time spent in Raleigh. The 2011-12 biennium of the General Assembly convened on January 26, 2011 and adjourned for good on July 3, 2012. In between those dates were two regular sessions – the "long" session in 2011 and the "short" session in 2012 – plus several special sessions devoted to redistricting, veto overrides, or other matters. If you add up all the days in which the General Assembly held session over the past two years, you get 138 days. That's the shortest biennium since 1979-80. But if instead of counting the number of days the state legislature conducted business you count the number of calendar days between the time a session starts and the time it concludes, you get 224 calendar days. By that measure, the 2011-12 biennium was the shortest since 1985-86. Even so, many other state legislatures do their business more quickly than that. Florida's legislature meets 60 calendar days per year in regular session. Georgia's legislature meets for 40 legislative days per year. Virginia has 60-day regular sessions in even-numbered years and 30-day regular sessions in odd-numbered years.

Being a state legislator involves more than meeting in regular session, though. There are special sessions, committee meetings, constituent requests, and other duties. Legislatures also differ widely in staffing levels, facilities, and compensation. NCSL groups the 50 state legislatures into five color-coded categories, ranging from red (truly full-time legislators) to blue (truly part-time legislators), with light red, white, and light blue in between. By this rating, North Carolina is in the middle "white" category, along with most of our neighbors. But two states roughly comparable to North Carolina in population and policy challenges, Georgia and Indiana, are light-blue states. They have retained more of the citizen-legislature tradition than we have.[8]

To the extent government reformers have focused on the state's judicial branch, they have tended to focus on the process by which judges rise to the appellate courts. North Carolina is one of 22 states where partisan or nonpartisan elections are used to elect members of supreme and appellate courts. Of those states, 14 list judges on the ballot without party labels while eight states hold partisan elections. Until 2002, North Carolina held partisan elections. That was the year that Democratic leaders, concerned that Republicans were increasing their share of appellate judicial offices, removed party labels from the ballot. The same 2002 legislature created a government funding system for Court of Appeals and Supreme Court candidates. In return for limiting their campaign fundraising and expenditures, candidates receive state funds. These rules have no effect on independent expenditures for or against judicial candidates, which are becoming more common.

How do the other 28 states pick their appellate judges? Some follow a federal model in which governors appoint judges subject to legislative confirmation. Others have legislatures pick judges. Another model, commonly known as the Missouri Plan, is in place in 13 states. It has governors pick judges from among judicial candidates approved by a commission, usually but not always dominated by their respective state bar associations. Finally, 10 states use a hybrid of these ideas – such as governors picking commission-approved judges, who later run statewide in retention elections.[9]

In summary, none of the major features of North Carolina's governmental system is unique or unprecedented. But it would be fair to consider some of them uncommon by national standards. We have an extraordinarily weak governor. We don't limit the length of legislative sessions. Our organizational chart is remarkably complicated, with a number of independently run executive agencies and huge governing boards for education and transportation programs that follow no discernible rhyme or reason. In another area, state-local relations, North Carolina is one of the most centralized states in the country. Counties and municipalities are creatures of state government, created to perform specific functions and still subject to significant oversight by the state's legislative branch (through local bills and centralized funding for education and other services), the executive branch (through budgetary and financial means), and the voting public (through bond and tax referenda).

If you compare the size, scope, and cost of North Carolina government, then you have to take the state-local dynamic into consideration. In some states, counties operate their own road systems and are the primary funders of public schools. Neither is the case in our state. Combining state and local operations together reveals that North Carolina has about 7 percent more public employees per capita than the average state does, even though our overall government expenditures aren't above the average.[10] That's one signal that the operating system of North Carolina government is inefficient. Another is that we simply have so many major state agencies and departments, often with overlapping jurisdictions and unclear lines of accountability to the voting public.

North Carolina 1.0: A Colony of the Crown

The confusing, cumbersome nature of North Carolina's state government reflects both design and accident. Without question, the framers of past constitutions intended the office of governor to be weak, and to give the legislature significant authority over local governments and the University of North Carolina. On the other hand, structures originally designed for a 19th or 20th century society have remained in place despite changing conditions. It no longer makes sense, for example, to regulate the insurance industry separate from the rest of the financial sector, or to entrust the former job to an elected official and the latter job to appointed officials.

The state's traditional suspicion of strong chief executives is rooted in the colonial period. After an abortive effort by his father to organize the sprawling territory south of Virginia into an English colony in the 1630s, King Charles II made a second try in the 1660s. With the Stuart monarchy recently restored after decades of civil war and unrest, Charles II decided to reward eight key supporters and political allies by making them the Lords Proprietors of the newly re-chartered Province of Carolina. The leader of the colonial proprietors was Anthony Ashley Cooper, the first Earl of Shaftesbury and future Lord Chancellor of England. A founder of the Whig Party who later ran afoul of the Stuart monarchy, Cooper employed a young aide named John Locke to help him with affairs of state, including colonial administration. Locke helped Cooper draw up the *Fundamental Constitutions of Carolina* in 1669. It was an odd document, and much of its elaborate governing structure was never actually implemented. It did grant more freedom of religion than was typical in the colonies, a tradition that continued in the 18th century and helped to attract immigrants from Virginia and other colonies and countries with stronger and more intrusive state-established churches.

By the beginning of the 1700s, the northern and southern parts of the Carolina colony still shared a common government, but they differed significantly in politics, economy, and culture. As prospective planters and African slaves continued to arrive in the southern part of the Carolina colony, especially around Charleston, the northern part attracted other kinds of immigrants. While there were certainly slave plantations along the Albemarle and Pamlico sounds, there was also a steady stream of Quakers, Calvinists, and other religious dissidents. Many of them founded small farms rather than owning or working on large plantations.

By 1712, North Carolina and South Carolina were clearly distinguishable entities and often described as such. The proprietors back in England were proving themselves to be variously inattentive or inept. By 1719, most Carolinians were fed up. They revolted against proprietary rule and chose their own leaders. The royal governor of King George I sided with the colonists. By 1729, the Crown had bought out seven of the eight proprietors and the Province of North Carolina became a separate royal colony, with its capital at Edenton. The seat of colonial government would later move to Wilmington, and finally to New Bern.[11]

North Carolina 2.0: A New State Government

As a royal colony, North Carolina's government combined an elected legislature with a governor appointed by the king. Over the decades, there was an increasing level of conflict between the two branches – as well as between the royal governor and the general population. These conflicts arose from economic, regional, and religious differences. By the early 1770s, for example, many Carolinians who lived in the Piedmont came to believe that colonial officials tied to then-Gov. William Tryon were exploiting them through unjust taxes and subverting their equal rights as citizens through unwarranted fines, shady land deals, and corrupt appointments to county governments. Mecklenburg, Anson, Rowan, Orange, and other counties were also growing in population but not in legislative representation, which westerners saw (correctly) as unfair.[12]

In addition, the eastern elites were mostly of English extraction, members of the established Anglican Church, and connected either to Tidewater Virginia or South Carolina's Lowcountry by family and commercial ties. By contrast, the westerners were disproportionately Scotch-Irish and mostly Baptist or Presbyterian. They had more ties to Pennsylvania and Maryland than to the colonial government in coastal Carolina. They also resented policies that intruded on their religious liberty. Gov. Tryon, for example, had pushed for two laws that strengthened the Anglican Church – one that appropriated tax money to the church and another stipulating that only Anglican ministers could perform state-recognized marriages. For every marriage that Presbyterian or Baptist ministers performed, they were fined. Another decision that enraged many westerners was royal opposition to the creation of an educational institution in Charlotte, the original Queen's College. Its original charter stipulated that the president of the college would be an Anglican, but allowed that other teachers might be Presbyterians. Because Anglican teachers were scarce in the backcountry, even the college presidency was likely to be filled by a Presbyterian, or left vacant. Local supporters got this college charter through the colonial legislature, but King George III twice vetoed the idea, fearing the potential cultural and political consequences of authorizing a college that would, in effect, be run by Presbyterians. (Local leaders thumbed their noses at the king and opened the Charlotte school, anyway. It was known as Queen's Museum and later Liberty Hall.)[13] After Gov. Tryon jailed one of the leaders of the western faction, legislator Herman Husband, in early 1771, the Carolina backcountry erupted in anger. Gov. Tryon mobilized the colonial militia. On May 16, 1771, they clashed with about 2,000 Regulators at the Battle of Alamance. The Regulators were crushed.[14]

When the American Revolution broke out, these and similar events were on the minds of those delegates to the Fifth Provincial Congress who gathered in late 1776 at the town of Halifax to draw up North Carolina's first state constitution. Among them were politicians who had originally sided with Tryon and other royal governors and then become disenchanted, as well as delegates from communities that had felt the heavy hand of royal oppression. One of the Mecklenburg delegates, for example, was Hezekiah Alexander, founder and treasurer of the controversial Queen's College. Another was Cornelius Harnett, a Wilmington merchant with a lengthy career in local and colonial politics. The presiding officer was Richard Caswell, an early hero of the Revolution. These men were determined to avoid any recurrence of gubernatorial tyranny, as were most of the other delegates. Their Constitution of 1776 put the new state legislature firmly in charge. The General Assembly appointed all executive and judicial officials. The governor (initially Richard Caswell himself) was allowed only three one-year terms within six years, and most of his decisions were subject to approval by a seven-member Council of State chosen by the legislature.[15]

North Carolina 3.0: A New Balance of Power

While the 1776 constitution provided for legislative supremacy, that wasn't quite the same thing as popular sovereignty. The electorate consisted entirely of men, and both voting and serving in office were subject to property-ownership rules. Interestingly, the original state constitution did not discriminate by race when it came to the franchise. If free, blacks enjoyed the same voting rights as whites. Thousands of black North Carolinians routinely voted throughout the late 1700s and early 1800s. Of course, the vast majority of black residents were enslaved, bound either to domestic service or the cruelty of the plantations. They enjoyed none of the rights of citizenship.

Another reason why the legislature did not truly bring popular sovereignty was that its membership was apportioned by locality, not population. Each county elected one state senator and two members of the state house. Half a dozen municipalities also sent one member each to the state house. Not surprisingly, then, the governmental map of North Carolina was gerrymandered to keep the easterners in power. In 1800, there were 36 counties to the south and east of Raleigh, vs. 23 counties to the west. Some northeastern counties such as Camden and Pasquotank were narrow slivers of land, while western counties such as Rowan, Lincoln, and Burke sprawled over large expanses of land that attracted a steady stream of settlers every year. During the early 19th century, the population in counties west of Raleigh grew three times as fast as that of the eastern counties. But their political representation did not grow apace.[16]

Eventually the demands for reform by new leaders in the Piedmont and west grew too strong to ignore. In 1835, a state convention met to consider major revisions to North Carolina's governing structure. While the result was not a brand new constitution, the resulting amendments to the 1776 constitution, ratified by a statewide vote of the people, constituted a significant rewrite. They fixed the number of state senators at 50 and the number of state house members at 120. Senators were elected from newly drawn districts encompassing roughly equivalent values of taxable property. The convention apportioned half of the house seats by locality, one member per county, and the other half roughly by population. Separately, the legislature began to approve the creation of new counties in the west, which also reduced the effects of previous gerrymandering and provided residents greater proximity to county courts. Under the 1835 governmental rewrite, the office of the governor came out from under the thumb of the legislature. For the first time, North Carolina voters would directly elect their governors, to two-year terms. Another boon to popular sovereignty was a new process for removing executive or judicial officials via impeachment for misdeeds or a determination of disability. On the other hand, free blacks lost their voting rights under the new system, an ominous sign of things to come.[17]

North Carolina 4.0: A Reconstructed State

During the 1840s and 1850s, North Carolina's new operating system proved to be an improvement in most respects. Still, many state leaders believed that the system should be further refined to clarify the relationship between the legislature and governor, as well as the relationship between Raleigh and local governments. We'll never know what may have arisen from this debate, because secession and civil war muscled it aside in the 1860s. After the Confederacy was defeated in 1865, the U.S. Congress required Southern states to reconstitute themselves before being restored to full membership in the federal union. In North Carolina, the result was the constitutional convention of 1868. Led by Republicans, it drafted a radically different state constitution. The office of governor was strengthened in some ways, including four-year terms and greater autonomy. But for the first time, members of the Council of State were subject to direct election and the powers and jurisdiction of the state's judiciary were clearly defined, both actions that took power away from the legislature while also limiting gubernatorial power. State senate districts were redrawn on the basis of population. The state legislature lost its longtime control over county governments and the University of North Carolina. The constitution also explicitly required the state to fund public schools and other programs previously left to legislative discretion.[18]

The Constitution of 1868 was approved by a Reconstruction electorate. After the former Democrats recovered their political rights and returned to power in 1870, they tried to throw the constitution out. But voters rejected a proposed new constitutional convention. So legislators resorted to specific amendments they knew voters would approve. These included restoring control of UNC, local governments, and the courts to the legislature. Over the next few decades, much of the debate over constitutional amendments concerned race and voting rights. Eventually, the racists won the struggle.

The Final Rewrite

Aside from issues related to segregation, there wasn't a great deal of pressure for constitutional reforms until the 1930s. The onset of the Great Depression led to massive economic dislocations and the bankruptcy of many local governments. During the administration of Gov. Max Gardner (1929-1933), the General Assembly enacted major changes to the structure of North Carolina government – centralizing the finance and operation of public schools and road systems, shifting the fiscal system away from property taxes, and reorganizing state agencies. But these actions did not require constitutional amendment. In 1933, the legislature sought to follow up the reforms with a brand new state constitution. It would have given North Carolina governors the veto power for the first time, given local governments more control over their affairs, and established an appointed State Board of Education to oversee public education, among other things. But the proposed constitution never made it to the voters, although one of its major provisions, establishing the State Board of Education, eventually passed via constitutional amendment.

The next attempt to rewrite North Carolina's state constitution occurred in the 1950s during the administration of Gov. Luther Hodges. A commission recommended that the new constitution expand the state senate to 60 members and give the state judiciary more autonomy, among other things. Like its 1933 predecessor, the 1959 constitution failed to make it to the voters but inspired individual amendments that voters subsequently approved. Increasing interest in bringing North Carolina's constitution into the modern, Civil Rights era and resolving longstanding tensions and contradictions in the text finally led to a 1967 study commission and a series of sweeping amendments ratified by the voters in 1971. Most of the current structure of North Carolina government was enshrined in this Constitution of 1971, including its finance and fiscal policies.[19] But it would still take another two decades to expand the power of the governor, by allowing successive terms (1977) and the veto power (1996).

The Case for Fundamental Reform

As the preceding historical account demonstrates, the details and peculiarities of today's operating system for North Carolina government have deep roots. Nor were the framers' intentions without merit. Using popular elections to keep public officials on a short leash and ensuring that governors don't ride roughshod over the other branches of government are worthy goals. But most states have found ways to accomplish the same goals without going to the extreme of electing ten different executive officers. Most states also give governors more power over state spending, give legislators more power over gubernatorial appointments, limit the length of legislative sessions, and better align the oversight of public schools, colleges, and universities with the electoral cycle, and thus with the will of the voters. It is also important to recognize that some of today's constraints on gubernatorial power are vestigial. We no longer have royal governments imposed by faraway monarchs. And modern means of communication and transportation make it possible for state lawmakers to check and balance the executive branch without holding lengthy legislative sessions or denying the governor basic tools of management.

Our current operating system also aligns poorly with the realities of North Carolina in the 21st century. Why is there an entire department devoted to boosting and regulating agriculture, while other industries critical to North Carolina's economy – such as manufacturing, finance, and health care – are subject to a bewildering array of subsidies and rules administered by a variety of different agencies? Why does the governor exercise substantial control over the State Board of Education, exercise joint control of the State Board of Community Colleges and the various UNC boards of trustees with the legislature, and have essentially no control over the UNC Board of Governors? Why do State Board of Education members serve eight-year terms, community college board members six-year terms, and UNC board members four-year terms? Why does North Carolina have a State Board of Transportation at all, given that most states have only advisory boards or no boards at all and seem to derive at least as much value for each transportation dollar spent?

I would submit that North Carolina can maintain a healthy set of checks and balances in state government while cleaning up the state's organizational chart, shortening the statewide ballot, and giving voters more information with which to hold their public officials accountable for the performance of their duties and the expenditure of funds. Here are some places to start:

The Executive Branch

- Expand the governor's veto power by allowing him to strike line items and reduce funding for individual programs and agencies. Studies show that states that give their governors the power of item-reduction veto tend to exercise more fiscal restraint, all other things being equal. The same research suggests that line-item veto authority alone, while potentially valuable for other reasons, does not have much effect on state spending over time.[20]

- Reduce the number of separately elected executive offices to four – governor, lieutenant governor, attorney general, and state treasurer.

Furthermore, follow the lead of states such as Arizona, Oregon, and Utah by giving the lieutenant governor the administrative and regulatory duties of the secretary of state, rather than simply having the lieutenant governor serve on boards, preside ceremoniously over the state senate, and prepare a future run for governor. As for the state treasurer, expand the office's duties to include those of state auditor and state controller, making it similar to the elected comptrollers in Texas and New York. The four elected executives – governor, lieutenant governor/secretary of state, attorney general, and state treasurer/auditor – would still constitute the Council of State and exercise its current authority over state property and other matters.

- Merge the existing departments of Agriculture, Labor, and Commerce into a new Department of Commerce and Consumer Services. Group like-functions together – economic development and marketing activities, for example, and the regulation of banks, insurers, and other financial institutions.

- Reorganize the governance of public education in North Carolina to make it consistent, comprehensible, and efficient. Eliminate the elected state superintendent of public instruction and let the State Board of Education hire the state superintendent, just as other appointed boards hire the presidents of the UNC and community college systems. Give the governor half of all appointments to the UNC Board of Governors, State Board of Education, and State Board of Community Colleges, with the General Assembly selecting the remaining half of all appointments. Make all terms of service four years, staggered so that an incoming governor or new legislative majority, just elected by voters, can begin to shape education policy without inordinate delay. In 2012, the Republican-led General Assembly essentially engineered such an outcome by refusing to confirm Democratic Gov. Perdue's appointees to fill expired terms on the State Board of Education. That left incoming Gov. McCrory with more control over new board members. Right outcome, but the situation deserves a permanent fix for future governors and lawmakers of any party.[21]

- Reduce the size of the State Board of Transportation and limit its role to offering general policy and advice to the governor and secretary of Transportation. It should have no authority over project approval, which should reflect formulas devised by professionals and approved by elected state lawmakers. About half of the states have no formal transportation boards at all, and most of the rest have small boards of between three and eight members.[22]

Legislative Branch

- Require confirmation by at least one chamber of the General Assembly of all gubernatorial appointments to Cabinet-level posts. Because the preceding recommendations have the effect of increasing the power of state governors, legislative confirmation would be a reasonable compensation to check the executive branch. It is also commonplace elsewhere. More than half of the states require some form of legislative confirmation for secretaries of Commerce, Health & Human Services, and Transportation, for example. Another way to balance the power of a stronger governor would be to rethink the succession rule adopted in 1977. At the very least the limit of two terms as governor should be a lifetime limit, not just a limit on consecutive terms.

- Strengthen legislative oversight of administrative and regulatory agencies. As discussed elsewhere in this book, regulators should be required to cite specific statutory authority for any proposed rule. The legislature's Rules Review Commission should be given additional authority to ensure that elected lawmakers, not unelected officials, decide what North Carolina's health, safety, and economic policies should be.

- Move North Carolina further towards a citizen-legislature model. For starters, that means following the lead of Texas, Georgia, Virginia, and Indiana by adopting a formal limit on the length of legislative sessions. One benefit of a session limit to lawmakers is that it allows them more time to work in their personal occupations or professions if they wish, in effect raising their hourly rate of compensation. If additional adjustments in legislative pay are desired, I suggest that they be combined with legislative term limits, as are already in place in Florida, Michigan, Ohio, Arizona, and 11 other states.[23]

- Reform the redistricting process. Voters should select their legislative representatives, rather than having legislators select their voters. The concept of popular sovereignty requires that the allocation of House and Senate seats by party ought not differ substantially from the number of votes each party's candidates collectively receive statewide. On several occasions in the past, Democrat-drawn legislative maps resulted in Democratic control despite the fact that Republicans had actually won a majority of votes cast. In 2012, while Republican candidates did in fact receive more votes than Democratic candidates did, their resulting majorities in the House and Senate were exaggerated by new legislative maps.[24] Lawmakers of both parties should consider the fact that Democrats had refused to reform redistricting in the past because they assumed they would always be in control when it came time to draw the maps. If Democrats had adopted a different process, as a sort of "insurance policy," they'd be better off today. Republicans would be well advised to take out their own insurance policy before 2020. There are several different models for reform, including redistributing commissions and mathematical formulas to reduce the potential for partisan manipulation or incumbency protection.

Judicial Branch

- Abandon the current system for electing judges to North Carolina's Supreme Court and Court of Appeals. It is really the worst of all possible worlds – nonpartisan elections that aren't really free from partisanship. By depriving voters of a valuable piece of information (party labels) and using so-called public financing to discourage judicial candidates from running real campaigns, the system pushes judicial politics into the world of super PACs and other independent-expenditure groups. I think the best answer is to restore real elections – partisan elections funded solely by voluntary contributions. The current taxpayer-financing system for judges and some Council of State offices should be abolished as a violation of political freedom and a misuse of public funds.

- If policymakers choose not to restore real elections for appellate judges, the second-best answer would be to emulate the federal model by having governors appoint the judges, subject to legislative confirmation and perhaps a subsequent retention election by voters. North Carolina should not adopt anything like the Missouri Plan, which gives undue influence to unelected, unaccountable special-interest groups.

Other Reforms

- Restore voter sovereignty over the issuance of public debt. North Carolina state and local governments currently have more than $53 billion in official, on-the-books debt (plus a similar amount of unfunded liabilities for state retiree benefits and other obligations). An increasing share of the public debt was never approved by voter referendum, as is generally required by the state constitution. Policymakers have evaded the referendum requirement by issuing certificates of participation (COPs) and other "special obligation" debt that does not technically pledge the full faith and credit of the government to bondholders, but in practice guarantees repayment with an implicit promise to tap general revenues. Special-obligation debt now far exceeds general-obligation debt on the state's balance sheet.

  All bonds, regardless of whether they legally pledge the full faith and credit of the state or localities, should be subject to voter referendum. The current practice of distinguishing between general-obligation debt requiring referenda and special-obligation debt not requiring referenda is too easy to abuse. While academic researchers disagree about the extent to which such limits hold down the overall amount of state debt, there appears to be no question that referendum requirements or other limits on general-obligation bonds increase the share of total debt held in special obligations such as certificates of participation or revenue bonds, a pattern we have seen in North Carolina over the past two decades.[25]

- Eliminate the risk of major budget shortfalls. Fiscal emergencies are rarely a time of calm, rational decision-making. In the past, unanticipated budget gaps have resulted in large, economically destructive tax increases or across-the-board budget cuts that lumped effective programs in with ineffective programs. One straightforward fix would be to impose a new requirement on the governor and legislature: The governor's proposed General Fund budget for the coming fiscal year, and the final budget approved by the legislature, can spend only as much General Fund revenue as has already been received during the previous calendar year. For example, a 2013-14 General Fund budget proposed during the 2013 legislative session could only spend up to the amount of General Fund revenue collected from January to December of 2012. This idea was originally proposed in the early 1990s – and if the General Assembly had adopted it then, much subsequent fiscal and political turmoil would have been avoided.

Conclusion: A New Separation and Balance of Powers

North Carolina's traditional policies of weak governors, overlapping and confusing governance structures, long ballots, and fiscal machinations are no longer suited to the needs of our state, if they ever were. Some of my recommendations would obviously require constitutional amendments, or function more effectively if enshrined in the constitution. Other recommendations can be implemented by legislation or executive order.

Some defenders of the current system will be reticent to strengthen the office of governor. But keep in mind that North Carolina's governors are exceedingly weak by national standards. As far as I can determine, even the adoption of all of my recommendations would make our state's governor only about average in institutional authority, not truly powerful like governors in New York, Massachusetts, and New Jersey are. The reality is that if you are a fiscal conservative, you should heed the findings of academic research suggesting that giving governors significant budgeting and veto power tends to result in better government at lower cost.

Under the current model, North Carolina's executive branch has 17 Cabinet-level secretaries and Council of State members. Under the proposed North Carolina 6.0 operating system, that number would drop to 12. The benefits wouldn't simply be fiscal. By putting functions such as consumer protection, economic development, and financial-service regulation clearly under the authority of the governor, the system would give North Carolina voters a specific politician to hold responsible – someone whose name they actually recognize. And by allowing both governors and lawmakers to appoint members to all three governance boards for North Carolina public education, the system would facilitate greater coordination between education policymaking (a responsibility of the legislative branch) and education administration (a responsibility of the executive branch).

The most compelling argument for reform is to strengthen the public's sovereignty over their government. As the second section of the state constitution's Declaration of Rights puts it, "All political power is vested in and derived from the people; all government of right originates from the people, is founded upon their will only, and is instituted solely for the good of the whole." State government does not exist to empower politicians or employ the politically connected. It exists to perform basic public services, services that would be impossible or inordinately costly for private citizens to procure for themselves through voluntary means. It has an obligation to deliver these services as effectively and efficiently as possible. A new operating system for North Carolina government would help to satisfy that obligation.

Endnotes

1. John L. Sanders, "Our Constitutions: A Historical Perspective," in *The Constitution of North Carolina: Its History and Content*, Raleigh: Office of the Secretary of State, July 1, 1989, p. 15.

2. John Hood, *Our Best Foot Forward: An Investment Plan for North Carolina's Economic Recovery*, Raleigh: John Locke Foundation, 2012, pp. 15-16.

3. See, for example, "August 2012 Poll Results," Civitas Institute, http://www.nccivitas.org/2012/august-2012-poll-results.

4. CNN exit poll, http://www.cnn.com/election/2012/results/state/NC/governor.

5. Thad Beyle, "Gubernatorial Power: The Institutional Power Ratings for the 50 Governors of the United States," http://www.unc.edu/~beyle/gubnewpwr.html, updated July 2008.

6. Richard A. Clucas, "Principal–Agent Theory and the Power of State House Speakers," *Legislative Studies Quarterly*, Volume 26, 2001, pp. 319–38.

7. "Legislative Session Length," National Conference of State Legislatures, http://www.ncsl.org/legislatures-elections/legislatures/legislative-session-length.aspx.

8. "Full and Part-Time Legislatures," National Conference of State Legislatures, http://www.ncsl.org/legislatures-elections/legislatures/full-and-part-time-legislatures.aspx.

9. Brian Fitzpatrick and Stephen Ware, "How Does Your State Select Its Judges?" *Inside ALEC*, March 2011, pp 9-12.

10. Data on full-time equivalent employees obtained from "2010 State and Local Government," U.S. Census Bureau, http://www.census.gov/govs/apes.

11. Hugh T. Lefler and Albert R. Newsome, *North Carolina: The History of a Southern State*, University of North Carolina Press, 1973.

12. William S. Powell, *North Carolina: A History*, Chapel Hill: University of North Carolina Press, 1988, pp. 48-55.

13. Dan L. Morrill, "A History of Charlotte and Mecklenburg County," http://danandmary.com/historyofcharlotteabs.htm.

14. Marjoleine Kars, *Breaking Loose Together: The Regulator Rebellion in Pre-Revolutionary North Carolina*, University of North Carolina Press, 2002

15. Sanders, p. 1.

16. David R. Goldfield, "History," in Douglas M. Orr Jr. and Alfred W. Stuart, editors, *The North Carolina Atlas: Portrait for a New Century*, Chapel Hill: University of North Carolina Press, 2000, pp. 53-55.

17. Sanders, p. 2.

18. Sanders, p. 3.

19. Sanders, pp. 7-12.

20. See W. Mark Crain and James C. Miller, "Budget Process and Spending Growth," *William & Mary Law Review*, Vol. 31, Issue 4, 1990, pp. 1021-1046. Glenn Abneya and Thomas P. Lautha, "The Item Veto and Fiscal Responsibility," *Journal of Politics*, Vol. 59, Issue 3, August 1997, pp. 882-892. David Van Den Berg, "Veto Politics: Can a line-item veto reduce spending?" *Regional Focus*, Federal Reserve Bank of Richmond, Spring 2009, pp. 29-30.

21. "New policy needed to give new governors control of state education board," *Winston-Salem Journal*, November 12, 2012.

22. David Hartgen, "Distributing Transportation Funds," John Locke Foundation Spotlight No. 385, April 6, 2010.

23. "The Term Limited States," National Conference of State Legislatures, http://www.ncsl.org/legislatures-elections/legisdata/chart-of-term-limits-states.aspx.

24. Mitch Kokai, "New Election Maps Help GOP Build Legislative Majorities," *Carolina Journal Online*, November 7, 2012, http://www.carolinajournal.com/exclusives/display_exclusive.html?id=9650.

25. See Robert Krol, "The Role of Fiscal and Political Institutions in Limiting the Size of State Government," *The Cato Journal*, Vol. 27, No. 3, Fall 2007. James Poterba, "Budget Institutions and Fiscal Policy in the U.S. States," *The American Economic Review*, Vol. 86, No. 2, May 1996.

Conclusion

❊❊❊❊❊❊❊❊❊❊❊❊❊❊❊❊❊❊

Restoring a Tradition of Freedom

by John Hood

More than two decades ago, a group of North Carolina business and civic leaders founded the John Locke Foundation to "work for truth, for freedom, and for the future of North Carolina." As a public policy think tank, JLF has issued hundreds of reports, studies, and issue briefs on virtually every subject of interest to state and local policymakers. JLF has also published many thousands of news articles, columns, and newspaper op-eds making the case for fundamental reform of North Carolina government based on the principles of competition, innovation, and personal freedom and responsibility.

"All work," wrote Richard Weaver, "is a bringing of the ideal from potentiality into actuality." Taking this to heart, JLF hasn't just spent its time pondering the abstract or debating ideals. Our work has been firmly rooted in practicality, how best to translate the timeless wisdom of free-market conservatism into specific recommendations for reducing the size, scope, and cost of government while improving the quality of core public services.

In a sense, this book is the culmination of more than 20 years of intellectual experimentation, careful study, and continuous discussion across political and ideological lines by current and former members of the JLF staff. By no means is the book intended to be an exhaustive exploration of North Carolina public policy. You'll find a wider set of issues covered in our biennial *Agenda* briefing books, for example. This work is focused on six key subjects: tax reform, budget reform, education reform, regulatory reform, health care reform, and constitutional reform. Each chapter contains a tremendous and valuable amount of background and detail. But the reform agenda laid out in *First in Freedom* can be summarized in the following recommendations:

• North Carolina should tax consumption, rather than total income, to fund most of state government's General Fund programs. We propose two options. Our "first-best" plan replaces the state's current taxes on personal income, corporate income, retail sales, and estates with a flat 8.5 percent tax on all household income that is neither saved nor given away to charity. Our "second-best" plan leaves the state sales tax in place, albeit at a lower rate of 4.5 percent, and adopts the consumed-income tax model at a 6 percent flat rate. These consumption-based tax models would improve the transparency and efficiency of North Carolina's tax system, while dramatically increasing the rate of job creation over the next five years.

• The state legislature should approve and submit for voter approval a constitutional amendment, a Taxpayer Bill of Rights, to cap the annual growth rate of state spending to a combination of inflation and population growth. Any state revenue growth beyond this cap should either be used to build up the state's savings reserves or refunded to taxpayers.

• North Carolina should expand parental choice and competition in elementary and secondary education by adopting several complementary reforms. A tax-credit scholarship program would offer dollar-for-dollar credits for contributions to nonprofit organizations that would, in turn, provide private school scholarships targeted toward North Carolina elementary and secondary students from low- or moderate-income households. An education savings account program would allow all North Carolina families to take tax deductions for money they spend or save on their children's educational needs, from preschool education to higher education, while offering low-income students in low-performing public schools the additional option of transferring to private providers and having a portion of their state appropriation deposited in their ESAs. North Carolina should also promote competition in public education by improving the governance, regulatory, and funding provisions of the current charter school law.

• Even after the implementation of a comprehensive school choice agenda, most North Carolina students will continue to enroll in district-run public schools. Their administration, efficiency, and effectiveness can be significantly enhanced by reforming the state's curriculum, standardized testing, teacher compensation, teacher tenure, and funding policies. North Carolina should devise its own, more rigorous curriculum rather than adopt the Common Core standards, and administer independent, nationally normed tests in reading, math, and other core subjects. The state should change its teacher compensation system to give school districts more flexibility, reduce the reliance on factors such as National Board Certification and graduate degree completion with scant empirical support, and increase the reliance on factors such as high demand subjects, challenging student populations, and value-added performance. Tenure should either be abolished or limited to a smaller number of high-performing teachers. On the funding system, North Carolina should collapse most allotment categories into a single, per-pupil allotment and give school districts the flexibility to use the allotted funds as needed. The state should retain supplemental allotments for special needs and small or low wealth districts, but make them simpler and fairer.

• On regulatory reform, state policymakers can build on the progress made during the 2011-12 legislative session by adopting some important next steps. The regulatory process should become far more transparent. Specific legislative approval should be required to adopt any regulation with a large economic impact, and the legislature's Rules Review Commission should be empowered to exercise greater oversight to make sure that executive branch agencies carry out — but do not make — the state's public policies. All regulations should have to meet a legitimate cost-benefit test, both before adoption and in periodic reviews afterwards. The particular challenges posed to small business in complying with state regulation should be formally considered and accommodated.

• North Carolina faces two big decisions regarding President Obama's health care plan. The state should reject both the expansion of Medicaid and the creation of a state-administered insurance exchange. The costs, fiscal and otherwise, of assisting Washington in the implementation of a flawed strategy for health care reform far outweigh any benefits. Instead, state policymakers should focus on policies such as licensing and regulatory reform to reduce costs without diminishing quality of care, while working diligently to control costs within Medicaid and the state employee health plan.

• The operating system of North Carolina state government needs an update. The legislature should approve and submit to voters a set of constitutional amendments to clean up the state's organizational chart, shorten the ballot, and provide for efficient, accountable government. The number of statewide elected executives should be limited to four: governor, lieutenant governor (also acting as secretary of state), attorney general, and state treasurer (also acting as state auditor and controller). North Carolina's governor should receive the power of item reduction veto. The legislature should receive the power to confirm gubernatorial appointments to Cabinet level offices, as well as additional authority to ensure that regulatory agencies do not exceed their legal authority. The governor and legislature should share responsibility for appointing all three educational governing boards: the State Board of Education, the State Board of Community Colleges, and the University of North Carolina Board of Governors. The state should move further toward a "citizen legislature" model, with formal session limits and an independent process for drawing electoral districts. For selecting members of the Supreme Court and Court of Appeals, North Carolina should restore real, partisan, privately funded general elections. Failing that, the next-best idea would be gubernatorial appointment with legislative confirmation and subsequent retention elections. Finally, the fiscal operations of state government should be improved by restoring the right of the people to vote on all significant issuances of state debt, and by limiting General Fund budgets to no more than the amount of General Fund revenue collected in the previous calendar year.

In offering these recommendations, JLF seeks to play a constructive role in the coming policy debates about North Carolina's biggest fiscal, economic, and social challenges. That's our job. We welcome questions, comments, even spirited rebuttals. Our goal is to make North Carolina "first in freedom" again. If you share this goal, we make of you two final requests. First, after reading this book, please share it with a family member, friend, or colleague. Second, please consider supporting JLF's work in advancing these and other policy recommendations for North Carolina. You can make a tax deductible contribution to: The John Locke Foundation, 200 West Morgan Street, Raleigh, NC 27601, or at www.JohnLocke.org.

About the Authors

◇◇◇◇◇◇◇◇◇◇◇◇◇◇◇◇◇◇◇◇

Roy Cordato is Vice President for Research and resident scholar at the John Locke Foundation. From 1993-2000 he served as the Lundy Professor of Business Philosophy at Campbell University in Buies Creek, N.C. He has also held positions at the Institute for Research on the Economics of Taxation (IRET) in Washington, D.C., University of Hartford, Auburn University, and Johns Hopkins University. His articles have appeared in a number of economics journals and law reviews as well as *The Christian Science Monitor, The Washington Times, Investor's Business Daily, National Review Online, The Washington Examiner, Tax Notes* and many other newspapers and magazines. Cordato holds an M.A. in urban and regional economics from the University of Hartford and a Ph.D. in economics from George Mason University. He also holds a Bachelor of Music Education from the Hartt School of Music.

Fergus Hodgson (@FergHodgson) is a former Director of JLF's Fiscal Policy Studies and currently a Policy Advisor with The Future of Freedom Foundation. He also hosts a weekly show, "The Stateless Man," with the Overseas Radio Network. Previously, he worked with both the American Institute for Economic Research and the Frontier Centre for Public Policy. His commentaries have appeared in newspapers and magazines in the United States, Canada, and New Zealand, including the *Sacramento Bee, The Charlotte Observer,* and *The Washington Times.* He has also contributed to online outlets such as *The Daily Caller, World Net Daily,* Fox News Latino, and LibertyBlog.org. Hodgson graduated from Boston University with a Bachelor of Arts in Economics. He then completed a second major in political science and taught macroeconomics with the University of Waikato, New Zealand.

Terry Stoops is the Director of Research and Education Studies at the John Locke Foundation. Before joining JLF, he worked as the program assistant for the Child Welfare Education Programs at the University of Pittsburgh. After crossing the Mason-Dixon Line, he taught English at Spotsylvania High School and served as an adjunct instructor in professional communication at the University of Mary Washington. He was a research assistant in the Department of Leadership, Foundations, and Policy at the Curry

School of Education, University of Virginia. Stoops earned a bachelor's degree in speech communication from Clarion University and a master's degree in Administrative and Policy Studies from the University of Pittsburgh, School of Education. He received a Ph.D. in Social Foundations of Education from the University of Virginia, Curry School of Education.

Jon Sanders (twitter.com/jonpsanders) is Director of Regulatory Studies at the John Locke Foundation. A regular columnist for TownHall.com, Sanders has also been published in *The Wall Street Journal*, *National Review*, ABC News online, *FrontPage Magazine*, the *San Francisco Chronicle*, *The Freeman: Ideas on Liberty*, *The Philadelphia Inquirer* and numerous newspapers throughout North Carolina. A native of Garner, N.C., Sanders has been an adjunct instructor in economics at North Carolina State University, and holds a master's degree in economics with a minor in statistics and a bachelors degree in English literature and language from N.C. State.

Sean Riley is Director of the Health and Human Services Task Force at the American Legislative Exchange Council. He has previously served as a Ronald Reagan Fellow with the Goldwater Institute, legal extern with the U.S. Senate, and extern with the U.S. District Court of Arizona. He holds a bachelor's degree in finance and received his J.D. from the James E. Rogers School of Law at the University of Arizona.

John Hood is President and Chairman of the John Locke Foundation. In addition to his duties at JLF, Hood is a syndicated columnist for the *Winston-Salem Journal*, *High Point Enterprise*, *Gaston Gazette*, *Durham Herald-Sun*, and 50 other North Carolina newspapers. Hood appears as a weekly panelist on the statewide TV show NC SPIN. Hood writes and comments frequently on politics and policy issues for national media. His articles have appeared in both magazines and newspapers, including *Readers' Digest*, *The New Republic*, *National Review*, *Military History*, *National Affairs*, *Reason*, *The Wall Street Journal*, *USA Today*, and *The Chicago Tribune*. His TV appearances include CNN, CNBC, "NBC Nightly News," and Fox News. He is the author of six books, including *Our Best Foot Forward: An Investment Plan for North Carolina's Economic Recovery*, published in 2011. Hood received his degree in journalism from the University of North Carolina at Chapel Hill.